The Ice Age

The Ice Age

Bailing Out the Welfare State in the Era of Austerity

Diego López Garrido

Translation

Jane R. Welsh

LONDON PUBLISHING PARTNERSHIP

The Ice Age: Bailing Out the Welfare State in the Era of Austerity
First published as *La Edad de Hielo* by RBA Libros, Spain (2014)

Published by London Publishing Partnership
www.londonpublishingpartnership.co.uk

ISBN: 978-1-907994-44-9 (pbk)

A catalogue record for this book is available from the British Library

This book has been composed in Minion Pro and printed on
FSC certified paper

Copyedited and typeset by
Riverside Publishing Solutions, Salisbury, Wiltshire

Printed in the United Kingdom by
Hobbs the Printers Ltd

FSC
www.fsc.org
MIX
Paper from
responsible sources
FSC® C020438

FOR MASUKA, MY WIFE,
FOR MY CHILDREN, DIEGO, MARÍA, JAIME AND ÁLVARO
(ORIGINATOR OF THE TITLE)
AND FOR THE BAY OF CÁDIZ, OPPOSITE WHICH I WROTE MUCH
OF THIS BOOK.

Contents

Foreword xi
by Nicolás Sartorius
Introduction xv

Part I The Great Crisis 1

Chapter 1 The Thirty-year Crisis 3
The Keynes Era 5
The Neo-Liberal Era 7
Anti-State policy 8
Financial capitalism 8
The tax revolution 11
The Washington Consensus 12
Less tax. More sovereign debt 13
A powerful, self-reliant financial market 16
Borrow 17
The financial 'Moloch' 19
The Bubble Bursts 21

Chapter 2 The Crash 23
The Financial Crisis (2007–2008) 23
Lehman Brothers 24
Contagion 25
The abyss 26
Keynesian Policies to Beat the Crisis (2009) 28
Monetary policy 29
Fiscal policy 33
The London and Pittsburgh G-20 meetings 37
The Growth Crisis 37
The European Sovereign Debt Crisis 39

Part II The Reaction 41

Chapter 3 The Failure of Austerity 43
Schuld (Blame, Debt) (2010) 43
The Vehicles of Austerity (2011) 50
Greece 51
Ireland 53
Portugal 55
Spain and Italy 55
The golden rule 57
Austerity Does Not Work (2012) 58
Economic recession. More debt. More unemployment 59

Turning to Keynes Again (2013) 60
Winter. Paralysis in the EU 60
Spring. The battle 63
Summer. Waiting for Germany 71
Autumn. Swords drawn 75
Consolidation of a Dual Model of Growth: Europe and the United States (2014) 78

Chapter 4 The European Central Bank and the Federal Reserve Take on the Crisis 81
The European Central Bank 82
The structural constraints of European monetary policy 82
Trichet and the counter-inflationary obsession 85
Draghi tackles the banking crisis 87
The unprecedented OMT bond-buying programme 90
The 'currency war' 91
Interest rates again 92
Helpless in the face of the credit-crunch 93
A spectre is haunting Europe: deflation 94
Now what? 95
The Mighty FED of Ben Bernanke 96
QE1. QE2. QE3 96
Communicating the exit strategy 98
Good news, bad news 99
Farewell to Bernanke and QE3 100
The New Role of Central Banks 102

Part III The Legacy of a Crisis 105

Chapter 5 The Assault on the Welfare State 107
The European Social Model Hit Hard 107
The Four Horsemen of the Apocalypse 110
Unemployment 110
Underemployment 111
Poverty 113
Inequality, the challenge of our times 114
The Washington Non-Consensus 117
Upstairs, downstairs 117
Obamacare 119
Financing welfare 119

Chapter 6 Debt, Tax Crisis and Tax Evasion 122
A Culture of Debt 122
National debt 123
Private debt 125
Internal devaluation 126
Exit options 127
Taxing Times 129
The debate about income taxes 131
The increase in value-added tax 132

The reduction in corporate income tax: fiscal devaluation 132
Wealth tax, M.I.A. 134
The Tax Avoidance Industry. The Pieces of the Plot 135
The perpetrators: runaway capitalists 137
The necessary collaborators: the opaque tax havens 138
The accomplices: the banks and financial institutions 144
The desperate politics of step-by-step 146
Multinationals and Their Sophisticated Tax Avoidance Schemes 149
The rotten apples 150
The empire strikes back 152
Europe: eppur si muove 154
Progressive Taxes Make a Comeback 157
Without Taxes, There's No Paradise 160

Chapter 7 The Hegemony of Financial Power 163
At the Heart of the Crisis and of the Fraud 163
When banks stopped being banks 163
Financial irregularities 165
Bailing out the Banks 167
The Dodd-Frank Act and the Volcker Rule, the New Regulation of the American Financial System 169
Too big to fail 170
The FED, the highest supervisory authority 171
Shadow banking 171
10 December 2013: the Volcker Rule is born 172
Tough to implement 173
The controllers' moment 174
European Banking Union Is Still on the Horizon 175
Oversight 176
The disappointing reform of the banking resolution mechanism 176
From bail-out to bail-in. Saving taxpayers from the sins of the banks 177
Banking union without the Volcker Rule (for the time being) 178
Basel III and Capital Requirements 179
The Power of the Financial Markets 182
Banks take over from banks 184
The other banks ... in the shadows 185
Financial innovation and systemic risk 186
Control Over Financial Power 187
Can the financial powers be controlled by the political powers? 187
The minimum reforms required 188
The Financial Transaction Tax, an Instrument to Curb Financial Power 190

Conclusion: The Ice Age Will Not Last Forever 195
Notes 200
Bibliography 223
Further Reading 231

Foreword

By Nicolás Sartorius

The great crisis that we have been suffering from for seven years has been like an earthquake which has disrupted all our lives. Suddenly, everything has changed. This was particularly true in the Western hemisphere, where millions of people, who had enjoyed many years of good living, were brutally affected in the form of layoffs, business closures, loss of wages, pensions and savings; evictions from their homes, cuts in social spending, increased poverty and social exclusion. Everyone has wondered what happened, where the source of so much misery was, how we had got to this point and what the remedy to this unfortunate situation could be. The bewilderment, confusion and sleight-of-hand that led to this calamity are considerable. I am reminded of a poem by Antonio Machado, who died 75 years ago. Writing of Spain at that time (and it could apply to so many countries now) he said that 'they made us poor, emaciated and drunken, so our hands could not feel the wound'. In fact, 'they' are doing everything possible to avoid our feeling the wound.

However, there are always clear-minded people who help us to feel the wound and to propose appropriate remedies. This is precisely what Diego López Garrido does in his splendid book, *The Ice Age*. This is an accurate and hard-hitting analysis, with plenty of data, which rigorously and dispassionately dissects the genesis and development of the greatest crisis of Western society since that suffered in the 1930s, which led to fascism and war. Garrido helps us understand what is happening to us and who was responsible. Once I finished reading the book, I remembered President Clinton's famous election slogan, 'it's the economy, stupid'. Well, in this case you might say, *a fortiori*, 'it's capitalism, stupid'. The author is a politician with practical experience, an economist and a professor of Constitutional Law, who has witnessed the crisis as an insider in the European Union—which he has always strongly defended.

His account of this incredible story begins in the Nixon era, when the Gold Standard was abandoned as a result of the financial needs of the Vietnam War, and thus began that dizzying escalation in the 'private' creation of money, that 'industry without a product', of money on top of money, which like a huge toxic cloud has ended up descending upon the world. It then continued with deregulation, privatization, the liberalization of Reagan and Thatcher and their Conservative revolution (which coincided, not coincidentally, with the collapse of the USSR and the socialist block). Later it continued with the reforms of Clinton, when banks were allowed to become what Chancellor Helmut Schmidt called the 'financial industry'. This was an industry dedicated not so much to fulfilling the mission of granting credit to the productive economy as to an outrageously selfish, high risk game of speculation involving incomprehensible products, which were allowed to dominate the whole economy.

When the financial crisis broke out, it was not the banks—or building societies—who paid the bill, but as if by magic and with help from governments, private debt became sovereign debt—which has to be paid for by our children and our grandchildren, because of the 'too big to fail' mantra, which we are, unfortunately, 'too weak to resist'. This corollary is examined brilliantly by the author. From finance, the crisis metastasizes across the real economy; debt became a millstone for states; credit stopped flowing, causing less investment, higher unemployment, lower growth, less demand, and so on—chasing its own tail in a downward spiral. The medicine that has been prescribed by the European Union is the mantra of austerity which, in my opinion, is the macroeconomic expression of the class struggle—this time riddled with geographical components in which the rich are winning by a landslide, as the American billionaire Warren Buffet has remarked. Using indisputable data, the author analyzes the three main forms this 'looting' takes: the socialization of losses incurred due to converting private debt into sovereign debt; the reduction in wages, pensions and salaries; and finally, massive tax evasion and capital flight to tax havens, tax cuts for the wealthy and an increase in VAT. This latter change sends the individual tax burden of the less wealthy soaring disproportionately, thanks to the greater propensity to consume among this group.

What is especially interesting is the comparative analysis by the author between the approach that the Obama administration has taken to address the crisis—versus the EU approach, dominated by the conservative Chancellor Angela Merkel. While in America great blood transfusions are made to the sickly patient via liquidity injections by the FED; at the same time, in the EU leeches are applied, via austerity—drawing blood, which leaves the patient increasingly anaemic. At the same time, and so that this sickly patient does not end up dying, the ECB lends unlimited money to banks at a 1% interest rate so that they can lend it to the member states at 4% or 5%, which obviously increases the debt of the states and the power of the banks. The result is that monetary policy is largely in the hands of private banks. The fascinating thing about the story is that this has been done without the European Central Bank imposing any conditions on banks to make them lend their money to companies and individuals to facilitate job creation. This mechanism is so irrational that some of these huge amounts of money received by the financial system is re-deposited by the banks with the ECB itself, and thus a kind of financial 'mortmain' is created, in this case not in the form of church lands as before, but money—so essential for the economy to bounce back from the crisis. Maybe we should think again about a modern type of Ecclesiastical Confiscation.

The conclusion drawn from this analysis (if we exclude the possibility of evil and stupidity), is that the EU has been caught off-guard by the crisis and has not been able to catch up in time through a lack of political will. Not all member states have fared as badly as others of course, because some were creditors (with Germany leading the way)—and some were debtors (the South of Europe). As the author reminds us, we still do not have an economic union, or a common fiscal policy, or a European Treasury, or mutualization of debt, or an ECB as lender of last resort to member states, or Europe-wide social policy. Instead we have only the monetary policy of the ECB, whose primary mission is price stability, when that is not the problem. On the contrary, the real risk is deflation. Meanwhile the central drama is mass unemployment: 12% of the Euro area and 26% in Spain; while in the USA, with other policies and instruments it is almost half that.

To pursue certain economic policies, in this case austerity at all costs, required some historical aspirations of the liberal-conservative forces: breaking the power of unions through labour laws that weaken collective bargaining and facilitate dismissal; shelving the Welfare State under the premise that it is unsustainable; allowing the 'tax revolt' of the wealthy, multinational corporations, etc., and toughening laws against demonstrations and migrants. This is analyzed with remarkable rigor in this book. Because it seems clear that under the current tax system, with tax havens, the black economy and the thousand ways to avoid taxes, maintaining the Welfare State is enormously challenging. So it is absolutely right for the author to posit the fiscal issue as one of the strategies to redress the situation from the point of view of progress and common decency. The other basic axes are defined by López Garrido as clamping down on and reducing financial capital, remaking and modernizing the Welfare State, and restoring political control. For what is meant when we say that the big banks are 'systemic' and that therefore they cannot be allowed to fail? I am afraid that what is behind that oft-repeated statement is that 'the system' is the financial system and not democracy or citizens. That is, they can ignore 20 million people on the unemployment lists, because they are not part of 'the system', but not a big bank because it *is* part of it. When this is the case, there is something we are not doing right. Admittedly, it is not without a certain internal logic, because we have reached the point where the power of the global financial system that unites many states is no longer dependent only on the taxes of their citizens, but on the credits of 'markets'. That is, they have gone from creditor-taxpayer via tax based on democratic representation and control of the state by citizens, to the creditor-market through loans and debt on the basis of the current power of the financial system. One need only examine who is in possession of Spanish government debt, roughly one trillion euros, almost 100% of GDP. Almost 20% is held by six Spanish banks. Well over half of all the tax burden in the country. This is the reason we can say that we are witnessing a depletion of democracy. This is why people on the street say 'this is not a crisis, it's daylight robbery'. It may sound demagogic, but they have a point.

After reading this book it can be better understood that the problem is that finance and the economy have been globalized—while politics has not. Between capital and labour, capital has won out. Although Nicholas Sarkozy said that capitalism had to be 're-established', what is actually happening is that financial capitalism is re-establishing politics. And this is so largely because the reaction to the Great Crisis by progressive political and trade union forces has been extremely weak: lethargy demonstrating once again that political and social failures always start with intellectual resignation—giving in to the 'third way' of Blair, Clinton, Schröder and *tutti quanti*, which proved to be dead-ends.

Diego López Garrido is a clear-thinking person and therefore not prone to despondency. He does not limit himself to hard-hitting analysis of the situation, but also offers an entire programme of recovery rooted in a decent and progressive political thought from and for the citizens. This is democracy. It has been summarized previously, but I cannot resist highlighting it again; controlling financial capital and restoring its function to giving credit to the productive economy; restoring taxation for member states so that they answer to citizens and not the markets; remodelling the Welfare State, and returning power to politics. This is a democracy which, as the author notes cannot simply be national, but must also European.

Introduction

This book argues that the great economic crisis has transformed itself into a new era for the European economy—a kind of new Ice Age. This is not likely to be a temporary change in the economic and social situation, but rather a 'new normal', characterized by three structural factors which will come to define the Western economies in the next decade:

- The profound erosion of the welfare state and four powerful phenomena: unemployment, underemployment, poverty and inequality.
- The castration of the power of taxation of the State. Tax evasion and avoidance, especially by transnational corporations and the 'super-rich' makes it impossible to maintain the investment and expenditure necessary for citizens to enjoy fundamental social rights. This is coupled with the increasingly unbalanced nature of tax laws, to the detriment of the middle classes.
- The fearsome consolidation of private financial power. This spawned the great crisis, however, the (bank and non-bank) financial system continues to dominate the global economy, subjecting it to systemic risk that has not disappeared.

Overcoming its 'freeze' is the most important challenge facing Europe and the United States, and its most progressive political forces. It can only be addressed through concerted action by states.

For now, Obama's America—more aggressively interventionist—has performed much better than the European Union which has anchored itself by spending too much time in its monolithic austerity phase. This book explores and compares the policies of the two economic superpowers and concludes that fiscal and monetary policies in the US have achieved much more encouraging results than the old and still uncoordinated Europe—despite it being the inventor of the Welfare State. The European social and economic model is in need of a real 'bailout'.

The book also examines the origins of this socioeconomic upheaval and the policies that have been implemented to combat it until early 2015. The comparative research on both sides of the Atlantic is an original contribution to the literature on the crisis. This study includes an analysis hitherto not carried out about the origin, development and possible future of the most dramatically significant economic event that current generations have experienced.

Furthermore, the work proposes the lines of economic and social policy needed to exit the Ice Age and build a cohesive society with the true values of the Western world.

Part I

THE GREAT CRISIS

1

The Thirty-year Crisis

On 9 August 2007, the French bank BNP Paribas suspended withdrawals from three of its funds.

For the Nobel laureate economist Paul Krugman, it was on that summer day that the first major financial crisis of the twenty-first century began to unfold. While in Beijing a week earlier, the Secretary of the Treasury Henry Paulson had stated emphatically that the problems with the housing and mortgage market had been 'completely contained'. This statement was similar to the assurances given in March by the Federal Reserve chairman, Ben Bernanke.

For a year after the demise of Bear Stearns, one of the largest investment banks in the world, and even for some time before the collapse of Lehman Brothers (15 September 2008), the position of the American authorities was uncompromising in that the economy was not in danger, despite the obvious difficulties with high-risk subprime mortgages.

In fact, the housing bubble had been teetering on the brink since 2005. The American markets were becoming aware of the trend towards recession. Prices, which between 1997 and 2006 had increased by 124%, started falling from the spring of the latter year. The interest rate charged on debt also grew in parallel. From 2004 to 2006, the Federal Reserve raised interest rates on federal funds to 5.25% to curb inflation. This increase contributed to the brake on and subsequent decline in housing prices, which had been boosted by artificially inflated loans.

By late 2007, the economy of the United States was already in recession. Subprime loans were finished in the eyes of the market, and this meant that demand for houses ground to a halt, as well as the confidence of the American consumer. Instead, what emerged was a chill which ran right through the body of Western capitalism.

On Thursday 18 September 2008, three days after the fall of Lehman Brothers, the Federal Reserve noticed a tremendous decrease in the region of USD 550 billion[1] in money market accounts. The Reserve decided to suspend trading in a matter of hours. Without a bailout, 'we won't have an economy on Monday', said its chairman Ben Bernanke to Congress. Mervyn King, governor of the Bank of England, warned: 'Not since the beginning of the First World War has our banking system been so close to collapse'.

Tim Geithner, president of the Federal Reserve Bank of New York, had already acknowledged in June 2008 the huge risk in investing in long-term financial assets with low liquidity, sustained by payment obligations in the short term. They were of low quality, highly vulnerable to periods of financial panic, because in many cases they had been created by a shadow banking system. Their products did not have the deposit protections to reduce such risk as existed in the traditional banking system.

The scope of these products, multiplied several times by their face value and 'globalized', meant that the crisis had a universal impact, terrorizing investors and drying up credit lines. It brought back memories of the crash of 1930 which sank the banks, as indebted as their debtor clients. The banks, in view of the steep fall in value of these subprime mortgages, did not know if what they now owed their depositors and their creditors was more than the assets they possessed. They did not know if there was a liquidity crisis or a solvency crisis because they had financed mortgages with short-term loans from the interbank market. Short-term loans to creditors who, overcome by fear, demanded their cancellation and refused to refinance them.

In addition, bankers had no way of knowing what was happening to other financial institutions. Trust, the foundation of the financial system, had evaporated. The banks refused to lend to each other, or demanded high interest rates in line with the level of risk assumed. The global credit markets went into what was termed the 'credit crunch'.

The aggressive nature of the crisis swept away many banks. Others considered 'too big to fail' would be bailed out through a process full of with high economic and political risks, which have yet to come to an end.

This crisis is not a brief blip of malpractice or the product of bad luck, or chance. Its origins lie in a structural base that started long ago. It is not possible to explain the crash of 2007 and 2008 without reference to the drastic political changes of the 1980s. Without Reagan's conservative revolution, which declared an end to the Keynesian approach to economic theory, we would not have ended up where we are today: a financial crisis that is distinctly American in origin and nature.

The Keynes Era

Students of Business Administration naturally study Nobel Prize winner Paul Samuelson's book. Samuelson's theories predominated until the 1970s in America and Europe. They explained what he termed the 'mixed economy', which he called 'neoclassical synthesis', i.e., the belief in the virtues of the market to allocate resources and the ability of governments to create macroeconomic conditions for the market to work: the provision of infrastructure and fair distribution of goods. This encapsulated the economic legacy of the Roosevelt era.

There is no doubt that the main political personality in the USA after the Second World War was, of course, Franklin Delano Roosevelt. The social-democratic policies of the New Deal spread during the 1940s, 1950s and 1960s. Roosevelt, who became president of the USA in 1933, implemented investment programmes in social services and social protection, as well as tax obligations, hitherto non-existent in America. There was at that time no tradition of direct taxation in America. In fact, income tax was declared unconstitutional in the late nineteenth century by the Supreme Court, and could not be applied by the Federal Government until the vital 16th amendment to the US Constitution was passed.

Later, the era of Lyndon B. Johnson (1963–1969), who inherited the presidency because of the assassination of John F. Kennedy, constituted perhaps the most progressive activism on the part of the State in the second half of the twentieth century in the USA in terms of civil and political rights, and in the still-limited Social Security System, through the launch of Medicare for the elderly and Medicaid for the poor. Poverty amongst the over 65s rapidly decreased.

Johnson's measures were reflected in total federal spending, with the creation of a fully-fledged tax system. When Roosevelt began his lengthy and controversial term, non-military federal spending accounted for 3% of GDP. The New Deal raised this to 10% in 1950; in 1970, it reached 12%; and in 1980, 16% (21% including military spending). And this was the situation when Ronald Reagan took office, as we shall see.

As regards Europe, an embryonic 'social policies' system had started emerging in the last few decades of the nineteenth century, and theories about the Welfare State had been bandied about since the twenties and thirties, the era of Herman Heller, the social democratic activist and eminent scholar on the theory of the state.

Europe after the Second World War had a dazzling political figure, a mixture of scientist and politician in the mould of Weber: John Maynard Keynes, the leading figure in support of the New Deal and unabashed critic of what he called 'casino capitalism', i.e., the predatory short-termism of the financial markets (see his General Theory, chapter 12).

Throughout the three post-war decades, the world was ruled monetarily by the Bretton Woods System, an idea championed by Keynes and supervised by the USA and its powerful currency. This was quite inevitable, as noted by Aldo Giannuli.[2] France and the UK were unable to continue to back their currency with gold reserves, in the way they had done until the Second World War. Therefore, the Bretton Woods conference (held between 1 and 22 of July, 1944) denominated the dollar as the international reserve currency. Only the USA could ensure immediate convertibility of the dollar into gold at a fixed price of an ounce of gold (28.35 grams) for USD 35.

Bretton Woods gave birth to two determining organizations for international trade and economic policy: the International Monetary Fund and the World Bank. It would be completed with the GATT (General Agreement on Tariffs and Trade), anticipating an emerging globalization and helping the growth of the global economy in the post-war decades.

These were the years of the 'Fordist' compromise between capital and labour. Luciano Gallino has shown that between 1960 and 1980 companies in major industrial countries recorded a decline in profits, a consistent increase in real wages and reduced working hours. They saw the introduction of national systems of social protection, especially in the field of healthcare.[3]

The economy of the two post-war decades, moreover, was notable for producer confidence that their goods would have a guaranteed market.[4]

During the same period, the public sector in industrialized countries expanded considerably and generated deficits because expenses grew more than tax revenues, especially in Europe. According to the European Commission, public expenditure in the EU rose from 35% of GDP in 1970 to a maximum of 53% of GDP in 1993.

As Lord Robert Skidelsky, Keynes' excellent biographer says, during the 30 years after World War II until the oil crisis of the 1970s, Keynesian demand-side economics took the lead. His philosophy formulated in 1936, which could be summarized as the attempt to maintain full employment and a regular and balanced growth of the economy, formed part of the toolbox of all governments—to the point that Nixon himself even said 'we are all Keynesians now'.

That statement sounds very cynical from someone who would definitively put an end in 1971 to the convertibility of the dollar (something which had already been mooted in 1968 by Lyndon B. Johnson), and who was ultimately responsible for devaluing it. This was the pathway to the colossal extravagance that led to the Vietnam War, financed by industrial quantities of dollars that were largely spent abroad and obviously could not be backed by the Fort Knox reserves.

Nixon's decision destroyed the Bretton Woods monetary system of fixed exchange rates and controls on the movement of capital. In the words of Richard Duncan, the nature of the currency changed. The result was a proliferation of credit that not only transformed the size and structure of the American economy, but also changed the economic system itself. The production of goods was no longer driven by savings and investment, as it had been before. Artificial and massive credit creation replaced the accumulation of capital, and became the engine of the Western economy to the extent that, in 50 years, the amount of credit has increased fifty-fold.

The Neo-Liberal Era

Against this background, it is no coincidence that the 1970s represented, in the Western world, the decline of the golden age of the Welfare State. Those were the years of stagflation, along with the misfortune of having two oil crises in 1973 and 1979—a time of Euro-pessimism.

It was obvious that productivity had experienced a decline, giving rise to the perfect circumstances in which to unleash a conservative reaction in the economic and political spheres, as well as the cultural and religious ones.

Short-lived president, Democrat and human rights defender Jimmy Carter (1977–1981), began to chip away at one of the achievements of the Keynesian Era: taxes on capital. This was the first sign of deregulation in key economic sectors (aviation, finance, transportation). This cleared the way for the idea that state intervention was harmful to prosperity and freedom. The Keynesian consensus was ending, and supply-side policies became fashionable.

What the new conservative wave confirmed among economic theorists was that a macro economy that could be influenced by government action, stimulus-based or not, was a virtual building lacking any foundation. Macroeconomics does not exist. The only reality is the self-regulating market. The millions of consumers, producers and traders are the real protagonists of the direction of the economy, because, it was said, they always act according to 'rational' expectations.

It was only a matter of time before the theories of market self-regulation, the self-styled scientific, 'rational expectations', converged with the monetarism of the Chicago School. And with a newly-minted capitalism.

Margaret Thatcher won the British general election in 1979, initiating a privatization movement via the dismantling of the Welfare State, with a bigger subsequent scope thanks to Ronald Reagan. In 1980, President Reagan beat Carter by a landslide, and the slogan 'America is back' gave a wide-ranging boost from the USA which the UK alone could not have achieved. Reagan broke the Rooseveltian aegis of European influence, and set out a new strategy with three pillars of iron: first, the decentralization of power from the Federal State—that is, its weakening—to the benefit of local authorities (states and municipalities), and private powers through what was called 'deregulation'; second, the power of finance; and third, the drastic reduction in taxation.

Anti-State policy

Thatcher and Reagan agreed that the government (the State) was the problem, not the solution. For this reason, it was necessary to limit it to meeting only a few public needs: justice, monetary policy, infrastructure and defence, for example. In addition, limits were also to be imposed on such policies with the aim of reducing spending.

The weakening of a State considered parasitic meant that of most public importance, the Welfare State, and, within it, the jewel in the crown, Social Security. The Neoliberal School has insistently reiterated: free or semi-free public services create a flawed relationship with the citizen, who becomes over-reliant on such services. They are not, therefore, a means of social cohesion, but a burden on competitiveness.

Thatcher failed in her quest to get rid of the British National Health Service; nor did she manage to exert a negative influence on the social security systems of continental European countries. Neither did Reagan manage to do away with the already fragmented and nascent American social security system. His cuts were focused on educational and energy infrastructure. Both failed in their objectives to restore growth and employment, because the policies, summarized simplistically as 'small government', were not adequate to address the problems that the eighties posed to Western governments.

However, they did succeed in imposing a devastating new public policy: deregulation. The economic policies of Reagan (Reaganomics) and Thatcher led the liberalization of economic activities, hitherto subject to the general interest represented by democratically elected institutions and defended by Thatcher's most bitter enemies: the unions.

In this suicidal strategy of disarmament of the State, the sector which took the lead, as a logical conclusion to its dizzying expansion at the time, was the financial sector, the money economy.

Financial capitalism

The second pillar of the conservative revolution of the 1980s was, in effect, the reckless growth of the new great economic power: the financial markets and their institutions.

Financial globalization meant—as a sine qua one—the absolute freedom of movement of capital, and thus overwhelmed the already significant freedom of international trade, leading to breakneck expansion over the past century. The Anglo-Saxon deregulation policies forced European governments (such as the French and German ones) faced with the real threat—which Mitterrand experienced in first person—of huge capital flight, to also allow absolute freedom of movement of capital in order to prevent a massive outflow of capital from these European countries.

Reagan dismantled the legacy of the Great Depression. It began with the Garn-St Germain Depository Institutions Act of 1982, which deregulated the savings and loan institutions and, as noted by Jeffrey D. Sachs,[5] provided the basis for immediate credit and mortgage crises. The walls between commercial banking and investment banking began to be broken down, a task later completed by Clinton in the early 1990s. This began a series of gifts to Wall Street that would continue from that date and be reciprocated by generous funding for election campaigns of the Reagan administration, and later ones, too. The alliance between Wall Street and successive presidencies continued unabated, largely thanks to the American system of financing of political parties, a free system based on private donations and without caps. This may explain why we have got to where we are with a financial sector devoid of any legal limits.

It is little wonder that within the financial sector, equality of earnings in the different social strata characteristic of the Keynesian era began to break down, a highly visible rupture which particularly benefited the leaders of that sector. The US government estimated that in 1980, company directors saw their salaries increase by 260%, while those of employees grew by only 50%.

All this added up in the USA to a policy of remuneration for creditors or lenders—that is to say, the financial sector—through high interest rates (up to 20% in 1980–1981), implemented by the Federal Reserve, and which formed part of a series of reforms included in the Economic Recovery Act (ERA).

The European Union, egged on by the International Monetary Fund, had to follow suit. The Treaty of Rome in 1957 established the four freedoms: free movement of goods, services, capital and people—the key factors of production. However, the free movement of capital remained paralyzed until Jacques Delors, President of the European Commission, promoted it in 1985 as part of the goal of an internal market.[6] Parallel to this movement by Delors, the French government through figures such as Michel Camdessus, Governor of the Bank of France, or Pierre Bérégovoy, the Finance minister had managed to build the 'Paris consensus' on the free movement of capital.

The movement towards a single European currency came about as the logical consequence. Following on from the liberalization of capital flows, it was untenable that every country in the then European Community should have a differing monetary policy and divergent interest rates. It would have unleashed a competitive struggle to set high interest rates to attract the financial markets, both within Community territory and abroad. It is easy to guess who set the tone for a strong currency, which everyone else had to follow: Germany. Its strong position had allowed it to withstand the test of reunification after the fall of the Berlin Wall.

The expansion of the financial sector was not only quantitative. Financial markets began to develop—through sophisticated products such as the futures markets, which multiplied exponentially the turnover of Western stock exchanges (in the forefront, Chicago, Wall Street and the City of London)—such a powerful movement that a whole raft of financial raiders were created, so sharply exposed in the famous novel by Tom Wolfe, The Bonfire of the Vanities, as well as in later Hollywood films.

The USA—like Spain—has always been a country with a home-owning culture. In the late 1970s and early 1980s, homeowners and mortgage borrowers benefited from rapid inflation and an accelerated growth in housing prices. Mortgages were a perfect way to save. With the rise in housing prices, owners could take out bigger and bigger mortgages against the rising value of their homes, even without any increase in their personal income. Bankers did not create obstacles, in spite of the illiquid nature of houses. In fact, the sophisticated financial innovation that was brewing would allow an alchemistic feat: the packaging of weighty mortgage securities, their distribution to investors, and thus converting houses into liquid cash overnight.

The policy of supporting homeowners has always been subsidized by the government, through the popular federal institutions Fannie Mae and Freddie Mac, the New Deal products for cheaper mortgages for Americans, and with the benefit of tax deductions. Ronald Reagan privatized this business via the Tax Reform Act of 1986.

This fundamental shift combined with the explosion in credit cards, which became usable for anything, anywhere. All this resulted in a much greater use of credit, which in the volatile economy of the 1980s exacted a high cost because defaults increased amongst many white collar workers who had greater access to credit cards. In spite of this, access to credit grew a great deal because, under the pressure of the credit card companies, the 'yuppies' were followed into the borrowing trend by lower income groups, which until then had practised more prudent behaviour with regard to debt and credit. The percentage of homeowners with credit cards grew from 35% in 1980 to 65% in 1991. The securitization of these loans from 1986 onwards became an apparently unlimited source of capital because they could be sold on to other investors. Thus, the 1980s saw the acceleration of financial engineering on Wall Street.

A veritable earthquake was being produced in the production system. A huge step had been taken from the manufacturing model as the core of Western economies, to the increase of credit and financial transactions, supported by the dazzling rise of information technology and telecommunications. In 1980, manufacturing accounted for 21% of GDP in the USA. Two decades later, in 2002, this industry had fallen to just 14% of GDP. In the intervening period, finance had taken its place. The turnaround was complete and absolute. The financial sector rose to represent 21% of GDP in 2002, from the 14% it represented in 1980.[7]

An economy with no basis in real goods, infrastructure or non-financial services was being created. An economy that could therefore grow without limits in tandem with the artificial creation of credit.

The tax revolution

The third element of the reaction in the 1980s against the Welfare State (re-distributor of profits and growth) was the socialization of losses as large public deficits, and the privatization of profits in the form of deep tax cuts for sectors of the population which were already better placed financially.

The Reagan presidency (1981–1989) was one of large deficits, largely due to the increase in defence spending and a significant decline in tax receipts later imitated by Bush Jr., even though, through the Tax Equity and Fiscal Responsibility Act, 1982, spending would be cut on Medicare, Medicaid and other benefits. The deficit, inevitably, became federal debt (in 1990 it reached USD 3.1 trillion) and all debt accumulates interest that has to be paid. That is how the USA went from being the largest creditor in the world to being the largest debtor. Debt also began to grow steadily in other developed countries, eventually becoming a ticking time bomb.

The other side of the coin—never a truer word was said—was the collapse in taxation of the biggest earners, big business, and multinational companies. This was done on the basis of the famous Arthur Laffer curve—never proven, scientifically or in practice—according to which, if there are high taxes on the rich, they will not invest: the less tax collected by the State, the less the economy and employment will grow, due to the lack of motivation on the part of these supposed investors.

To Reaganism, taxes were lethal to the goal of achieving short-term profits, to initiative and entrepreneurism in a free market, as had been highlighted during the recessions suffered in the previous decade. For Margaret Thatcher, progressive taxation constituted discrimination in favour of the poor (hence the infamous poll-tax, which ended up forcing her out of Downing Street).

In 1981, when Ronald Reagan took office in the White House, income tax paid by the very wealthy was at a rate of 75% (it had reached 94% in 1945). When Reagan left office in 1989, the maximum rate had fallen to 33%. In the UK, the change was even greater. In terms of income tax, the top rate went down from 83% to 40%, and corporation tax dropped from 52% to 33%.

All this is the corollary of a policy of the revitalization of capitalism and a deadening of the State and public expenditure, to the greater glory of the invisible hand of Adam Smith. It is the expression in tax terms of a monetary policy consisting of unprecedentedly high interest rates, and structural unemployment as the only way to curb inflation.

The Anglo-Saxon model of tax reform, aided by the weakness affecting most European socialist parties—Spain, which had just returned to democracy, was an exception—quickly spread. The Nordic countries, it is true, made their own adaptations. However, they did not avoid a transformation of the structure of their tax systems, even Sweden. The 1991 law gave rise to a new tax: taxes on corporations and capital gains stabilized at a rate of around 30%. The maximum income tax rate fell from 87% to 57%. Despite this, Sweden remained one of the most egalitarian countries in the world.

The conservative tax revolution changed, says Michel Albert, the true nature of the relationship between a state and its citizens; decades of constant increases in the tax burden, especially in industrialized nations, suffered a sudden reversal.[8] The term 'tax relief' became fashionable, not only in the political and administrative fields, but among the general public. It was a cultural transformation—'hegemony', as Gramsci would call it—that has not yet left us, and which explains the difficulty of governments in breaking free of this dynamic that leads us down the path of debt issuance, fearful of the slightest possibility of increasing the tax burden on the social groups with the greatest purchasing power.

The combination of the three essential components of the new post-industrial, twentieth-century capitalism: a weak state, powerful international financial markets and government debt financed preferably by a deficit, but not through progressive taxation, inevitably led to the global crisis of the twenty-first century. But first, the most neoliberal version of capitalism was to become even more firmly rooted after the fall of the Berlin Wall, as we will see.

The Washington Consensus

The 1990s, which started with the end of communism in Europe—the 'end of history', as Fukuyama put it—and with the approval of the Euro project, was the consolidation of what was called the 'Washington Consensus', undoubtedly because of the part the USA played in the change that ended the Keynesian era.

In fact, the terminology was coined in the wake of the situation of increasing conditions attached to loans, and economic policy requirements of developing countries when they needed to borrow from the IMF. In 1989, the World Bank economist John William specified the following requirements: budgetary discipline geared towards balance, a realignment of public spending, tax reform to get rid of progressive income tax, fixing the value of the currency based on trade fluctuations, a complete liberalization of trade and imports, openness to foreign investment, privatization of public enterprises, and broader deregulation. This is the doctrine of the Washington Consensus, which was arrived at with the establishment of the World Trade Organization (WTO) after the Marrakesh Agreement (15 April 1994), in which the abolition of barriers to free trade was stipulated; the jurisdiction of the WTO was extended in the areas of services, agriculture, textiles and health; and protection of intellectual property was imposed by Western countries, the USA especially.[9]

The lines drawn by this change in policy would not be substantially re-drawn when Bill Clinton entered the White House, or when socialist prime ministers headed European governments although, where it happened, the drift towards the destruction of the Welfare State slowed down.

As we shall see, the two main pillars of neo-liberalism—on the public side, the dismantling of progressive taxation and on the private side, an unregulated and de-regulated financial system—enshrined their economic hegemony.

Less tax. More sovereign debt

Studying the historical data from the OECD it can be observed that, in the period from 1967–1987, the percentage of GDP to developed states' income—from Europe, America and the Pacific—increased from 26.9% to 36.3% (in Europe, from 27.7% to 38.5%). That is, the tax burden rose no less than ten points in the twenty years from the time of construction of the Welfare State. In Spain, the increase reached almost 14 points (from 16.9% to 30.7% of GDP) because democracy took its first steps under the mantle of a frail Inland Revenue service, a remnant of the Franco dictatorship.

Looking at the period from 1987 to 2007, after two decades of dominance of the Washington Consensus we can note several things. In that period, average tax revenues of the States of the OECD, grew from 36.3% to 38% of GDP (in Europe, from 38.5% to 39.7%). This is an increase of just over one per cent in the tax burden in twenty years. In Spain, the increase in the tax burden is higher in these two decades and amounts to 33.1% in 2008 (six per cent below the

European average) because we started from further back after the reinstatement of democracy.

The contrast between the periods examined is stark. Over the first 20 years (until 1987), tax revenues rose ten points. Over the second twenty years (until 2007), they rose only slightly more than one per cent in the OECD area.

Besides this, there has been a profound change in tax structure because of 'international tax competition'. In the 1990s, the complete liberalization of capital flows in developed countries put pressure on governments—in order to prevent the relocation of companies—to reduce corporate taxation on income and capital gains and to decrease the progressive nature of personal income tax. This process is very well explained by José V. Sevilla.[10]

The European Union has always shown its inability to introduce progressive changes in the taxation of capital gains. Albert recalls that in 1989, the Commission had already tried to do so. A 15% deduction at origin for all purchases of financial assets by European residents was proposed.[11] However, what was proposed in February had to be abandoned in June, because Germany detected a massive capital flight to Luxembourg, by then a tax haven. The consequence? Zero deductions at source as standard. In the European Union, unanimity is the rule in financial matters, and states such as the UK and Luxembourg will always say 'no' to tax harmonization when it means any kind of increase in taxation.

The USA is a special case. Bush Sr., president from 1989–1993, committed the 'sin' of breaking his famous campaign promise—'Read my lips, no new taxes'—not to increase taxes. Bush's intention of reducing the growing deficit by USD 482 billion in five years, led him in 1990 to make the Congress vote in the Omnibus Budget and Reconciliation Act. Besides raising taxes based on the income of individuals, he did away with limits on deductions and indirect taxes. The law of 1990 secured the support of 47 Republicans in the House and 19 Republicans in the Senate.

The conservatives never forgave George HW Bush for agreeing to higher taxes. In fact, from then until the end of the first term of the current president, Obama, no Republican congressman voted in favour of raising personal income tax, apart from the exceptional 2012 pact.

Some lawmakers saw the doctrinal opposition to tax increases as a new form of ideological glue for Republicans after the Cold War; the Republican Party, which was the party of the balanced budget, became radically opposed to increases in taxes for two decades.[12] 'When I entered politics, the frame of reference was a balanced budget, as the principal conservative precept' said the former member of the House of Representatives James Leach, an Iowa Republican who was in the House from 1977 to 2007. 'Today it's the level of taxation'.

This ideology that led them to refuse to vote in favour of tax increases became dogma, even in cases where this was aimed at reducing the deficit. Hence no one will be surprised that that not one Republican congressman voted for the Clinton budget proposal.

During the Bush (Jr.) presidency, the situation became impossible to ignore. Not many know that Bush, albeit reluctantly, went so far as to propose a tax increase, given the size of the imbalance in the budget as a result of the stratospheric costs of the Iraq war. Again, a majority of Republicans voted 'no' to the initiative of their president. In contrast, in 2001 and 2003, the Republicans agreed to tax breaks for the rich that Bush proposed.

The tax cuts between 2001 and 2003 not only increased inequality within American society, but also failed to stimulate the economy and negatively influenced the deficit and debt. The Stiglitz Report concludes that Bush's decision narrowed the room for manoeuvre of fiscal policy faced with the rise in unemployment, making the task of monetary policy even more difficult.[13]

In short, over the past 30 years, the tax burden in the United States has been as follows: it decreased in the 1980s, the Reagan era; it increased in the 1990s, with Clinton, and it fell again, and by a substantial amount, with Bush Jr.

The tax cuts affect the federal level of government, those on higher incomes; but taxes have increased at state and local level, on the lowest incomes. So federal savings are maintained at the expense of those on lower incomes.

However, let us move on and look at the other major source of revenue: debt. And also, let us look at the two periods to which we have referred above in connection with taxes. From 1967 to 1987, the national debt in OECD countries rose from 35% of GDP to 55%, in round numbers (in the Euro area the average is similar). However, from 1987 to 2007, OECD debt jumped to 100% (in the Euro area up to 85%). These percentages are due to the source of all sovereign debt: the deficit.

What is clear from the above data is that, during the 20 years preceding the economic crisis, developed countries replaced taxation with debt, faced with their ongoing financial needs. That is, money that does not have to be paid back, replaced by money which increases the state's obligations to its creditors and which in turn increases public spending exponentially.

This is validated by the content of the OECD report: Économies en transition, 1989, which leaves no doubt as to the politically dominating trends in developed countries. In the private sector, the aim is to achieve a much greater liberalization of international capital movements. In the public sector, the aim is to prevent inflation and decrease the weight of public spending. This results in less taxation and spending. However, at the same time, the report—falling into an obvious contradiction—has no choice but to admit that the interest on debt is a heavy burden that runs the risk of 'creating an explosive situation' through the need to import capital to finance the deficits. However, it does not propose increases in tax; on the contrary, it complains that the tax burden is too great in many countries. The OECD report, then true to its neo-liberal orientation, advocated lowering marginal tax rates on income and, in turn, extending indirect taxes.[14]

A powerful, self-reliant financial market

If we start with the above assumptions—that is, the tax exemption for higher incomes and the very wealthy, the fiscal crisis of the state, in short—and if we move through the looking-glass to private finance, we find a new reality: the development of a mammoth financial system with hitherto unknown characteristics.

Only with some figures can we capture the extent of the phenomenon. In 1981, when the Reagan era began, financial assets amounted approximately to total world GDP. In 2007, when the crisis occurred, these assets represented four times world GDP, expressed mainly as debt underwritten by banks—in the legitimate or shadow-banking system—by individuals and states. In the last twenty years, global GDP has grown at a rate of 3%, while financial assets have done so by 8%.

Transactions on global financial markets which corresponded in 1991 to 15 times the world's GDP had increased to 75 times of world GDP by 2007. In 2007, 80% of these transactions were purely speculative in nature, separate from the real economy.

The instruments called 'derivatives' represented 12 times world GDP at the end of 2007.[15]

This spectacular growth in the financial economy is not accidental. It has a political origin and is undoubtedly linked to two determining factors: the release of any impediment to the movement of capital, and the invention of the most sophisticated financial products that had ever been seen. In this way, the fault lines that began in the decade of Reagan and Thatcher have continued to deepen, with greater intensity.

The *iter* of the process leading up to the Great Depression went like this: first, total liberalization of capital; second, massive development of new financial products; third, unchallenged dominance of the financial power hubs of the planet.

In 1978, a follower of Keynes, James Tobin, Yale professor, now more known worldwide for his famous tax than for winning the Nobel Prize, predicted that excessive capital mobility would make any monetary or fiscal policy impossible in the future. Hence the tax on financial transactions was conceived as a way to control capital flows, rather than for the purpose of increasing revenue by the State.

Thus, in the final decade of the twentieth century, the exact opposite of what was proposed by Tobin happened. Not only were no controls on capital movements re-imposed, but both Clinton administrations had a major impact on the most important aspect of deregulation, that of the financial sector, which had always enjoyed special protection.

The Glass-Steagall Act, which had been created by the New Deal, and which established the clear separation between commercial banks (deposit-based) and investment banking (involved in higher risk projects), was repealed in 1999 by the Financial Services Modernisation Act, under President Bill Clinton.

Clinton's back-pedalling entailed many things. It made it possible for certain high-risk financial transactions to be placed off balance sheet; to conduct derivatives trading outside the stock market for speculative purposes; and to carry out major mergers and acquisitions. In short, it was possible to develop the type of activities that would bring us to the crisis. The regulators of the stock exchange also gave investment banks the ability to disproportionately increase the risk to their capital (their 'leverage').

The consequences were immediate. Risky operations made use of the deposits by individuals and families, and the era of global private debt was upon us.

Borrow

This is the title that Louis Hyman gave to a fascinating account of how personal credit created the American middle class and almost tipped the nation into bankruptcy[16] (and the Western world, we should add), because the Great Depression was spawned, developed and hatched, without any doubt, by the powerful US financial machinery.

Private debt flooded the markets. If in 1989 the debt of homeowners in the United States was 48% of GDP, in 2007 it had risen to 100%. Something similar happened in other sectors. Businesses increased their debt from 53% to 76% of GDP. The US financial sector itself used the purchase of debt as a way to engage in other operations. In the same period, the debt grew from 22% to 117% of GDP. The Federal Reserve helped by lowering interest rates after 2001.

A key technique to achieving these dizzying numbers was called 'securitization' of mortgages and other debts. The securitization of mortgages consisted in the packaging of different mortgages (packaged as bonds). Then, these packages were sold off, basically guaranteed by the mortgage holders' debt. These were called CDOs (collateralized debt obligations). The financial innovation consisted in creating a legal entity providing such securities (off balance sheet) which, in turn, sold them on in tranches depending on the risk (and therefore the level of profit from the interest). These products were blessed by the ratings agencies, which gave AAA ratings to 'senior' tranches with preferential repayment rights in the case of default or insolvency. Such investments were successful because they enjoyed better levels of return than ordinary bonds.

The technique of securitization was inflated with the emergence of CDS (credit default swaps). The CDS insures the risk against default of the packaged mortgage securities that the banks had distributed to many investors in exchange for juicy commissions. It should be noted that the mortgage securities sold encapsulated high interest rates, but the houses were always worth more. Ratings agencies gave high ratings to what was actually risky debt, given the possibility of acquiring CDSs. During the twentieth century, mortgage default insurance was covered by Fannie Mae and Freddie Mac. In the twenty-first century that place would be taken by the leading insurance company, AIG, which would not have sufficient capital backing after the crisis.

The strategy that the market launched involved first the creation of risk, and then the distribution of that risk to the rest of the world, i.e., also to Europe, which would leave it open to being struck by the imminent crisis.

We were witnessing an infinite cascade of indebtedness, based on the short-termism of obtaining profit—nothing to do with the tradition of long-term investment in real estate mortgages, which produced slow-growing returns. Each change meant an increase in the nominal value of the asset and the payment of the respective commission.

The thesis of the present governor of the Central Bank of India, Raghuram G. Rajan, is that low interest rates for population groups with low social status, driven by government lending agencies, was the way the political class could offer something valuable, quickly, to Americans with stagnant or diminishing incomes.[17] Affordable housing would not require years of waiting, as would have been necessary if the goals were, for example, education and health. This was without doubt the aim of the Clinton administration: 'Financing strategies, fuelled by creativity'. Thus the minimum required for a government guarantee on the initial deposit on a mortgage was reduced, thereby increasing the size of the mortgage that could be taken out.

Not even the crisis in technology market shares in 2000 (the dot-com bubble) could put a halt to this blind rush. Interest rates were at low levels and borrowing capacity continued to increase. Mortgages gave greater returns to investors than Treasury Bills. The solvency of the debtor began to be irrelevant in markets keen to invest short-term; and for debtors, many in precarious employment, the opportunity to become a homeowner and benefit from a loan of nearly 100% of the value of the house, which was being 're-valued' almost every day, was impossible to resist. The same speculative bubble pattern was repeated in Europe.

The abundance of investors willing to meet the voracious demand for consumer loans was due to the presence in the markets of new agents who burst onto the scene. During the first decade of the new century, the demand by American and European families and companies for money and goods was covered amply by funding from the oil-rich countries, with plenty of savings which were partly invested abroad, especially in the USA. European banks, especially German ones, also financed the American debt.

Alongside this monumental private and national debt had grown a giant speculative entity, fuelled by it: global financial power.

The financial 'Moloch'

The name 'Moloch', an ancient god, has been used figuratively in British literature since the work of John Milton, *Paradise Lost* (1667), to refer to a person or thing that requires a costly sacrifice; it seems a wholly appropriate name to refer to the financial system, the gold-worshipping god that in the end really leads to costly sacrifices. This creature was engendered by the financial agents who squared the circle of achieving maximum benefit with minimum risk.

Securitization and the subsequent sale of debt allowed financial institutions to disperse risk geographically, but above all, and this is the key, made it possible for such assets—many of them toxic—not to be reflected in the accounts of banks, thus enabling them to avoid keeping capital reserves to back them.

This is how something crucial was achieved, that is to say, endlessly expandable creditworthiness. Lending institutions could lend more and more. Once the capital requirements for lenders were reduced, interest rates could go down, enabling more loans—and therefore more debt—to be made available to a wider range of, and higher-risk, borrowers. This had never happened before (Hyman): the supply created the demand. In 1990, only 1% of credit cards were securitized; in 1996, 45% were, which means that financial investors outside the banks were the ones becoming lenders. In turn, companies like First USA, Capital One, and Advantage Corporation acted as intermediaries with other equity investors, protected by the AAA rating that the rating agencies granted to these increasingly high-risk investments.

Meanwhile, many big American companies faced serious difficulties in getting banks to lend them money. In effect, the latter preferred to engage in the more lucrative gambling in subprime mortgages on homes with increasing value (keeping the privilege of tax deductions) and credit cards, securitized and with the risk dispersed throughout the world. The formula of securitization made it possible for any investor anywhere to participate in the buying and selling of bonds or debt. Always supported, as stated previously, by the maximum rating given by Standard and Poor's, Moody's or Fitch, all competing to attract customers to whom they could bring good news.

The certainty of managers of large financial corporations that governments would never let them fail, because otherwise, their failure would cause a 'systemic' catastrophe, has been deemed by analysts to be one of the adverse factors. This is the case because such dynamics drove managers to fail to take adequate precautions, and embark on high-risk adventures. If they did well, the high risk brought a return; and if they were wrong, it was the government who assumed the burden of risk. This idea was proposed to the 'system' by Alan Greenspan in his speeches and his actions (for example, in his laxity with the 'tech bubble' in the spring of 2000), or in the low interest rates that filled the market with liquidity.

Alan Greenspan, who assumed the leadership of the Federal Reserve in 1987, was the person who most encouraged self-regulation of financial markets, which had no reason, in his view, to do wrong. He also encouraged them to make use of derivatives, i.e., imaginative financial innovations to decrease risk. And if there were problems, the FED was prepared to mitigate the consequences, favouring lending entities that did not have to worry about playing a dangerous game: taking short-term loans themselves, and then granting them long-term to creditors. This was Greenspan's incredible message.[18] He probably thought that financial innovation added to the pull of the US savings market exerted on the rest of the world. The Western financial world paid heed.

This is how in the aftermath of banking deregulation and financial globalization, what has been called 'the shadow banking system' developed, through credit institutions and investment funds characterized by their aggressiveness, their commitment to high-risk and the corresponding high profits, being allowed to roam freely in the stock market jungle and reduce financial activity to that of a bookmaker.

The borrowing capacity of this shadow banking was huge, because leveraging was widely used, allowing for example a million dollars of capital to create 30 or 40 million of credit (and debt) for the entity, without any supervision by the supposed regulatory bodies.

The international financial system obtained exorbitant profits, armed with speculative instruments and the *ex novo* creation of new money, i.e., debt.

In the USA, which spearheaded this inexorable rise, the profits of the financial sector between 1950 and 1980 accounted for around 10% of all corporate profits. This proportion doubled during the 1990s and reached 34% (!) in the first decade of this century. The same was true—albeit one step behind—of labour income of the sector: from 3% to 7%.[19] In 2007, the year of highest profits in the financial sector, this came to 47% of all corporate profits in the USA.

The obscene salaries of senior executives of banks and other entities, which are still maintained and have even increased (note the doubling of the salary of the chief executive officer [CEO] of J.P. Morgan in 2014)—are the best evidence of the speculative approach by the financial system. Something particularly applicable to investment banking, always so keenly supported by Alan Greenspan, who for years had allocated more than half of its net profits to executive pay, through different means (salaries, bonuses, stock options, etc.). No amount of investment in the real economy would allow such compensation, which shows that the activity of such investment banking is largely speculative. It is no wonder that in 2008, the top five investment banks in the world, all American, would disappear as legally independent entities.[20] Just a year earlier, its executives were handed bonuses of billions of dollars.

Financial institutions had become, before the crisis they themselves caused, the leading sector in generating growth and profits. Before, it was not so. From 1948 to 1980, revenues in the financial sector were similar to those of other industries.[21] Again, we see how the 1980s marked a before and after in the capitalist economy.

The same is true of another date: 2007. That year, the most glaring and damaging failure of the financial sector was laid bare. And so, paradoxically, was its dominance.

The Bubble Bursts

The price of homes in the USA between 1996 and 2006 grew as much as they had done in the previous 100 years. No one noticed that the appreciation of housing (close to 15% at one point), together with a labour market in decline, was a potentially explosive situation. Property revaluation and bullish sentiment were the product of pure speculation.

However, what no one wanted to see finally became apparent. In the course of one day in 2006, prices started to fall, because the instability of the job market was becoming evident. This effect was transferred to the housing market when the supply of new housing swamped demand because of overbuilding, high prices and increasingly higher mortgage interest rates, which discouraged the hitherto inexhaustible buyers.[22]

Rating agencies insisted on irresponsibly maintaining AAA ratings for the assets of mortgage debt. Insurers demanded yet more securities to guarantee the debt-laden bonds, unable to prevent the collapse of the insurance giant AIG, kept afloat only by the United States government.

No data, not even the increase in the deficit in the USA (in 2006 it was 6.5%) and that of the corresponding debt, seemed to affect the monetary authorities and international organizations. Alan Greenspan believed that the deficit was not worrying, nor the debt either.[24] The IMF remained undaunted. Its semi-annual report of April 2007 (World Economic Outlook) noted that risks to the global economy had been reduced to a very low level and there was no reason to worry too much.

What happened in 2007 in the USA was that the debt accumulated over 30 years, USD 50 trillion (in 1964, it was a billion) and which had generated enormous economic activity in its wake and had also changed the production system by developing an all-powerful financial industry, could not be repaid—the dream of artificial wealth built on debt and credit, which, as Richard Duncan says, had replaced real money, had vanished.[25] That credit could no longer be extended. This was the final cause of the Great Crisis.

The crisis started from subprime mortgages. However, the insidious growth of the financial system in the 1980s and 1990s meant that the earthquake with its epicentre on Wall Street was rapidly spreading through the economies of developed countries. European countries were especially hard-hit, leading to a painful ordeal of financial crisis, economic crisis, sovereign debt crisis, social crisis and political crisis.

However, the responsibility for the catastrophe remained, and remains, intact, opaque and inviolate, with the ability to become a real power that challenges democratic institutions: financial power, or what is euphemistically called 'the markets'. The crisis is itself a financial crisis, with a public dimension and a private one—that is its true nature. If we do not clearly understand this, we will not be able to overcome it.

2

The Crash

The Financial Crisis (2007–2008)

Nobody expected it, but the conditions for an epic crisis which had been building up, as we have seen, over three decades, eventually emerged in the form of financial shockwaves. In the summer of 2007, the default rate of subprime loans exceeded 15%, compared with the 5% average of mortgages in general. It was estimated that between two and three million American borrowers lost their homes. Wynne Godley of the Levy Institute declared, 'The debt of American households is unsustainable'.[1]

According to François Morin, this was the starting-point of the first seizing up of liquidity.[2] Securities linked to high-risk mortgages—by definition, long-term—began to lose liquidity (and value) in ever-increasing steps, putting serious strains on hedge funds, whose short-term creditors were pressing them to repay loans.

In June 2007, the investment bank Bear Stearns had announced the death of two of its hedge funds, which had invested in subprime mortgages (Ramport and HGSF). Lenders demanded the immediate repayment of their loans. It was the beginning of a series of breakdowns in the granting of low-quality mortgages. The United States economy moved into recession in late 2007, and unemployment began to rise.

In Europe, the financial environment was moving in a similar direction. On 13 September 2007 it was revealed that the hitherto reliable Newcastle bank, Northern Rock, had requested the help of the Bank of England, which was immediately granted. Northern Rock followed a business model similar to the American one, obtaining a large proportion of its funding from the markets (70%), subsequently investing this in toxic securities. The deposits of individuals represented only 30% of funding, hence the drop in finance from the non-banking sector would have a decisive effect on it.

In October, the Swiss bank UBS was the one to announce huge losses, for reasons similar to those of Northern Rock. Next, the loss of 3,100 million at Citigroup was uncovered, in addition to the liquidity crisis in the banks of Iceland (Landsbanki, Kaupthing and Glitnir) now nationalized, as well as the Irish crisis. On 7 February 2008 Northern Rock would also be nationalized. Private debt became national debt. This is the rescue model that would be followed during the Great Financial Crisis, changing its nature as snakes shed their skin: economic crisis, sovereign debt crisis, and in the background to all these crises, a social crisis.

A chain reaction in terms of a crisis of confidence that was bound to end very badly had been set off in the interbank market. Demand for business sank and risk aversion grew. Liquidity dried up and the crisis had begun and was now in full flow.

Lehman Brothers

In March 2008, international banking announced asset losses to the tune of USD 260 billion. The powerful investment banks, particularly those not linked to commercial banks, were about to go through an ordeal. The 'Big Five'—Lehman Brothers, Merrill Lynch, Morgan Stanley, Goldman Sachs and Bear Stearns, had a serious problem. Not being ordinary commercial banks, they could not benefit from the protection of the Federal Reserve as lender of last resort. Their creditors had no deposit insurance. As Roubini points out, being less regulated, they tended to be more highly leveraged and were therefore more dependent upon short-term funding to maintain immediate liquidity.

Throughout 2008, the big five were to disappear. The first was Bear Stearns. Liquid assets took flight and everything else was sold at a knock-down price to J.P. Morgan, with the invaluable help of the Federal Reserve which, for the first time since 1929, illegally accepted a rescue to which only commercial deposit banks had a right.

Creditors of Bear Stearns were fully compensated. It was understood that the action was absolutely vital to avoid contaminating other financial players who had acquired risky assets, i.e., to avoid panic. The same thing happened with Goldman Sachs and Morgan Stanley. Merrill Lynch, the other big one, was acquired for USD 50 billion by Bank of America. Almost nobody noticed. Similarly, the government protected the creditors of Fannie Mae and Freddie Mac, nationalizing these companies on 7 September. It made sense. They were the two major companies designed to guarantee home loans to individuals, amounting to six trillion dollars, including of course a considerable quantity of junk loans.

However, this behaviour was not repeated with Lehman Brothers. Lehman lenders lost confidence and demanded adjustments and new guarantees that Lehman could not give.

This time, the Bush administration said no. The government and Wall Street would have nothing to do with buying Lehman Brothers. So on 15 September, the Treasury secretary Henry J. Paulson allowed Lehman Brothers to fail, and it declared itself bankrupt and filed for Chapter 11 bankruptcy—the biggest in American history. Lehman Brothers acted like a tsunami of USD 700 billion. On 17 September, AIG, the number one American insurer, was swamped by that wave. Here, a twist of fate decided that AIG was too big to fail. Paulson, with some reluctance, pumped USD 85 billion into AIG. It would finally reach USD 182 billion, all guaranteed by the American taxpayer, who subsequently owned AIG. It was a rescue, not so much for AIG but for the banks that had purchased insurance from that company, and who could have been penalized. AIG had in their accounts credit default insurance to the tune of USD 440 billion.

Contagion

These events resulted in a collapse of confidence in the financial system through a parallel economic and psychological process, disproportionate to the entity of Lehman Brothers and other companies, but nonetheless real. Due to the paralysis in credit markets, the Federal government had to confront all kinds of excessive liquidity and solvency problems in the US financial markets. The Federal Reserve and the government decided to extend the underwriting and protection of debt from banks and other financial institutions to hitherto unknown lengths; it also helped with loans to non-financial companies. It was all worth it to placate jittery public opinion.

That black September in America (which ended with the bankruptcy of the Washington Mutual and Wachovia banks) was duplicated in Europe: public money for Glitnir Bank in Iceland; for Hypo Real Estate Group in Germany and the Franco-Belgian financial group Dexia. Nationalization for the Fortis Group, in the Netherlands and Belgium; for Royal Bank of Scotland, Bradford and Bingley, HBOS and Lloyds TSB, in Great Britain; and for Bank Roskilde, in Denmark. On Tuesday 30 September, Ireland, faced with the inability of its banks to help the international capital markets and to avoid financial collapse, decided unilaterally to guarantee the deposits of all large entities.

It was quite natural that this contagion should occur, since the toxic disease of American real estate loans, as well as non-real estate loans, had been sold on to financial markets and European banks in the preceding decades. The transmission of instability had been facilitated by the liberalization and deregulation of capital movements, enacted via legislation in the 1990s. The likelihood of contamination had been set in motion.

The crisis spread to emerging economies, which also suffered from the drying up of market liquidity. As Jacques Adda explained, the shock wave created by the dislocation of the American financial system and the international diffusion of the banking crisis dramatically worsened the recession in which the world economy found itself.[3]

Towards the end of 2008, the icing on the cake of the paralysis in credit was the consequence of losses in financial wealth. Loss of consumer confidence caused the collapse of production. All of this would create a vicious circle of business closures and unemployment. In one year (2007–2008), the mortgage crisis had become a systemic crisis.

The abyss

Given the inability of financial markets to get out of the crisis by themselves, intervention by government bodies took place, albeit unevenly and not sufficiently coordinated.

The International Monetary Fund warned on 28 July of the impact of the financial crisis on the real economy. The losses incurred to date by the credit market crisis exceeded EUR 250 billion. Eurozone GDP had fallen by 0.2% in the second quarter of 2008 (annualized quarterly rate). This was the first negative figure for the whole area since the crisis of 1992–1993, and the first decline in GDP since the launch of the Euro. Until then, the Eurozone had never found itself on the brink of recession. Many European economies such as Italy, Ireland, Denmark and the UK were heading in that direction. Germany and France had already registered negative growth in the second quarter.

For starters, massive injections of liquidity. The ECB injected EUR 30 billion into the financial markets, all on the one day, 15 September, and a total of EUR 70 billion on the next; the Bank of England did the same: GDP 50 billion on 15 September, and GDP 20 billion the next day. The two central banks mentioned, along with the Federal Reserve, the Bank of Japan, Bank of Canada and the Swiss National Bank coordinated a series of measures to alleviate the high pressures on the markets in short-term dollar supply to address the shortage of dollar funding worldwide. They agreed to put up to USD 180 billion of this key currency into the system.

As for the ECB, it announced that it would continue providing relief for as long as necessary, to a European banking system devoid of liquidity, already paralyzed by the unwillingness of financial institutions to lend to each other on the interbank market and knowing that the US banking crisis had already irreversibly infected the European banks. However, the ECB—supposedly to prevent high inflation—kept interest rates high, thus contributing to the rise in value of the Euribor and the fall in European stock markets.

For its part, on Monday 29 September the Federal Reserve pumped USD 630 billion into the financial system—an unprecedented move aimed at central banks around the world, among which the first recipient was the ECB, at a critical time for European banks. It received USD 120 billion, followed by the Bank of Japan (USD 60 billion) and the Bank of England (USD 40 billion).

The period of time from 15 September (with the announcement of the bankruptcy of Lehman Brothers) until 19 October 2008 (the day of the meeting of the European Council) is probably the most turbulent and dramatic in recent Western economic history, and it has two important dates: 6 October, when the US House of Representatives (after an initial rejection), approved the bailout (the Paulson Plan, drawn up by the Bush Administration), following its approval in the Senate; and 12 October, when the Eurogroup agreed concerted action to rescue the European financial system.

The Paulson Plan meant a rescue operation amounting to USD 700 billion to buy toxic loans from banks at the taxpayer's expense. That was the initial idea. Then, it shifted towards bank recapitalization, with the possibility of the Treasury Department acquiring the capital of the entities that participated in the plan, in a kind of partial nationalization.

On that same 6 October, the FED expanded its supply of liquidity by paying interest on the bank reserves that banks are required to deposit with the central bank. The FED also announced its intention to purchase short-term corporate debt through the Commercial Paper Funding Facility. The monetary authority would seek to provide liquidity through purchases, by intervening directly in the markets for three-month debt issued by companies to meet their current funding needs.

Immediately after the decision of the FED, the USA, the Eurozone and some other countries made a surprise half-point interest rate reduction (8 October).

Sarkozy's initiative, in his capacity as head of state of the country holding the rotating presidency of the European Union in the second half of 2008, was to hold an emergency meeting of the Eurozone leaders on Sunday 12 October in Paris. The extraordinary summit was to define 'a joint action plan to address the current financial crisis'.

At the Paris summit, Eurozone leaders agreed a rescue plan to unblock the financial system, 'ensure the liquidity of financial institutions' and 'provide additional capital resources to ensure proper functioning of the economy'. It was all about providing liquidity to the system, ensuring the adequate functioning of the interbank market, at that point still crippled by a lack of trust between institutions; increasing the resources of the banks by providing solvency through direct state involvement, and recapitalizing troubled banks with public funds.

In short, the measures consisted of the member states providing guarantees for any new debt until the end of 2009, and buying up the capital of banks, if necessary. In total, the Union guaranteed EUR 1 trillion, 700 billion of which EUR 840 billion came from Germany and France. It was not an action by the Union as such, but by the member states. From that moment, each country launched major programmes that tripled the Paulson bailout plan.

The European Council on 15 and 16 October 2008 was, in a way, the culmination of that frantic month when the financial world peered into the abyss. The Council, in its conclusions, validated the Eurogroup agreement and aimed even higher with a categorical and grandiloquent phrase: 'The European Union must act in relevant forums in favour of a "real and comprehensive" reform of the international financial system'. Six years later, we are still waiting for that to come true.

The same could be said of the outcomes of the meeting held on 18 October in Washington. There, President Bush reaffirmed with Sarkozy and Barroso their joint intention to recapitalize banks and financial institutions with unlimited liquidity, to give guarantees on deposits, to facilitate credit to businesses, to repurchase the toxic US property bonds and securities, and to get together with the G-20 to agree upon more regulation of the ratings agencies, hedge funds and tax havens. These principles would provide the basis for the reforms endorsed by the Finance Ministers of the EU on 10 November. On 15 November, the G-20 summit took place in Washington, with an American president more 'lame duck' than ever. The meeting reiterated the consensus on the causes of the crisis, apportioning blame between market agents and regulators. The highlight of the summit and the most positive aspect—which Spain attended for the first time ever—were these three objectives: the use of fiscal measures to stimulate domestic demand to rapid effect, the strengthening of financial regulation, and the rejection of protectionism.

Any specific reform was put off until the April 2009 summit in London. On the horizon the recession could already be seen, and the financial system appeared, even more clearly, not fit for purpose.

Keynesian Policies to Beat the Crisis (2009)

In the third quarter of 2008, for the first time in its short history, the Eurozone went into recession. However, it seemed that there was no recession, in view of surveys which were then published by the major regional and international financial institutions, which were constantly changing.

The ECB predicted in September 2008 that the Eurozone GDP would grow 1.2% in 2009. In December, the ECB reversed its earlier estimate and warned that the economy would shrink by 1%. In January 2009, finally, the Commission predicted a decline of 1.8% of GDP in the European Union for 2009.[4]

The ferocity of the economic downturn in Europe was completely unexpected, and those who should have been more rigorous in their assessments were found wanting. That may be why the economic policies adopted by the West in the worst year of the crisis, 2009, continued to insist upon solving the plight of the financial system, rather than the real economy. The latter suffered the sudden unavailability of short-term credit, which is essential for the smooth functioning of small and medium enterprises.

The anti-crisis policies were typically dual in nature: monetary, applied by central banks; and fiscal, led by governments. Both appeared much focused, again, on the emergency and panic in the financial world. We will look separately at them by analyzing the different ways in which they were addressed by the United States and the European Union. The first had a broader approach, to provide credit directly to commercial and industrial companies, whilst the EU put its focus on saving the banks—a huge strategic difference that would also lead to very different results, to the detriment of those who chose the worse option: Europe.

Monetary policy

According to many economists, the president of the Federal Reserve, Bernanke, revolutionized monetary policy through a series of interventions in the financial system that few understand even today. Bernanke went through a whole range of measures, from the conventional—cutting the interest rate to zero, for example—to those that were unprecedented, leading to a 'massive expansion in the power of the Federal Reserve on the economy'.[5]

The Federal Reserve, unlike the ECB, certainly showed remarkable activism in support of the American financial system, rescuing both institutions without liquidity and those lacking solvency, even though this meant taking on significant risks. The Federal Reserve went to the limits of its own legal status after taking on a feature of fiscal policy proper to government—spending money—exchanging government bonds for toxic assets and even acquiring toxic assets and including them in its balance sheet. It was the unorthodox way the Federal Reserve, sometimes in partnership with other central banks, sought to prevent the financial crisis from spinning out of control.

One of the objectives—not the only one, as in the EU—was to provide liquidity to the stressed and paralysed banks, commercial as well as investment, hence the invention of dozens of financial instruments, loan facilitators, too numerous to list here. There was only one limit: the bank applying for fresh money had to provide assets of sufficient quality as guarantees. The opening up of the FED was well-defined in terms of corporate bonds, commercial loans secured by real estate and general short-term commercial debt.

Bernanke's bold monetary policy—which only in a few aspects continued that of Greenspan—pursued a crucial purpose: to open up credit to the real economy, something which failed in its entirety.

From late 2008, the Federal Reserve—and other central banks—flooded financial markets with billions of dollars, to enable the recovery of fluidity in the markets in the short term or very short term; such was the drought in virtually all banks and financial institutions. A Federal Reserve traditionally considered as a lender of last resort, was rightly dubbed by Roubini 'lender of first, last and only resort'.[6] Joseph Stiglitz described it differently: 'The Federal Reserve had gone from the banker of bankers to be the banker of the nation.'[7]

Perhaps the most powerful tool used by Bernanke to address the crisis in the financial system has been a programme called Quantitative Easing (QE), which Paul Krugman re-named 'Qualitative Easing', launched in late 2008. With QE, the intervention of the central bank has a broader perspective with operations on the open market. Its purpose was to open up opportunities for long-term credit to companies that had to pay a very high interest rate, unlike the privilege of near-zero interest in funding provided by the FED to financial institutions.

Banks had—and have—a secure business. They take money out of central banks essentially interest-free and invest it in Treasury bills at 3–4%, at no risk. With Quantitative Easing (QE1 in 2009 and QE2 in 2010) Bernanke acted as follows: government long-term debt was bought, i.e., Treasury bonds, and massive amounts of liquidity were simultaneously injected into the market because the FED was paying for the bonds simply by printing money and not by selling what it had on its balance sheet, as it did before. This was the monetization of debt. Since the bonds have been purchased from banks, they have cash income. The liquidity allows banks to create credit. It decreases the easy appetite of banks for Treasury Bills and facilitates credit to the business sector.

This policy was announced on 25 November 2008, at the same time as the bulk purchase by the FED of other assets and mortgages; i.e., those toxic securities that were present at the outbreak of the crisis. In the month of March 2009 alone, the FED announced an expansion of asset purchases of up to USD 1 trillion, 750 billion. Among them, a trillion dollars was for mortgages and USD 300 billion for long term T-Bills. It was all part of quantitative easing. These interventions meant a change in the nature of the central bank: they created an artificial market for unwanted assets.

The balance sheet of the FED was transformed. From USD 900 billion in assets in 2007, almost exclusively composed of US government debt, in the summer of 2009 the balance sheet of the FED jumped to nearly 2.4 trillion. It was now financing most mortgages. Some of these assets were secure (e.g., the debt of Fannie Mae and Freddie Mac), but others were unsafe, such as derivatives of real estate mortgages, credit card debt and loans for purchase of cars all of which were potentially toxic.[8] There was something that the FED did not undertake in its unconventional monetary policy: the purchase of damaged shares on the stock market, something which was done on a massive scale by the authorities in Hong Kong in 1998, and the Bank of Japan in 2002, and, on a smaller scale and more selectively, in 2009.

Bernanke's message was clear: the FED will do everything necessary to prevent the financial crisis from spinning out of control. Draghi would say the same much later (in summer 2012). However, Bernanke practised what he preached, braving what has been called 'moral hazard', i.e., the conviction of the markets that if things go wrong, they will be bailed out by the state, contradicting what he told Frank Borman, the head of Eastern Airlines in the 1980s: 'Capitalism without bankruptcy is like Christianity without hell'.[9] The US monetary policy left too many banks unpunished, and they were therefore unfairly saved by the taxpayer.

As stated by Duncan, once the FED lowered the interest rate to almost zero, QE was the only policy left to stimulate the economy. QE1 was intended to allow the financial sector to reduce its indebtedness (leverage). As a result, the debt in this sector of the economy—not others—fell by 15% (2.5 billion) between November 2008 and March 2010. The sector also saw its assets revalued due to increased demand. It was good for the liquidity of the stock market, the so-called 'market sentiment'. Moreover, QE was used to wipe clean part of the US budget deficit, which is no longer covered by the current account deficit that America had enjoyed thanks to their trade relations with the rest of the world before the crisis.

And now we move on to the 'conventional' monetary policy. The crisis should have had an unavoidable response in terms of the setting of interest rates. Central banks should have lowered them. That is what they did in 2008 and 2009, not always with results that were encouraging for stimulating consumption or investment. The FED did so with conviction and forcefulness. It unceremoniously cut borrowing costs from 5.25% to 1% in a few months, when the crisis first began to become apparent. In December 2008 it was effectively at 1%, and then declined further to close to 0%.

In this and other aspects of monetary policy, the decisions of the Federal Reserve were different from those adopted by the European Central Bank, whose reluctance to lower the interest rate has already been mentioned. In November

2008 it was still at 3.25%. It was not until April 2009 that the ECB lowered rates to 1.25%. The FED would set the rate in May at between 0 and 0.25%, which encouraged Trichet in turn to reduce it to 1%, which would be maintained throughout 2009. The ECB was always one step behind the Federal Reserve in taking these actions.

It is necessary to bear in mind the difference in legal status between the FED and the ECB. The FED was founded in 1913 to ensure the stability of financial markets. The BCE, on the other hand, can only lend to banks. Treaties prevent it from buying bonds from states via the direct issuance of debt. It must resort—and with great care—to the secondary market, if it wants to take debt from the market.

The ECB, an independent body, has by statute a single objective: price stability. This mandate was interpreted strictly until the crisis forced the ECB to the edge of that limit. And there it remained. It has never seemed to occur to the ECB that it ought to worry about the dire situation in the real economy in some European countries.

The ECB found it difficult to make its policy regarding collaterals more flexible, i.e., the guarantees required by the central bank for banks seeking liquidity. In February 2009, the ECB, incomprehensibly, adopted an ultraconservative policy on the valuation of assets accepted as collateral, lowering it by about 50%. This strategy was described as 'lazy' by the *Financial Times*, in view of the deflationary risks in the countries of the region.[11]

In May 2009, Trichet used his appearance at the meeting of the ECB in which the interest rate was lowered to 1%, to announce some measures wrested from Germany: the purchase of assets to the value of EUR 60 billion until June 30, 2010, and the extension to 12 months (from six) of the loan period to banks. The aim was to turn on the credit tap, which was still turned off despite massive injections of liquidity and billions in aid to the financial sector. The auction had an effect on the interbank market, to the point of opening up credit lines and causing the lowering of the Euribor.

Monetary policy played an important role in the American and European policy of containment of the financial crisis, or rather, salvation of the actors in the financial system. However, in September 2008 Bernanke had asked Congress for help to 'stabilize the situation' because, despite the efforts of the Federal Reserve, the Treasury and other agencies, global markets remained 'under extraordinary pressure' with huge risk, Bernanke added, 'to our financial markets'.[12] Bernanke was asking for 'urgent congressional action', or what is essentially the same thing, admitting the limits of monetary policy. He requested, ultimately, a rescue that only the executive and the legislature could decide. What the FED chairman was referring to was fiscal policy. That policy had to be set in motion to save the financial system.

Fiscal policy

In this area, differences also surfaced between the USA and Europe when it came to stemming the haemorrhaging in the financial system caused by the traumatic injury it had suffered through lack of foresight.

Both in the US and Europe, fiscal policy came slowly, in spite of there being enough signs to see that the perfect storm had been inevitable since 2007. We had to wait for an earthquake to occur with Lehman Brothers for there to be any political movement. And through it all, the fiscal policy did not materialize until late 2008 or early 2009. Who knows if perhaps greater diligence could have prevented such a disaster.

In the USA, the electoral calendar had a determining influence. The political situation did not become favourable to intervention until a new president, charismatic and elected by a landslide, succeeded Bush, by now worn down by the unpopular Iraq war and the noise and fury of the financial crisis. The most important of the measures of the Obama Administration, the American Recovery and Reinvestment Act (ARRA) of 2009, completely overshadowed the 2008 Paulson Plan, the Troubled Asset Relief Programme (TARF). This, as we saw, began as a means to buy toxic assets from banks, and 10 days after its approval by Congress, gave way to recapitalization, by of course over-valuing heavily damaged shares in order to deliberately keep the government in a minority and thus unable to participate in the management of the affected entities.

What happened after the Paulson Plan was that banks did not resume lending activity. The economy continued to decline, including employment and consumption, and questionable loans multiplied in the assets of the banks, whose shares fell further between late October 2008 and late February 2009. The two largest American banks, Citigroup and Bank of America, remained afloat thanks to the Bush government providing a state guarantee on most of their assets, the largest rescue operation in financial history. The case of Citigroup (which had lost 80% of its value since June 2007) is quoted as an example by Jacques Adda of the republican model. No change was ever demanded in terms of the management or board of the team of people who had led the bank to this precipice.[13]

The model imposed by the new Obama administration would submit the banks to more transparency and stricter rules, in terms of equity. Above all, Obama launched a stimulus programme at a cost of USD 789 billion (EUR 615 billion). The President was going to handle the most important public investment since the days of the New Deal of President Franklin D. Roosevelt.

In the course of this difficult negotiation, the Democrats had to abandon about USD 30 billion of social spending in the spirit of compromise. The result was a plan that the left thought insufficient, and the right considered an irresponsible waste of money; a plan backed by 59% of the population (according to a Gallup poll for USA Today).

The ARRA covered a wide range of activities, expenditure on infrastructure and energy projects (USD 140 billion) and tax credits (USD 237 billion) for first-time home buyers and automobiles, as well as benefits for the unemployed, the elderly and other vulnerable sectors.

These measures did not significantly alter the spending decisions of individuals. Tax cuts were transformed into private savings and less private debt, but at the same time, more national debt. The debt just switched places. To this is added the problem that fiscal policy takes longer to produce effects than monetary policy.

In the Eurozone, monetary policy against the crisis could only be European. However, with fiscal policy the opposite occurred, with a management Adda described as 'anarchic'. European banks were exposed to a triple crisis, in chronological order: the American subprime mortgages, the European housing bubble (United Kingdom, Ireland and Spain) and sovereign debt, which was still to come.[14] According to the OECD (2009 estimates), the potential losses for European banks in 2007–2009 amounted to 1.6 trillion dollars (USD 600 billion only for the British banks) with a trillion's worth of losses for American banks (without taking into account the non-banking financial institutions).

The banking crisis was managed from a national viewpoint in its various dimensions: deposit protection (the Commission had to update a directive in March 2009, after almost all countries had placed the protection limit at the EUR 100,000 mark); the injection of public capital (UK, Ireland, Holland, France, Belgium, Germany); the purchase of toxic assets (Belgium, Netherlands, Germany); and the guarantee of banking assets (Ireland, UK, France, Belgium, Spain). In all these cases there were no European standards; they were developed later. This was yet more proof of the weakness of the regulation of the financial community, which explained why before the crisis in Greece hit, the banking crisis had still not been resolved in the European Union.

The only measure of fiscal policy stimulus that the Union, as such, launched to combat the financial crisis was the European Economic Recovery Plan (EERP), that the Commission presented on 26 November 2008 and which the European Council adopted at its meeting on 11 and 12 December, a budgetary push of about EUR 200 billion (1.5% of EU GDP at the time). This effort was divided among the Member States (1.2% of European GDP, approximately) and the EU itself, which contributed the remaining 0.3% to EUR 30 billion from the EU budget and EIB.

This meeting of the European Council signalled the start of the debate, which would continue throughout 2009, consisting of two options to deepen the stimulus measures knowing that they almost certainly meant a growing deficit, or to start making adjustments in view of the fear of uncontrolled debt. Two figures embodied these positions: the newly elected Barack Obama and Angela Merkel, the chancellor of a coalition government of the right and the left.

Obama, with an unemployment figure of 6.7%, was flying the flag for the ARRA, a more aggressive policy of spending, although still not enough for some economists who thought that a stimulus plan close to 4% of GDP of the United States was necessary to really help the economy and not just the financial sector.

Germany started the year 2009 by adopting a second anti-crisis plan totalling EUR 50 billion, which added to the EUR 35 billion approved two months previously.[15]

The German plan is an example of the ones being implemented by each of the EU countries, which, in March 2009 were valued at EUR 400 billion by the European Commission. These plans, coupled with increased public spending to pay unemployment benefits, were equivalent to 3.3% of EU GDP.

That same month, Geithner, US Treasury Secretary, announced a new plan to mobilize up to a trillion dollars with help from the private sector, aimed at cleaning up the contaminated banks' balance sheets, without taking direct control of them.

In contrast to Geithner, throughout 2009 Angela Merkel continued to lay increasing emphasis on warning of the overwhelming increase in the deficit and the corresponding debt. Thus, in April, Merkel stated that Germany could not afford to continue encouraging domestic consumption. For the German chancellor, it was an economy with too much debt, with a population in decline, unwilling to promote domestic demand at the expense of export strength. The German strategy was to get through the crisis trying not to lose too much industrial capacity in order to be well prepared when the recovery eventually arrived. It was not only the chancellor warning about this. This warning was also given by Germany's social-democratic finance minister in the coalition government, Steinbrück, linking the increase in debt to inflation.

Part of Merkel's strategy was her criticism of the management of the crisis by the central banks, especially the entry into unknown territory which involved the implementation of the printing of money.[16]

The German influence was evident in the Ecofin. Finance ministers from the EU were increasingly concerned about the budgetary impact of fiscal stimuli. In a report on the implementation of the EERP, the Ecofin (8 June) estimated that the stimulus measures would amount to 5% of EU GDP, and that this constituted a limit that should not be exceeded. And they said this despite the economic disaster in terms of unemployment and output (e.g., in April 2009, the industrial collapse of the Eurozone had reached 21.6% in a year, an all-time record).

The German attitude had a lot to do with the general elections that the Christian Democrats would win and the Social Democrats would lose. Merkel called on the G-8 (on 8 and 9 June) for a containment of public spending, compatible with a tax-reduction policy.

For now, the official European position was that the stimulus should be maintained until the crisis ended. That was also the position of the IMF, convinced that the global economy would emerge from the crisis in late 2009. The then managing director Strauss-Kahn explained this emphatically in the autumn meeting in Istanbul. The objective: no increase in unemployment.

That was also the position of the G-20 meeting in September: the group saw the need to extend economic stimulus plans until 2010, to avoid a sluggish recovery. The parallel meeting of the Eurogroup went further, surprisingly. It was suggested that measures to increase economic momentum should not be withdrawn until 2011, given the fragility of the situation.

This posture meshed with that of the European Commission, favouring the maintenance of the policy of stimulus until the much hoped-for end of the crisis should arrive.

A political event changed the situation and the attitude of the EU to this dilemma of fiscal stimuli or reduction in spending. In the German elections of October Angela Merkel won and formed a government with the Liberals. The discourse hardened, except for one small detail: the tax cuts remained, amounting to EUR 24 billion, which would come to an end in 2013.

Merkel had admitted that the only way to meet the challenge of budgetary consolidation was by encouraging growth.[17] We would never hear her say that again. The Bundesbank did not waste a minute in urging the new government to reduce the public deficit. Alex Weber, its president, stated in a speech in Berlin (29 October): 'The financial policy in Germany and the rest of the Eurozone should be looking for an exit strategy from the expansionary stimulus measures'.

There is no doubt that the elections also launched an austerity message, which was picked up on by central banks, by definition anti-inflationary, at their meeting in November at the headquarters of the Bank for International Settlements (Basel). Trichet ruled that, once public intervention had prevented 'an extremely threatening depression', it was time to decide 'the right time' to begin 'a gradual withdrawal' of crisis measures.

The contrast with the United States was extreme. In early December, Obama announced new economic stimulus measures with investments in infrastructure at a speech delivered at the Brookings Institute in Washington. Days later, the US Congress House of Representatives, meeting a year and three months after the fall of Lehman Brothers, took the first legislative step to approve financial sector reform aimed at tightening control over it.

The London and Pittsburgh G-20 meetings

The obsession of governments with bailing out the banks, and the short-term nature of any decision adopted in a state of shock, was naturally transmitted to the 'G' groups which met during the critical year of 2009. These meetings gave birth to a greatly strengthened G-20, in principle, as the embryonic beginning of a kind of global government. After the dramatic 2008 meeting in Washington, there were two G-20 summits in 2009: one in London (April) and one in Pittsburgh (October).

The G-20 in London had as its official targets stability, economic growth and global employment, the guarantee of a coordinated fiscal stimulus, a jumpstart for trade and a rejection of protectionism. However, the bulk of the decisions of the G-20 that were assessed as positive were in relation to the strengthening of financial regulation and supervision on an international level.[18]

As for the Pittsburgh Summit, the final declaration contained a policy statement that was gone with the wind in a few months: 'We will avoid any premature withdrawal of stimulus' and, when necessary, it will be done in a 'cooperative and coordinated' manner.

Policies on the financial system had been skewed from the start. Political authorities had acted with absolute determination, burning bridges when it was a question of saving banks and salvaging such a financially- and banking-based economy. However, this decisiveness and willpower were conspicuous by their absence when change in their irresponsible behaviour was demanded from the banks, or when 'real, comprehensive reform of the financial system' is mentioned, as the European Council proclaimed in such an overstated way.

The Growth Crisis

In October 2009, the IMF noted that the losses of the banking sector in the world amounted to 3.6 trillion dollars. However, at that time, they had succeeded in stopping the crisis in the financial system. This was termed 'the great stabilization'. It was the natural consequence of ferocious rescue measures—tax and monetary—such as those just described, which were developed in 2008 and 2009. Efforts were concentrated on the financial system and trying to save it. No governments did the same, especially the European ones, with the real economy.

The real economy (production and employment) had reached rock-bottom. Family wealth had atrophied. According to World Bank estimates, the global economy had contracted by 2.1% in 2009, an unprecedented decline not seen since before 1945. In the OECD area, the economic contraction reached 4.7% from the first quarter of 2008 to the second quarter of 2009.[19] The fall in world trade was another sign of the severity of the crisis; according to the World Trade Organization (WTO), the global volume of trade in goods and services decreased by 12% in 2009.

Unemployment increased rapidly. Continuing on with the OECD data, the unemployment rate rose to 8.7% in early 2010. This meant 17 million more jobless than in 2008. In the USA alone, nine million jobs had been lost. More jobs were destroyed than were created, especially among young people: the employment rate among 15- and 24-year-olds dropped more than eight points. One young person in four was unemployed in France and Italy; more than two in five in Spain.

In late 2009, virtually all OECD countries were coming out of recession, but the recovery was too small to change the dreadful unemployment rate (Keely and Love).[20] Naturally, these overall figures vary significantly if we look at the data at country level and per sector. In Ireland and Spain, hard hit by the collapse of the construction sector, the effects triggered an ever-quicker weakening of the job market. In Ireland, the unemployment rate rose from 4.8% to 13.2%; in Spain, from 8.6% to 19.7% (!). By contrast, in Germany the employment rate remained stable, although it continued to decrease slightly, and in Japan the unemployment rate went up from 3.7% to 5.1%. While services did not lose much employment in proportional terms, the durable goods sector was clearly affected. For example, the automobile industry, by definition globalized, was damaged by the fall in international trade.

What is surprising, however, is the resilience of employment in the financial sector in comparative terms, despite its being the origin of the cause of the crisis. There is a good reason for this: the effort of the taxpayer was targeted at supporting financial agents, and not other sectors.

There were not many opportunities to broach the problems in the real economy, amongst other reasons because, when it seemed that the financial machinery had revived, another serious crisis loomed on the horizon necessitating an immediate reaction on the part of governments and the European Union. As well as the financial crisis and the politically-neglected economic crisis, there was a third one, which was the result of the enormous effort made by public finance to help private finance.

The European Sovereign Debt Crisis

In the US, the deficit incurred by the Federal Government to deal with the financial shock became a rising national debt of gargantuan proportions. In 2009, federal spending reached 25% of GDP (much lower than the percentages of the European welfare state). Federal tax revenues accounted for only 14.9% of GDP, the lowest rate since 1950. Spending soared with stimulus programmes and automatic stabilizers such as unemployment insurance. Tax revenues collapsed abruptly, both because of lower corporate profits, and because some tax cuts were part of the same stimulus programmes. This resulted in a budget deficit of around 10% of GDP, i.e., 1.4 trillion. An impossible amount to finance, because not enough money was coming from international investors.

Duncan believes that the deficit prevented the US from falling into depression in 2009. In this hypothetical case, rather than contracting by 3.5%, the economy would have shrunk by 15%; unemployment would have been at 20%, and would have been worse in the year 2010.[21]

Why could the US afford such a restorative deficit in the short term? How was it able to have such a big expansion of federal debt, USD 4.4 trillion between 2006 and 2010, and make up for the inability to pay off a large part of the private debt? The answer is because the FED monetized the debt, without creating inflation problems. With QE1 and QE2, the FED monetized much of the debt as described above. By creating money, by printing money. This, therefore, is why the official interest rate in the USA was so low.

What happened was that the maintenance of public spending was favourable to entrepreneurship and private consumption. It therefore favoured employment and additional demand.[22]

The European Union and its Member States, in particular those belonging to the Eurozone, were not able to behave like the US. National debt, produced in Europe for the same reasons as in the USA, could not be funded above a certain level. Treaties prohibit the monetization of debt, at least in a direct way, by the ECB. But this is the only central bank that makes monetary policy in the Eurozone. So the rapid increases in national debt in this area during the crisis gave rise to high or very high market interest rates, according to investor confidence that a given country would be able to repay loans made to it. Those investors who lost trust sold their sovereign bonds. Ed Yardeni in the 1980s called them 'bond vigilantes'.[23] Investors who had Greek bonds in 2009 got rid of them as a consequence of this mistrust, and this was the beginning of the sovereign debt crisis, which was not limited to Greece. Then came Portugal and Ireland. And then Spain and Italy came under attack from speculators—and they were all without central banks to defend them.

Underlying the sovereign debt crisis is the substitution of private debt by national debt, and the latter is in the end what has to be answered for. National debt took on the bail-out money for the banks and assumed the consequent deficits, and ended up being a substitute for the 'lender of last resort' that the European Central Bank is not.

This is the critical point of the crisis in Europe, which has not yet been resolved. In late 2009, the architectural issues of the Economic and Monetary Union surfaced like an erupting volcano. The Euro countries had—and have—to answer alone for their financial commitments, but they could not manage the sovereign debt that they issued, because monetary policy is made by the ECB, and that bank cannot be the lender of last resort. Hence the feeling of insecurity regarding their solvency that certain debts transmitted to international investors, to the point of causing the first crisis of the Euro, if it can be called that.

In late 2009, the share of national debt in the Eurozone had increased by almost 15 points of GDP, and the budget deficit had increased from 1% to 6% of GDP on average. The situation in Greece was dramatic, its national debt approaching 130% of GDP and its deficit 16%—by any reckoning an unsustainable situation that manifested itself when, because of a single event—a debt restructuring announced by the Emirate of Dubai—the interest rate of Greek debt soared. The outcome is known. In early 2010 a bail-out programme for Greece was approved and set in motion on 23 January, and increased several days later.

Given this serious situation, the EU had to react. And at that moment a qualitatively different phase of the crisis in Europe was set in motion. It is when the member states got together to arrange an 'exit strategy'. There were two things that needed to be done: a radical change in the architecture of economic governance in the Union, and the creation of an economic policy that Brussels would have to manage as a result of the new architecture. This would be the answer that the Union would develop, between 2010 and 2013, to unfreeze the economy of Europe, and Europe itself.

However, in defining and implementing this strategy, the Union became engaged in a real internal struggle. A challenge arose between two ideological positions: that of a balanced, inflexible budget built on drastically curtailing public expenditure; and the vision that, in contrast, considers financial intervention and public stimulus by the State and the Union essential for the economy. This debate, implicit or explicit in the complicated decision-making in the Union, is not over yet.

Part II

THE REACTION

3

The Failure of Austerity

The *Report on the State of the European Union* by the Fundación Alternativas (a Spanish Socialist Party think-tank) and the Friedrich Ebert Stiftung (Foundation), which I had the honour of directing, defined the state of the European Union in early 2013 as 'The failure of austerity'.[1]

This assertion was what best described the overall strategy: the one approved and launched, prematurely, by the EU, at the time when the collapse of Greece was spreading panic among Western governments.

Austerity developed between 2010 and 2013 to become the mother of all solutions to a crisis that began with the total failure of the financial system in terms of the management of the economy, followed by a sudden recession and the near collapse of employment, and ending with a takeover by the state, in the form of debt, of the cost of the wreckage. The simplistic and elementary reaction was austerity, as a way of making citizens (who were actually the victims of the crisis) pay and take the blame for others.

Schuld (Blame, Debt) (2010)

In the German and Dutch languages the word *Schuld* has an ambivalent meaning. Dictionaries define its first meaning as 'fault'. From there, other words are also offered as alternatives, demonstrating the amazing constructive ability of the German language. For example, *schuldige*: 'guilty' or, in criminal law, *Schuldprinzip* 'principle of guilt'.

Continuing on, the second meaning of *Schuld* is 'debt', i.e., the debtor position in an economic relationship; therefore, *Schulden* means 'to owe' or 'to be in debt', and *Schuldener* is 'debtor'.

These two meanings—'guilt' and 'debt'—are closely linked in the Calvinist tradition. Being in debt is like being guilty of that debt. Therefore, it is worthy of 'punishment'. 'Crime and Punishment' is used as an expression, *Schuld und Sühne*. The punishment is to pay the debt with interest.

The use of a single Germanic term for 'guilt' and 'debt' is not a fluke. Neither is the negative connotation implied by debt, which forms part of the theory of 'ordoliberalism' (the social market economy), a term used to describe the underlying ideology of liberal capitalism typical of the successful Federal Republic of Germany, born of World War II. The First World War was financed by debt, not taxes; the subsequent disastrous inflation experienced at that time explains the German aversion towards inflation.

The Freiburg School of economists, dominant in post-war Germany, was the creator of the 'social market economy' (*Sozialmarkwirtschaft*) concept which, together with certain principles related to the Welfare State, embraces the dogma of monetary control as an independent mechanism to ensure stability that will slow the growth of debt. This means combating inflation and recession, and defending a policy of order and stability (*Ordnungspolitik*).[2]

The concept is enshrined in the Basic Law of Bonn (1949). The main instrument for obtaining this result is the Bundesbank, an organization clearly independent of political authority. Commercial banking is another essential element spearheading sustainable financing of industry, which in the case of Germany has always been export oriented and has kept costs and wages low. Growth was determined by the external market, hence the need for monetary stability.

The ordoliberal principles were incorporated into the convergence criteria of the Maastricht Treaty, expressed in the Stability and Growth Pact. From this came the powerful European Central Bank, the spitting image of the Bundesbank, monopolistically focused on achieving price stability. This went along with the powerful competition policy, applied with an iron fist by the European Commission. In this framework, a reunified Germany was able to accept the disappearance of the Deutschmark and its replacement by the Euro.

The rest of the Eurozone countries had to make an effort to reduce the deficit to enter a club guaranteeing stability and, consequently, very low interest debt. Here you can see the root of the financial crisis, mainly caused by the housing bubble, which was fed by very cheap and unlimited money (debt), as we have seen.

The countries (Germany and others) that in this context were and are creditors are necessary collaborators in the financial crisis, to continue using that terminology. However, in the Calvinist culture that for Max Weber is the source of capitalism, savers—converted into creditors—are not sinners, are not guilty (*schuldig*). The guilty parties are the debtors (*Schuldner*). Hence, a 'golden rule' regarding balanced budgets or a constitutional brake on debt (*Schulden-bremser*) has to be introduced for all EU countries in order to tackle the crisis, as reflected in the standards of the Fiscal Compact.

If member states have borrowed and got into debt, the only possible policy is a strict diet of austerity in order to remedy the situation. If they do not, they have to suffer economic sanctions.[3] This is the policy that has either been applied or attempted in the EU in recent years. In all member states at once, with results that could not be clearer and which we shall soon examine.

However, what is this so-called 'austerity' as an economic policy that has dominated in Europe—not in America—and which supposedly offers a solution to the crisis? Mark Blyth gives a fairly acceptable definition: austerity is a form of voluntary deflation by which the economy adjusts by reducing wages, prices and government spending to restore competitiveness. It is assumed that this is achieved by cutting the state budget and, therefore, the deficit and debt. Proponents of austerity believe that 'market confidence'—a rather vague concept—is achieved, because this way, the government does not absorb capital through debt issuance (the 'crowding out' effect).[4] From this questionable point of view, if the State does not issue bonds, private investment is stimulated.

The other more logical reason to justify a policy of austerity is that it does not increase the burden of national debt. However, when the crisis hit there was already a considerable amount of outstanding government debt in Europe and the USA, because that is the policy that was followed in both areas in the past 30 years, as was stated in Chapter 1 of this book. Western governments had had recourse to the financial markets rather than taxing those on higher incomes, a decision which rebounded on society as a whole. This was something which had been fostered in the Eurozone since the launch of the euro and the corresponding sharp decline in interest rates. This acted as an impetus to borrow, not save, and there was a huge imbalance in external deficits: in 2007, before the crisis, Greece reached 15% of GDP; Spain, 10%, and Portugal, 9%. The exception was, again, Germany. The Social Democratic government of Gerhard Schröder and his policy of strong wage compression resulted in a surplus of 75% of GDP in 2007. The divergence between Germany and the so-called 'peripheral countries' contributed largely to deepening imbalances in the Eurozone. German exports were double those of France or Spain in relation to GDP.

Guillaume Duval notes that the Stability and Growth Pact did not anticipate control of private debt nor deficits or external surpluses.[5] The real estate bubble burst, and at the same time, national debt. The State—or rather, the taxpayers—absorbed the banking crisis, thus transmogrified into a sovereign debt crisis. To this growing amount of debt must be added the unbearable burden of interest, with a growing risk premium.

The reaction to this deterioration in public finances, after a year of Keynesianism, was austerity. This was particularly true of the Union because, apart from ideological factors—almost all governments were conservative governments—the Union did not have available the necessary fiscal policy instruments (there is no European Treasury), or monetary instruments (the ECB cannot accept any asset as a guarantee to grant credit). The USA, however, does possess these abilities.[6]

In any case, the pressure to turn towards a rigorous policy came from many angles in the more advanced countries. Neil Irwin signals 6 February 2010 as the start of such a policy, at the meeting of the Group of Seven finance ministers from the advanced countries, held in the remote Canadian Arctic. Nowhere more appropriate than that icy enclave to approve an abrupt shift from stimulus to austerity.

Irwin says: 'The leaders of the world economy together agreed that their greatest challenge had shifted. The economy seemed to be healing, and for them it was time to stop worrying about pushing growth. No more stimulus'.[7]

It is not easy to know on what the Group of Seven based such an optimistic diagnosis. GDP growth in the EU in the last quarter of 2009 was 1%, described as 'disappointing' by the monetary authorities, which contributed to unexpected stagnation in Germany. In reality, it had not improved at all after only just starting to move out of the worst recession in the history of the European Union. The Commission's 2010 report attested to this fact.

Of no use were emphatic statements that some prime ministers of leftwing governments—United Kingdom, Greece, Norway and Spain—gave, defying the financial markets, at a conference in London in February 2010. Gordon Brown said the following: 'the agenda of the European Union must be growth and employment this year'. JL Rodríguez Zapatero said: 'Do not fall into the trap of causing the paralysis of credit. We will cut the deficit when economic recovery is under way, but not at the expense of social cohesion', adding: 'these budget deficits are being incurred to save those who now demand budget cuts. What a paradox'.[8]

Nevertheless, the shift towards austerity was inexorable. During the Spanish presidency of the EU the Union would adopt the new 2020 Strategy for growth and jobs, and yet, its actions diverged from this direction towards stimulus. On 11 February 2010, the heads of state and government of the Union gave an unrealistic objective to an already shaky Greece, namely to achieve a deficit of 4% for the same year.

The Ecofin Council of 16 March was crucial. Finance ministers gave approval to a draconian austerity plan presented by George Papandreou, who placed the deficit target at 8.7%, more realistic than the preposterous 4%; but they could not agree on a programme of assistance due to the opposition of Germany. The most significant aspect was, however, the agreement to steadily remove the plans supporting the real economy that European countries had been following since 2008 in response to the crisis.

The chronological order of the exit strategy was significant: first, measures to support the real economy would be withdrawn; then the measures for the employment market; and finally—without any time limit—measures to support the financial sector, but only when credit was undoubtedly flowing back into businesses.

On 25 March, the Euro summit reaffirmed its commitment to the stability of the common currency. This meant in practice that member states would have to take on the burden of the financial crisis, aided by bilateral loans from the EU, which were looming on the horizon in the light of the Greek case.

In April, the markets demanded between 5% and 6% more interest on ten-year bonds from Greece than from Germany. Greece could not finance itself from the markets and the government had no choice but to seek assistance from the EU and the International Monetary Fund.

There was not at that time a formalized mechanism for such assistance. The success of the Euro from its inception—the creation of 16 million jobs, inflation below 2%, very low long-term interest rates, deficit of 0.6% of GDP in 2007—had made it unnecessary to think about that eventuality. So the EU had to improvise an ad hoc formula in the form of bilateral loans subject, of course, to strict conditions. That is, 'austerity'.

The European Union, frightened by its dependence on the markets and without an ECB to defend it, championed the argument for putting an end to stimulus packages. Jean-Claude Trichet, making a virtue of necessity, sided with Schauble, in the forefront of the conservative charge calling for immediate debt reduction. He thus took a different path from that of the United States, which was reluctant to change economic policy stimulus without evidence of a clear recovery in the public sector.

Seeing is believing: Neoclassical Europe, and Keynesian America. For once, the Union convinced Canada and the brand new pushover Prime Minister David Cameron, leaving the United States isolated. This was the sombre new slogan: 'expansionary fiscal consolidation', a contradiction in terms.

On 9 May, chaired by the finance vice-president of the Spanish government, the famous Ecofin meeting took place: this would lead to an abrupt change in economic policy starting with an initial cut of 1.5 points of GDP, without the compensation of an equivalent tax increase on higher incomes, which would have been fair from any point of view. From that point onwards, the finance ministers of the Euro constantly repeated the mantra of 'fiscal sustainability' and 'structural reforms'.

The June summit of the G-20 in Toronto consolidated the change in direction. Leaders prioritized the message of deficit reduction over that of growth. Despite acknowledging that the economic recovery was 'fragile' and 'uneven' and that unemployment remained at 'unstable levels in several countries', the G-20 decreed an end to fiscal stimulus to revive the economy. Cutting the deficit was imposed in the final communiqué. Emerging countries, with lower deficits, were opposed. However, President Obama himself sent a letter to the G-20 leaders pledging to reduce the deficit (then 11%) by half in 2013, and to 3% in 2015. He did not say how.

In short, the Eurogroup meeting in Luxembourg on 7 June approved an 'orientation for fiscal policies of the Member States in the Euro area', in which the basic content of the doctrine called 'austerity' was accurately set out. Ministers fully recognized the priority of immediately halting and reversing the increase in the debt ratio, which in 2009 had increased in the Eurozone to 78.7% of GDP. The Eurogroup agreed to continue with the 2010 fiscal targets as a way of 'giving credibility to consolidation strategies' and thus allowing 'a rapid return to levels consistent with true deficit reduction in the level of national debt in all member states, which is necessary to ensure that the economic recovery is not jeopardized'.

As we can see, there was blind faith in this policy: the restructuring of budget expenditure; debt reduction; return to growth. Recovery was expected in 2011, as occurred briefly, before receding in 2012. In hindsight today, four years later, the misinterpretation of pursuing an illusory growth is acknowledged by the IMF. The depressing effects of the cuts as the only anti-crisis measure were not sufficiently taken into account.

It is true that the fiscal adjustment recommended in the declaration proposed a mix of spending cuts and tax measures, and that each government should decide these for itself. But the Eurogroup document of 7 June—coinciding with the ECB—recommended spending cuts rather than tax increases and, as to these, said nothing about the fundamental ideological option of raising either direct (progressive) or indirect (regressive) taxes. It also recommended 'structural reforms', an expression which referred to the policy of making savings on pensions and other changes to facilitate dismissal in the employment market.

The European institutions and governments were fully aware that the withdrawal of fiscal stimuli would lead to contraction. The ECB estimated that in 2011, 2012 and 2013 European GDP would be cut by 0.5 points, but considered nonetheless that the fiscal adjustment represented long-term benefits. An opinion that was based on faith alone, because the bank itself admitted that the stimuli had propelled the European economy forward by 1.1% in 2009 and would do so by 0.8% in 2010.

In an outbreak of team spirit, everything was put down to the fact that the fiscal consolidation effort was the only thing which had given confidence to the financial markets (Ecofin of 30 September and 1 October 2010).

The belief in the miracle-working effects of austerity was shared outside the common currency area. In November 2010, David Cameron's government presented the biggest budget cuts in the UK, and pledged to divide the deficit by five in five years, to 2.1%. The plan included swinging cuts in social services, the loss of half a million civil service jobs, and raising the retirement age to 66 years of age.

To the radical stance of the Union in favour of budget restructuring now had to be added the International Monetary Fund. The IMF preferred to cut spending rather than raise taxes (IMF Report for Summit Autumn 2010).

In terms of the withdrawal of stimuli there was one exception: the banks. One of the post-crisis measures adopted by the European Commission was allowing aid of up to EUR 500,000 in the public sector (legally, sums below EUR 200,000 are not considered to count as state aid), and imposing no limit on aid to financial institutions in crisis. The former remained in force from 2009 to 2010; aid to banks continues to the present day, although conditions have hardened.

Indeed, the European Commission continues to allow national governments to give public support to financial institutions which, under normal conditions, is prohibited by the treaties. The rationale is that credit has not yet been normalized.

Almost the only argument that has yet been put forward—and continues to be put forward—in the core countries of the Euro is that the root of the Euro's difficulties does not lie in the problems of the financial system where the crisis originated, which have not yet been resolved—but in the explosion in interest in sovereign debt in peripheral countries (statements of Angela Merkel in Davos, January 2011). Paul Krugman notes in this regard that the Greek disaster turned into a new kind of crisis: not of failed banks, but of failed governments, uncompetitive and over-indebted, 'guilty' and unable to finance themselves on the markets. For this reason, all the official emphasis leaned towards the cleaning up of public accounts at any cost; except that for creditor countries, Eurobonds were not a solution.

The strategic shift towards cutting public spending highlighted the awareness of all the Euro countries of how the debt crisis threatened to engulf the Euro itself. A logical conclusion, because the economies in the Eurozone, and the financial sector in particular, are strongly interconnected and interdependent.

The initial question posed with Greece teetering on the brink—joined later by Portugal and Ireland—was to decide who had to bear the costs of the crisis.

In a supposed debt crisis—private debt first, and then public—those principally affected are creditors and debtors. However, as the crisis extends into a full monetary zone (the European), political considerations become involved making the full picture more complex. In this context, the choice of austerity is not neutral. It involves shifting the burden of proof of liability onto the debtor of last resort, which is the state; and, as such, the citizens. These people, as taxpayers, pay for the excesses of the financial system; and as recipients of social benefits, the needy in particular find their welfare rights damaged, as a result of the state dramatically reducing its expenses and not offsetting this via taxes on the better-off, all of which has occurred during this crisis.

In 'the crisis within the crisis' that developed in the Union to decide how it would respond to liquidity risks or insolvency in the Eurozone, there were four essential options: either the funding effort would be made by the creditors, European banks for the most part, giving up some of their debt; or it would be made by investors, refinancers of debt, thanks to a monetary policy of low interest rates enforced by a belligerent ECB; the third option was that it would be made by the debtor countries through more stringent austerity; or, ultimately, the Union (creditor countries) working in solidarity by issuing Eurobonds and reaching agreement on a more expansionary policy. Austerity won the day, because those with the weakest hand were obviously those with the highest debt burden, and were therefore the most dependent. What still divides the Eurozone was clearly demonstrated.

All this turmoil started to be experienced in Europe as the spectre of sovereign default appeared. The plight of some debtor countries, to varying degrees, was what made it politically possible for the creditor countries to impose uncompromising austerity, without any concessions to stimulus measures.

The year 2010 was the year in which the concept of the austerity policy was established under the conditions listed above, and in which it achieved hegemony over stimulus. However, economic and legal instruments were needed to impose it on theoretically sovereign countries, disinclined to support supranational austerity dominated by the most economically powerful countries. 2011 was the year that culminated in decisions that have facilitated the implementation of difficult and, in my opinion, unbalanced budgetary constraints.

The Vehicles of Austerity (2011)

For the second time in community history, the Stability and Growth Pact (SGP) was seriously applied. The first was before the launch of the Euro, because countries aspiring to join the system had to meet the Maastricht criteria, in particular the limit of 3% of GDP deficit and limiting national debt to 60% of GDP.

After this, it turned a blind eye since some of the non-compliant countries—Germany and France in 2003—were too powerful to sanction. From 2010, with the adoption of a recognized fiscal rigour, the SGP was revived. The previous year (2009) overall Eurozone deficit had deteriorated from 4.3% to 6.3% of GDP, as a natural consequence of the triggering of automatic stabilizers in each country (mainly unemployment payments, as would be expected in social democracies). This led to the opening of excessive deficit procedures in most member states and recommendations aimed at ending that situation as soon as possible. It meant that in 2011 'fiscal consolidation' had to begin decisively, i.e., the path towards getting the deficit below 3%. The Eurogroup believed that recovery would begin in 2011, so this was the right moment to rapidly decrease budgetary expenditure and hence, deficits. Both economic and political penalties were threatened in the case of non-compliance with these guidelines, and this time they would be carried out.[9] All this prompted the Euro to choose the straight and narrow path as far as possible, because what would happen next, as is well known, was that the over-the-top temporary deficit reduction targets were not achieved, and had to be rendered more flexible in almost all the countries concerned.

However, the main threat to countries in trouble was not so much the European Commission as the financial markets, since they already clearly doubted that the debts owed to them would be repaid. The immediate effect was a steady rise in interest rates on the debt issued.

Greece

The markets looked at the short-term. The 'Greek tragedy' in a country which represented 2.3% of GDP in the Eurozone, but whose real deficit (which the previous Conservative government had hidden from Brussels) was 13%, and whose debt was to a great extent in the hands of European banks, especially German ones, spread to the Eurozone creating the first crisis there.

The Union, with Germany and France at the forefront, decided to keep Greece in the Eurozone, but did not have the support of the European Central Bank. The treaty does not allow a country to be bailed out by the ECB. Hence they opted for 'coordinated bilateral loans' that were decided unanimously in the Eurozone, although under 'strict conditions', i.e., stringent austerity controlled by the famous Troika: the European Commission, the European Central Bank and the IMF, which provided a minority of the funding. Interest rate conditions were tough because they had to be, to encourage a return of the markets to Greece, as explained at the Eurogroup summit on 25 March 2010. For example, for a three-year loan to Greece, the interest would be around 5%.[10]

This was the beginning of a tortuous path of successive rescue plans with encounters and clashes between Brussels and Athens, which still continue; constant give and take on the deficit targets and 'structural reforms', particularly on taxes, the employment market, business, public health and the efficiency of the civil service.[11]

In 2011, Greece went through yet another serious crisis. Tax revenues and social security contributions plummeted amid falling demand and a decrease in investor confidence. The budget deficit was worse; GDP contracted by 7%. The new crisis led to harsh adjustment plans, to mass privatization, to socially regressive measures. They resulted in violent social protests and a political crisis that swept away Prime Minister Papandreou, replaced by the technocrat and former vice president of the ECB, Lucas Papademos. The Greek economy suffered a recession of –6.1% in 2011.

The job market added to these worsening prospects. Unemployment came to about 23%, with 45% of young people unemployed. The desired return on capital moved further and further away on the horizon. The payment of debt once more became unsustainable and the real possibility was looming—again—of a default.

The discussion about the possibility of restructuring flooded the European economical-political scene, because there was a grave fear of breaking the sacred principle of guaranteeing public debt, especially in the Eurozone. The solution to this impasse began to be seen when Germany—Merkel and Schauble—started to consider, as an exceptional and unique measure, debt relief to avoid bankrupting the Euro.

In any case, the harsh policies continued. On 20 and 21 February 2012, after months, the Eurogroup agreed on a second bailout for Greece that naturally included, as Olli Rehn (Commissioner for Economic Affairs) took care to emphasize, strict conditions and reinforcements to ensure effective control of the aid programme. The bailout included the comitment of the two major parties to meet these conditions.

The second bailout rose to EUR 130 billion, which in reality was EUR 164 billion because there were still EUR 34 billion outstanding from the first rescue. They decreased interest rates (3.5%) to achieve savings of EUR 3 trillion, 400 billion in exchange for stronger cessions in fiscal sovereignty. The aim was that borrowing descend from 160 to 120.5% of GDP in 2020. The debt relief for banks and private creditors—the workhorse of the agreement—exceeded 75% of the value of Greek debt, which meant savings of EUR 100 billion. The national central banks of the Eurozone participated in aid to the tune of EUR 1 trillion, 800 billion from the expected profits from investments in Greek government debt. The ECB participated in the operation accepting with guarantees, the Greek debt as collateral. The rescue package included further conditions.

Advancing to February 2015, as I write, Greece has a new government controlled by the party Syriza, from 25 January 2015, which is proposing a break with the logic of the bailouts. The proposal for a new stage is being made by Tsipras, the head of government, allied with a nationalist, xenophobic and anti-EU party.

The scenario is the following: on the one hand, there is the Government of Greece, which has immediate need of funds but repudiates enlarging its debt and bailout programme; on the other, the Union, including the ECB, demanding compliance to continue helping the country.

This book is finished coinciding with intense negotiations between the new Greek government and the Eurogroup (February 2015). On Friday 20th, an agreement was reached, Tsipras accepted the main requirements from Brussels: to honour Greece's financial obligations to all its creditors; the extension of the current programme four months more in order to negotiate a new rescue programme; no unilateral actions; supervision under the EU and ECB framework, and the IMF; and the necessary reforms.

The Greek case is the paradigm of the crisis. Hundreds of thousands of euros given to Greece from 2010 to avoid the fall of European creditor banks, which were only to be useful for refinancing the private debt into public debt and transmuting it into the hands of Eurozone governments and the ECB. They did not serve to stabilize the Greek economy. Among other things because of the deflationary conditions of the bailouts, consisting in depressing consumption, which made it sink further. It was a pointless debt.

Its compensation should have been—and was not—an investment programme; at the same time as internal reforms in the administration, anti-corruption measures, and the tax system—not fit for purpose—which Greece suffers from, along with a decrease in the over-expenditure on Defence.

That explains why the new finance minister Varoufakis reneged the debt, considering it an addiction, a drug. That's it exactly. The aim of the Greek Government is to abolish the bailout programme and replace it with a loan that does not have conditions attached to its economic policy. That is, more debt, although unconditional. But the bailout programme was imposed on Greece as it was not able to finance itself on the markets. Nobody was willing to lend to them at affordable interest rates. Only the Union, and naturally, with conditions which have hitherto been too hard on the Greek people.

Ireland

The next case of a country on the abyss, faced with default, was Ireland, but this case was different from that of Greece. In Ireland's case there had been no lies about the deficit and financial situation, nor the obvious squandering of public money that Greece had suffered in recent years and decades. The fall of Ireland—re-baptized as the 'Celtic Tiger' because of its great performance in GDP and its attraction of US companies due to reduced taxation—is a phenomenon linked to the housing market bubble fuelled by bank mortgages, in turn fed by aggressive lending on the US 'repo' markets during the first decade of the century. This resulted in a high level of private debt, using and abusing the very low interest rates that had permitted Ireland's entry into the Euro.

The most important player in the crash was the Anglo Irish Bank, absolutely staggering in a bank that had grown from having a turnover of EUR 42 million in 1987, to EUR 1 billion, 200 million in 2007.

The Anglo Irish Bank was nationalized and a 'bad bank' (National Asset Management Agency, NAMA) to which the toxic assets of all banks were transferred to, was created. It was a 'total bailout' in which taxpayers bought these assets at their book value and then returned them to the banks. The best model, according to Trichet.[12]

As usual, the bank debt was then guaranteed by taxpayers. Irish national debt, which was a healthy 25% of GDP in 2007, reached 125% in 2012, to which must be added property owner debt of 147%, and company debt of 210%. A debt that is almost double that of Greece.[14]

Ireland requested financial assistance on 22 November 2010, and this was approved by the Ecofin Council on 7 December. The total amount was EUR 85 million.

In Ireland the overall policy designed to help the financing needs of a Eurozone country that had got into difficulties was now applied. The Ecofin had approved the so-called European Financial Stability Facility (EFSF) (a company listed under Luxembourg law) at its often quoted meeting (due to the tensions experienced) of 9 May.

To this instrument was added the European Financial Stabilisation Mechanism,[15] more under the control of the Council and the Commission. Exceptionally, the United Kingdom, Denmark and Sweden, whose banks were affected by the Irish crisis, also offered bilateral loans.

The objective of the EFSF, in view of the situation in various Eurozone countries, was to raise capital in the markets at low interest rates, so as to grant credit in conjunction with the IMF to such countries, subject to 'strict political conditions' (Eurogroup statement of 7 June 2010). The limit was EUR 444 billion, an amount insufficient to rescue a big country like Italy or Spain, or to prevent speculative attacks. As Farlow says, the bailouts were intended more to address the symptom of the problem (sovereign debt) than the cause of it (bank debt).[16]

The reality of the three years (2010–2012) of austerity in Ireland was not positive. In 2012, national debt was at 108.2% of GDP; in 2007 it was 32%. Not to mention the cost of the NAMA programme (Irish investment programme), which explains the exponential increase in total debt in relation to the afore-mentioned GDP.[17] Today, Ireland can finance itself in the markets, but only after having suffered an enormous social cost.

Portugal

On 7 April 2011, at the same time as the difficulties of Greece and Ireland, Portugal requested a bailout from the Union. Prime Minister José Sócrates could not handle the pressure of the markets and ratings agencies. The interest rate on bonds (10%) was already unacceptable and the debt had acquired huge proportions (92.4% of GDP).

At the Ecofin meeting of 17 May a three-year bailout plan was approved, tougher than the one previously rejected by the Portuguese Parliament. The amount was EUR 78 billion, of which one third was disbursed by the IMF and the other two thirds were from the European Financial Stabilisation Mechanism (EFSM) and the European Financial Stability Facility (EFSF).

The whole raison d'être for the agreement was, of course, to impose a one-dimensional austerity plan without any kind of additional stimulus: fiscal consolidation (3% in 2013); structural reforms (in the health system, the judicial system and the civil service, together with a 'flexible' employment market); privatization, and the cleaning up of the financial sector (debt reduction and capitalization of the banks). The subsequent results of this rescue have been stormy, to say the least.

Despite the budgetary constraints of the Passos Coelho government, of tax increases and the sharp drop in interest rates (5.9% in 2013), the government, in March of that year, requested one more year—until 2015—to reach the 3% deficit target.

Spain and Italy

Faced with capital flight from the debt of these countries, the austerity policy came to Greece, Ireland and Portugal with Eurogroup-approved bailouts. Margaret Thatcher would have said: 'There is no alternative' (TINA). The only alternative was sovereign default, i.e., the breakup and discrediting of the Euro.

In Spain and Italy, the situation neither was, nor is easy to understand. In both cases, there was also capital flight and speculative attacks on debt. However, market funding remained possible.

Nearly all economists agree that the main problem in Spain was not the level of sovereign debt reached, around 60% of GDP in 2010, lower than that of other large countries—Germany, France and the UK. Nor the deficit, which did not exist. The problems were essentially on the one hand, the high ratio of private debt (170% of GDP), which was growing at 20% annually, due to a bloated construction sector in debt up to its eyeballs; and on the other hand, a part of the financial system—in particular, the savings banks (the Spanish equivalent of building societies), including Bankia, which went bankrupt in 2012 and had been nationalized—which were indebted in an opaque and undercapitalized way. The system was therefore completely dependent on the international interbank financial market, which had until then been overflowing with unlimited cheap money. Spanish banks had obtained money borrowed from German banks (approximately EUR 180 billion), from French banks (EUR 160 billion) and British ones (EUR 110 billion).

From 1997 to 2007, house prices in Spain rose by 115%. Spain, said John Mauldin, 'was the mother of all housing bubbles'.[18] However, it was not thus only in Spain. In the UK prices had grown by 140%, and in Ireland, 160%. In 2010, the Spanish residential construction sector represented 16% of GDP, with loans to developers that accounted for half of that GDP; the sector generated 14% of employment, and imported immigrant labour in huge quantities. So when the bubble burst, unemployment rose in two years from 8% to 25%, including 52% youth unemployment. Domestic demand plunged by 7% and GDP contracted by 6.3% in the first quarter of 2008 alone.[19]

In the summer of 2011 a dangerous situation arose for Spain. The interest that the markets demanded of the Treasury rose to a spread of 285 points over German bonds, because of the impasse in the Greek crisis. Spain did not have to ask for a bailout along the lines of Greece, Portugal and Ireland, but eventually applied for one for the banking sector a year later. On 7 June 2012, the ratings agency Fitch downgraded Spain's rating from A to BBB. On 11 June, a loan to recapitalize banks (savings banks) of up to EUR 100 billion was announced. However, Germany demanded that this credit should go directly to the Spanish government as guarantor and only indirectly to the savings banks. With this, the pathological link between bank insolvency and sovereign insolvency, rather than being dissolved, was strengthened. In fact, the level of national debt increased by 9.5% of GDP, reaching 90%.[20] It is now at 100%.

So the austerity policy, the 'Brussels consensus' formally arrived in Spain through a bailout for bank recapitalization which reinforced the demands of the Stability and Growth Pact. The Memorandum of Understanding (MOU) agreed upon required, in addition to the specific conditions for the banking sector (conditions both bank to bank and horizontally), macroeconomic adjustments: Spain would have to meet the commitments arising from the Excessive Deficit

Procedure, the recommendations of the European Semester and the macroeconomic imbalances procedure.

Italy was in the same boat as Spain, as regards market distrust and the risk premium, but the situation there was different. The problem in Italy was its high level of national debt (the third highest in the world) as against relatively low private debt. Italy had registered a poor growth figure along with a swiftly aging population. All of this explained the reluctance of the markets vis-à-vis the economic health of Italy and its stratospheric deficit. Italy ended up accepting the doctrine of austerity in the face of markets which considered it would be difficult for the country to meet its financial obligations.

What happened in Greece, Ireland, Portugal, Spain and Italy perfectly illustrates the mechanisms that creditor countries (and their banks) impose on debtors (and on their companies and on individuals) to ensure repayment of the debt. The vehicle is always a 'rescue'—or the threat of it—that borrowers accept through clenched teeth faced with the impossibility of finding financing in the markets. The medium is what the terminology of Brussels, Frankfurt and Berlin terms 'strict compliance', i.e., the demands for deficit and structural reforms (Welfare State restrictions). We have seen it in the aid programmes for Greece, Ireland and Portugal, and the subsequent bank bailout in Spain in 2012 whose Memorandum of Understanding (MOU) (which was never made known to the Spanish Parliament but only the German one) is a complete recipe for achieving that 'strict conditionality'.

The golden rule

The spectre of having to help Spain or Italy terrified the Eurozone countries. Not only that. A more powerful financial instrument had to be considered. The European Financial Stabilisation Mechanism (ESM), with a total effective capacity of EUR 500 billion approved by the European Council on 24 and 25 March, and operational from 1 July 2013, was not enough.[22]

Thus, at the European Council on 8 and 9 December 2011, the 26 participating countries (all of the EU except the UK) agreed to the introduction of an intergovernmental treaty (Fiscal Compact) which would make provision for a more automatic application of the excessive deficit procedure, the adoption of a balanced budget rule at the constitutional level or equivalent, and the recognition of the competency of the European Court of Justice. This was what unlocked the second aid package to Greece. The Eurogroup, meanwhile, established a link between the ESM and the Fiscal Pact, in order to reinforce respect for budgetary discipline. The fund would benefit only the signatories to the treaty. Germany agreed to strengthen the ESM in exchange for greater austerity commitments. This is what made Spain urgently approve an amendment to Article 135 of the Constitution, where the 'golden rule' of balanced budgets was incorporated, but unfortunately, without a parallel commitment to fiscal sustainability, which would have been necessary to ensure that the rule never impaired the social rights of the Welfare State.[23]

The European Council of 30 January 2012 gave final approval to the Treaty on Stability, Coordination and Governance (TSCG). It was not signed by either the UK or the Czech Republic. According to the treaty, which was signed on 2 March 2011 and entered into force on 1 January 2013, the budget deficit cannot exceed 0.5% of GDP. The limit could be surpassed in exceptional circumstances, such as a 'negative growth rate [sic] or a cumulative drop in production over a lengthy period'. This standard, incorporated into national legislation within a year, demanded the prior reform of Article 136 of the Treaty on the Functioning of the European Union.[24]

At the same session of the European Council, the treaty establishing the European Stability Mechanism to which we refer (ESM) was concluded.

The dual symbolism of the decision could not be clearer. The strategy was reaffirmed. The Union—in this case, referring to the creditor countries—would help the debtor countries facing serious difficulties only if they strictly followed a policy of austerity. Land for peace.

Austerity Does Not Work (2012)

The European economy suffered a slowdown in the second half of 2011, with bad omens for employment. László Andor, the Hungarian Commissioner for Employment, recognized the correlation between adjustment and unemployment. The commissioner noted that unemployment levels were increasing more rapidly precisely in countries undergoing a tough austerity regime. According to László Andor, this trend was particularly visible in Greece, Portugal and Ireland, but also in Spain, which had embarked in haste on a preventive programme of rigorous budgetary control.[25]

The European Union—or rather, the countries which had been relying on it as a shelter from the financial markets since the beginning of the crisis—adopted reductions in government spending as dogma, while at the same time it recommended that indebted states should not take on more debt. This is the main contradiction of the doctrine of austerity: on the one hand, without any concessions, a much larger budgetary constraint than any corresponding increase in taxes is proposed, with the supposed objective being to lower the debt burden. However, on the other hand, the dominant orthodoxy towards the creditor banks and the financial markets—the fear of their fear (the fear of default)—means that peripheral Europe assumes more government debt in two ways: firstly, via the bank bailout, i.e., the acceptance of responsibility for the private debt of troubled (too big to fail) banks that had slipped into the circus of perpetual leverage via international credits (the bubble); and secondly, the unfavourable differential in interest rates on sovereign debt, and on credits to companies, large, medium or small, of that same damaged periphery. The countries of southern Europe are discriminated against financially due, among other things, to the legal inability of the ECB to act as a lender of last resort.

Add to that the burden of the automatic stabilizers on the budget, and falling tax revenues. The result is declining state contribution to economic activity. It is estimated that one GDP point of budgetary restriction means a 1.5% decrease in economic activity, thus increasing the financial risk of the country in question.

Economic recession. More debt. More unemployment

In late 2012, the raw EU figures were devastating: an exceedingly high level of unemployment (10.8% of the workforce), a new recession (–0.3% of GDP) and an increase in national debt (up to 85%), which meant that European debt was growing faster than the economy.

These figures were worse in the Eurozone—between 2010 and 2013, austerity measures had the impact of a reduction of almost 7 per cent points of GDP, according to a study of three independent institutes, IM12 (Germany), AFCE (France) and WIFO (Austria)[26]—and much worse in countries like Greece, Ireland or Portugal, recipients of bail-outs from the Union.

There was no doubt that Draghi's words in the Spanish Congress of Deputies (the lower house of parliament) on 12 February 2013, signalling that the first positive results of the adjustment could already be observed, were not supported by the evidence.

The conclusion to be drawn is that the indiscriminate, one-dimensional austerity policy and deep cuts in Welfare State spending decreed by the EU, at the cost of avoiding any stimulus measures, had been a failure in every way, with nothing to make anyone think that the continuation of that policy was likely to create a more favourable situation, with credit on hold and household demand reduced. This was because to a large extent, this policy was to blame for such negative figures.[28] This has served only to increase the substantial differences in growth in income and employment across the European countries, the true disease of the Eurozone.[29]

Debt represents a particularly discouraging but very revealing outcome in terms of the loss of direction of a policy which has had a shrinking effect on growth while at the same time helping to increase indebtedness. In July 2013, Eurostat published an interesting article on its website on the 'Structure of the National debt of the Member States in 2012'. One of the main conclusions was that debt as measured by the Maastricht criteria saw an increase as a percentage of GDP in 21 States of the Union, almost all of it underwritten medium and long term.

The guarantees granted by the public sector should also be noted, almost all of which involve backing banks in difficulties. These are not classified as debt, but they can become debt if the banks fail and the guarantees are executed. Spain had a ratio of these guarantees close to 18% of GDP in 2012 after experiencing the largest annual increase (7.2% of GDP).[30]

Along with debt, the other bad result of 2012 was the worsening employment situation, in terms of quantity and quality, due to the steady increase in the number of unemployed persons (5.6 million more young people)[31] and the steady decline in household incomes. The annual income of each person, which was an average of EUR 26,500 in 2007 according to the European Commission, declined in 2012 to EUR 27,700. In other words, there was a loss of purchasing power of 3% (against a loss of 0.6% in the USA), which in the case of Greece was 18% and 20% in Ireland.

There is no alternative to admitting that unemployment had acquired a structural character in the region which is supposed to have the pursuit of full employment as one of its main aims.

The poor performance of this policy of rigidity was not exclusive to the Eurozone. The United Kingdom of Cameron and Osborne is the best example, despite the optimism of the Treasury in its 2012 report.[33]

Because of the strict policy of austerity (except for aid to the City) dictated by the coalition government, and the unstoppable rise in VAT, the disposable income of households had taken a significant hit. The response of Cameron and Osborne was to criticize the Eurozone for the economic ills of the British economy.[34]

Turning to Keynes Again (2013)

Winter. Paralysis in the EU

When the economic and financial world leaders gathered in Davos at the World Economic Forum, they knew that the times of recession, unemployment and lack of liquidity for investment or consumption would continue in 2013.

In a study just presented by the IMF, compiled by Olivier Blanchard and Daniel Leigh, errors were recognized in the growth forecasts and the fiscal consolidation plans in times of crisis. The study found that in developed economies, a stronger fiscal consolidation was associated with lower growth than expected, especially at the beginning of the crisis.

As Stiglitz noted, most of the participants in the Davos Forum celebrated above all the survival of the Euro thanks to the commitment of the ECB of intervening whenever necessary.[35] However, that complacency went hand-in-hand with a sense of deep uncertainty and with the realisation of the lack of a credible roadmap to provide a way out of the crisis. Apart from the exception that proves the rule, Germany,[36] Europe was the only significant region of the world where unemployment was growing (a million jobs were lost in the Eurozone in a year, i.e., 7.5 million jobless young people), a situation that had a lethal effect on potential safety nets. A new form of poverty was born, and was now threatening a quarter of the European population.

Of course, the situation of economic decline also affected the large EU countries—not only those subject to bailout programmes: Greece, Ireland and Portugal. Spain was also affected, with soaring unemployment and growing social exclusion,[37] in an economy that became smaller and smaller in response to the increasing demands made upon it; the same was true of Italy, paralyzed by endless political crises; and even France, despite verbal commitments from the president, who had promised to make 2013 the year of the struggle for employment.[38]

The large countries were not alone. The other Euro countries suffered similar difficulties, and this was noticeable, as evidenced by the World Economic Survey (WES) in April issued by the IFO Institute and the University of Munich. This was the case in Belgium, Holland, Denmark, Finland and Austria.[39] The similarities between northern Europe and the South are greater than is initially apparent. The monoculture of austerity ends up leaving everyone in the same condition: anaemic. Only in Germany and Estonia was the prevailing economic climate positive, and outside the Euro area, in Norway and Switzerland.

The British economy had experienced the weakest recovery among major countries in the period 2010–2011.[40] In spite of this, and pessimistic forecasts for 2013 that the government did not share, they stubbornly continued with austerity at all costs. The toughness of this policy was criticized by Olivier Blanchard, IMF chief economist, and in similar terms, by Nick Clegg, Liberal Democrat Deputy Prime Minister in the coalition government,[41] and even by the Tory mayor of London, Boris Johnson, who advocated investment in construction and transportation instead of continuing with the old 'rhetoric of austerity'.

The overall negative state of the UK and the Eurozone was not off-set by the so-called 'transition economies', nor was the reverse true. The growth of the economy and credit in Central Europe and the Baltic countries had slowed. Neither were the economies of Russia and Ukraine invulnerable to the Eurozone crisis.

USA. Doing things their way

In the USA, where the European model of austerity policy fortunately did not exist,[44] growth was put at 2.8% in 2012 after a review by the Bureau of Economic

Analysis. The stimulus policies enacted by Obama in taxation and by Bernanke in monetary matters, had borne fruit.

Obama, in his State of the Union address in February 2013, made a powerful speech to Congress. Its core message was about the re-activation of the economy and the strengthening of social programmes supported by taxes on the rich, those who had been favoured in the past by Bush Jr.'s fiscal policy. Obama suggested the idea, immediately rejected by Republicans, of raising the minimum wage of USD 7.25 to USD 9 an hour, and presented the proposal as part of a goal to increase stability and productivity.

It was a way to stimulate the economy without the federal government having to raise public spending. It was poorly received in the European liberal press, even though at that time the dominant fiscal policy was restrictive in all spheres.[45] The truth is that the results of both policies were as clear as day.

In the USA, private investment had increased steadily, something that had not happened in the Eurozone or in the UK. The explanation given by some in the USA was that the private sector had benefited from a banking system that did a better job of recapitalization than that orchestrated by European banks.[46]

Despite its economic activism, the USA then found itself face-to-face with a fierce political debate between Democrats and Republicans on the so-called sequester, i.e., the drastic and automatic reduction in public spending and defence on 1 March 2013, unless otherwise agreed, of two trillion dollars over 10 years, coupled with the removal of the tax breaks of the Bush era.[47]

This picture of the economy in early 2013 is summarized in one word: stagnation, with slight growth or recession, depending on each case. There was more of the latter in the European Union, and especially where the austerity policy had been particularly one-sided. However, such a diagnosis had no effect on the attitude of the European Commission.

Its vice-president Olli Rehn acknowledged recession and unemployment. He did it three months after predicting that in 2013 the Eurozone would grow.[48] Of course, the Commissioner reaffirmed that the policy being followed was the correct one.

Hermann Van Rompuy even said to those who were protesting this that, 'green shoots' of recovery were already being seen, something that had been repeated many times in the past without those words having any basis in reality.[49]

Angela Merkel restated[50] that the austerity policy was incompatible with new programmes of 'temporary stimulus' along the lines of those which had been implemented in 2009 all over the world to address the financial crisis.

However, stubborn resistance was useless against the strength of events. Economic activity was still flatlining. In the first quarter of 2013, despite the considerable increase in exports the economy contracted again, after fifteen months of recession, highlighting what was wrong with the expectations of the governments of European countries. National debt in the first quarter, according to Eurostat, amounted to 92.2% of GDP in the Euro area and 85.9% in the Union 27.[51] The Union suffered a longer recession than that experienced between 2008 and 2009. Uncertainty gripped the economic scene, and therefore politics. And, as Bernanke said, 'A growing uncertainty provides an incentive to delay investment until we have new information'. When in doubt, business is put on hold.[52]

But politics cannot wait, although this policy has remained as poorly defined as it was in 2013.

Spring. The battle

This is my name for the debate (subsequently to become open warfare) on the economic policy of the European Union, which started in the first half of 2013. It actually started as an academic debate about ideas, which led on to an intense struggle between countries, governments and parties. The terms were simple enough: either austerity or stimulus.

The view from Washington

It has to be said that in the USA, where an unexpected slowdown was suffered in the last quarter of 2012, albeit limited and short-term—the first in three years—the debate on austerity did not explode with the same virulence as in Europe, and this was so for two reasons. The first is due to the fact that, owing to lack of consensus, the famous sequester came into force on 1 March 2013, freezing credit to the tune of USD 85 billion, within the financial year ending 30 September 2013. This was followed by the automatic freezing of budgetary credits amounting to USD 109 billion, which would affect defence and other national programmes throughout the fiscal year beginning 1 October 2013.[53] The sequester formed part of the efforts to reduce the federal budget deficit by a trillion and a half dollars in the period 2012–2021. Obama had agreed to this in order to avoid the 'fiscal cliff' and breach the debt limit. The infamous sequester would be triggered if a better consensus were not achieved. Obama had to confront the opinions of many members of his own party, who complained that this would affect programmes like Medicare and Social Security, or infrastructure, the environment, innovation and education. In exchange, the Republicans gave in to an increase of 35% to 39.5% on the marginal rate of income tax for the very wealthy, which set the older factions of the GOP grumbling.

The second reason, and the more important one, as to why the debate about austerity in the USA was not as harsh, is that Obama's policies, especially regarding the Federal Reserve, had been geared towards expansive policies since the outbreak of the crisis. Regardless of the economic downturn suffered by the US in 2011 and 2012, its economic policy suffered no major disruption. The slowdown was attributed to some extent to the European sovereign debt crisis, whilst admitting that the reductions in discretionary federal spending (a result of the Republicans' having taken control of the House of Representatives in 2011) had had, as is generally agreed, an undeniable effect on the slowness of the economic recovery.[54] Unemployment was never at such alarming levels as in Europe. In October 2009 it reached the highest peak, with 10% unemployment. However, in February 2013, in contrast to Europe, the USA recorded the best employment statistics since December 2008, with unemployment down to 7.7% thanks to the private sector. Nonetheless, in the USA the despondency of young people seeking jobs has played a negative role, with many of them ceasing to be part of the active population.

The battle continues in the US, but not because of the strict austerity policy, which almost nobody considers necessary in a country where the price of government bonds is practically zero. What exists is a political debate—not so much economic—about the role of government in the economy and the tax system, in which there are two very clear partisan positions. On the one hand, Obama's stance on combining deficit reduction with increased spending on social programmes and infrastructure, as well as through targeted tax cuts, for which it is essential to tax the wealthy more heavily, something which Obama managed—only partly—in January 2013. On the other hand we have the position of the Republicans, opposed to any tax increases and obsessed with reducing public spending (despite this potentially sweeping away defence spending, which for Republicans has always been sacrosanct) and whose main intention is the repayment of debts, ahead of Social Security obligations.[55]

Two schools

The first manifestation of the debate on austerity in Europe has been in the field of academic think-tanks and the media.

In this area, the pro-austerity groups were reluctant to come out into the open, because the predominating orthodoxy was secured in practice by a dominant and compact 'friends of austerity' grouping made up of the ECB, the European Commission, the OECD, governments and other parts of the private sectors such as finance, particularly those closest to the Central European area.[56]

As an example of the language that was used until recently, it may be helpful to cite the study, released in late November 2012 by the Berenberg Bank and the Lisbon Council think-tank, on the reforms undertaken in countries such as

Portugal and Italy on their employment laws with reductions in protection in the fạce of dismissal. The report concluded that they were bearing fruit.[57]

The WSJ speech in its editorial on 10 January 2013 was repeated three months later (April 24) in an editorial that ended: 'Greece, Portugal, Spain, Romania and Italy cannot afford their current Welfare States';[58] the taxes that were necessary to support them, it said, misdirected money that could be invested in new businesses, innovation and the creation of employment.

Just one week later, there was the academic and political scandal caused by technical errors discovered in the famous book by Harvard economists Kenneth Rogoff and Carmen Reinhart, the hitherto undisputed bible of the 'friends of austerity'.

Reinhart and Rogoff—the latter, IMF chief economist between 2001 and 2003—published their study in 2010, coinciding with the sovereign debt crisis, before the bestseller *This Time is Different: Eight Centuries of Financial Folly*. Advocates of a return to austerity turned it into their great technical tool for the conversion of an opinion into scientific dogma, since it was assumed that the findings of the study were based on historical data on the effects of national debt on growth: with debt at over 90% of GDP, growth of 3% or 4% of GDP collapses, and precipitates recessions of 0.1%, according to Rogoff and Reinhart.[59]

Three professors from the University of Massachusetts Amherst, Robert Pollin, Michael Ash and Thomas Herndon, discovered that the findings of Rogoff and Reinhart were based on erroneous data and sprang from an erroneous methodology. The conclusions of the Massachusetts researchers were the total opposite: when debt exceeds 90%, the average growth is 2.2% of GDP, not 0.1%. They also concluded that, in reality, the relationship between growth and debt completely varies depending on the period and the country. It is not possible to know whether a decline in growth is the cause or the effect of high national debt. In the case of the financial crisis of 2007–2009, Pollin, Ash and Herndon believe that the growth in debt was the consequence, and that it stopped demand from sinking without inflation necessarily rising rapidly.[60] It is true that the USA was helped by low interest rates. Not so in Europe, where the interest on sovereign debt in southern countries soared, which is why in the Union panic gripped the markets and the advocates of austerity won over the governments of the most indebted countries.

According to the WSJ, the central issue was the main purpose of debt: financing expenditure and social security-related costs, which are then difficult to reduce.[61] Behold the Gordian knot.

The Rogoff and Reinhart business slanted the debate more in favour of the critics of austerity. However, it is true that their academic superiority was clear much earlier, when they established the uselessness of fiscal consolidation policies in lowering debt payments when there is no inflation or growth, the situation in which the Union found itself.[62] The fiscal deficit can only be reduced in a growing economy. And in a situation of mass unemployment, policies to encourage growth do not pose any significant risk to inflation, and do allow the expansion of demand. Contracting demand through fiscal consolidation is a dead end which can lead to damage to the economy, a prolonged depression and increased and unsustainable social unrest.[63]

Economists had been starting to think that austerity was not a short-term tactic to deal with a temporary crisis, but that it instead had structural effects which were difficult to reverse. This is the case with cuts in social spending. Not least because, as Wolfgang Münchau notes, for desperate governments it is quicker and easier to cut social spending than to increase taxes or cut payments to local government.[64] The economic crisis has been used as an excuse to destroy social policies. So much so that the constitutional courts have come out against those policies that clash with constitutional guarantees to these social rights. This is what has happened in Portugal with regard to the cuts in wages and pensions of public sector employees.

It is curious that the discussion on the politics of austerity has had more visibility in the Anglo-Saxon media than in the so-called Continental media. In the United States, regardless of newspapers like the WSJ adopting more conservative positions, the prevailing opinion has been critical of austerity. The New York Times (NYT) and its European edition, now called New York Times International (INYT), have been abundantly clear in warning that austerity and reforms cannot be carried out simultaneously in all countries, and in showing their incomprehension regarding Merkel's refusal to issue bonds backed by the Eurozone.[65]

The most prominent anti-austerity economist is the Nobel Prizewinner Paul Krugman. His constant reflection has revolved around the idea that, if austerity is practised at the same time by all economic operators, as has happened in the European Union, the result is recession, because the expenditure of one is the income of another.[66]

The *Financial Times* did not hesitate to describe as 'self-flagellating' the indiscriminate and uncoordinated policies of the 'high priests of fiscal consolidation'.[67] Columnists with considerable influence beyond the British Isles like Martin Wolff, the main economics editor and Wolfgang Münchau, voiced their opinions on the subject very clearly.[68]

Naturally, the greatest momentum against the policy conducted by Cameron and Osborne came from the progressive press, amongst which *The Guardian* stands out. Of course, it participated in the bitter debate that was taking place in the Western economic and political world, criticizing the short-term nature of Osborne's fiscal policies, but also the indecisiveness of the Labour opposition, which took a long time to decide that it would opt for higher taxes and less debt in the long term.[69]

The debate in the political arena

What in intellectual life was a reality by late 2012—the failure of austerity—did not develop quickly enough in the stormier ambit of real politics. The last piece of evidence we have for this is the Union budget for 2014–2020, which, for the first time, decreased credit destined for European expenditure for the next seven years. A show of austerity in an organization, the European Union, which has neither deficit nor debt.

Something which should be noted are the findings of other multilateral organizations such as the OECD, for which the 'structural reforms to restore competitiveness and fiscal sustainability' were not measures to be added to others, but nothing less than 'conditions' for a return to healthy growth after the crisis.[70]

These attitudes clearly began to change in spring 2013. In my view, mainly for four reasons, in order of increasing importance. First, the evolution just discussed in the academic and media debate. The second reason for the tipping point in the policy lies in the about-turn of the International Monetary Fund which, living up to its reputation and influenced by pessimistic data and the aforementioned work of Olivier Blanchard and Daniel Leigh, acknowledged another major error.[71] IMF economists, as has been noted, had underestimated the damage to growth, employment, consumption and investment inflicted by the policy of austerity. The damage was actually three times more severe than had been previously calculated. Experts had applied an incorrect fiscal multiplier: instead of destroying economic activity by 0.5 euros per euro not spent by the state, the correct figure was 1.5 euros subtracted from economic activity for every Euro not invested.[72] This explains why the forecasts given during the crisis—the famous green shoots—had always been so out of touch with reality. The truth is that the fiscal multiplier increases exponentially as the crisis becomes more serious.

After the first quarter of 2013, the IMF argument—and that of its twin, the World Bank—turned to a critique of Germany and the UK for tightening their belts too quickly.[73]

At the annual meeting of the finance ministers of the G-20 and the governors of the central banks, held on 18 and 19 April in Washington, Christine Lagarde said that the best way to create jobs was to encourage growth, words that clashed with the input of the IMF into the significant emergency loan programmes that imposed harsh measures on peripheral Europe.[74]

Suddenly, Olli Rehn, who, in a letter to the ministers, had already disowned the work of Blanchard and Leigh on fiscal multipliers, considering it 'not useful', continued to insist on the recovery of sound public finances. In this he had the backing of the President of the Commission, Jose Manuel Barroso.[75]

It is here that may be found the third reason that led to a change—or to the beginning of a change—in European economic policy, along lines so far only defended in the political arena by the European Socialist Party and, more emphatically, by socialist parties at the national level (usually those not in government at that time) and other progressive movements.

The accession of Socialist Hollande to the presidency of France, and the rise to power of the Italian left in the form of Letta was crucial to this.

Also, governments like the Dutch, and even the Polish, began to emphasize the need for flexibility in the adjustments and deficit schedules, for obvious reasons. To all of the countries in the process of reducing excessive deficits, it was quite clear that the budgetary targets could not be met.

Merkel's government and the Commission were in a defensive situation. The answer, as far as form was concerned, was to avoid the accursed word 'austerity', and in practice to accept longer periods to allow compliance with the deficit targets—without abandoning them—in exchange for significant structural reforms.[76] This is what Van Rompuy called 'austerity fatigue', which was already the feeling of millions of Europeans in response to the huge effort that had only succeeded in reducing the deficit in 2012 by worsening all other important areas: growth, employment and debt.[77]

In response, Olli Rehn (as he had already been saying since the beginning of the year) announced the intention of the Commission to recommend that the governments of the Union grant Spain two more years to reach the 3% deficit target (2016), France two more years (2015), although its deficit situation was much better than that of Spain, and a year to Holland, hitherto virtuous and exemplary. It was a full-blown correction, and confirmed the failure of austerity. As previously noted, the other side of the coin would be 'substantial structural reforms', in the words of Rehn, which for some, in France, was interpreted as a 'poisoned chalice' of liberalization measures.

At the London meeting of the G-7 (9 May), the USA and the IMF jointly called for a policy based on strengthening demand. Jack Lew, US Treasury Secretary, for his part called for a rebalancing in the Eurozone.[78]

The definitive blow to the policy of austerity was delivered by data for the first quarter of 2013, published on 15 May. The Eurozone suffered another fall in that period (0.2%) compared to the last quarter of 2012, and with it beat the sad record of the longest recession since the birth of the Euro; the fall also spread to 'northern countries' such as Holland and Finland.[79]

Unemployment reached 12.1% in the Eurozone, also its highest level. Even Germany managed only modest growth.

European data contrasted sharply with that of the USA, made public a day earlier. In 2009, the US deficit accounted for 10% of GDP. From the end of the recession during that year, the government budget deficit had improved by a trillion dollars each year. The figures provided by the neutral Congressional Budget Office estimated that the deficit for the fiscal year ending 30 September 2013 would fall to USD 642 billion (4% of GDP), better than expected in Washington.[80] It was proof of the success of Obama's economic strategy based on increasing some taxes and reducing civil and military programmes.

The other benchmark with which to compare Europe was Japan. At a time when the EU economies were experiencing a continuous decline, Japan grew by 3.5%, reacting to stimulus measures introduced by the new Prime Minister Shinzo Abe to end two decades of a flatlining economy and recession in 2011 and 2012. It essentially involved what are known as 'Abe's three arrows': expansionary monetary policy, fiscal spending and structural reforms.[81]

The data was incontrovertible.[82] Germany still refused to take steps before its general election, but Europe could not wait.[83] The growing dissatisfaction of the public at the apparent inability to tackle dreadful unemployment rates led to three important steps. The first, a Franco-German agreement, sponsored by President Van Rompuy, with a plan to tackle youth unemployment. As a result, France and Germany healed the wounds inflicted by a French Socialist Party document in which the 'selfish' Merkel policy was criticized with unusual harshness.

The second step was the meeting of 29 May, at which Ecofin gave the previously announced final seal of approval to three of its largest economies, France, Spain and Holland, allowing them more time to achieve the goal of a deficit of 3% of GDP. Poland, Slovenia, Belgium and Portugal were also given this opportunity. Likewise, Italy exited the excessive deficit procedure.[84] The main conditions imposed by Ecofin and the Commission were the following: reform of employment markets, the easing of business taxation and an extension of the retirement age. To all this, Hollande replied: 'The Commission is in no position to dictate policy to democratically elected governments'.[85] He was right. Indeed, governments maintained substantial room for manoeuvre in achieving the deficit target, i.e., opting for policies of less spending or higher taxation according to their political ideology.

The third step had bigger institutional effects: the June meeting of the European Council.

The European Council on 27 and 28 June: the draw

In addition to the requirements arising from the desperate situation of the European economy in general, the interest rates of individual countries were becoming more similar, with the exception of Germany: into the negative.

Blameless countries in compliance with the balanced budget, those keeping a close eye on their deficits, were being sucked into the victims' club of those affected by the adjustment policy the former had previously requested. This was the case of the Netherlands, Finland and Austria. Holland had to ask for more time to meet the deficit target, with its economy falling 1.8% in 2012. Finland had entered its third recession since the financial crisis, and unemployment had risen to 10.8%, the highest in four years, despite good figures on deficits and debt.[86] As for wealthy Austria, the bankruptcy in June of the construction company Alpine, the largest since World War II, led the coalition government to approve a stimulus package amounting to 0.5% of GDP, keeping the target of zero deficit for 2016.[87]

The new Western consensus, triumphing over the exhausted austerity policy, was simply stated at the G-8, in mid-June. The leaders declared that growth and employment, especially for young people and the long term unemployed, was their most urgent priority. They added to their agenda something truly important: the fight against tax evasion, which thus became the other side of the coin—a most appropriate expression—of a stimulus policy for the economy.

The progressive leaning towards a more balanced approach between deficit adjustment and demand stimuli had to be present at the June European Council. It was the only institution with enough power—if it so wills and agrees by consensus—to tackle youth unemployment and to ease policy in the direction of growth and therefore job creation, the two great needs of Europe.

In Spain, the importance of the summit led to an unprecedented event in the legislature: a (nearly) all party agreement between the government and the Socialist Party to adopt a common position in Brussels. This agreement was approved by the House of Representatives by an overwhelming majority of groups (all except the Plural Left and the Mixed Group).[88] The content of the proposal found a place in the European Council conclusions, except for the suggestion of direct recapitalization of the banks.

The European Council was neither excited nor disappointed, but there was considerable agreement in its further analysis, in the sense of taking it a step further, of opening up a new era of politics to fight the crisis.[89] The summit made progress on the Banking Union without defining it clearly enough, and adopted three big measures:

1. The quantification, for the first time, of EIB support to investments (EUR 150 billion) through loans to small and medium enterprises;
2. The setting up of a policy to combat unemployment, hitherto unmentioned in the Union, supported by a fund of EUR 8 billion—a quarter destined for Spain;

3. The approval once more (it had already been done the year before) of the sum of EUR 120 billion in what was called the Plan for Growth and Jobs.

The European Council played out the situation that had led to the 'Battle of Spring' between austerity and growth stimuli: a draw.

Summer. Waiting for Germany

Macroeconomic data for the third quarter of 2013 were also hybrids.[90] Public perception was that of the persistence of a real crisis, with the bailouts of Greece and Portugal openly threatening progress.

The millstone of chronic decline in lending to SMEs in the countries of southern Europe, and the absence of a European banking union, weighed heavily.[91]

Against this depressing backdrop, the pressure from the USA to return to the promotion of domestic consumption, financed by credit if necessary, acquired a greater ability to make way in the world: Japan ('Abenomics'), the UK (the creation of a subprime style mortgage market), China, Italy and France. An analyst as prestigious as Anatole Kaletsky dared to proclaim that, in view of these changes, the 'end of the era of austerity' was just around the corner.[92]

All eyes turned to Germany, and its insistence on placing the rapid reduction in debt at the top of its priorities, more so when the day after the Moscow summit of G-20, on 22 July, strong growth was announced in the Eurozone debt in the first months of 2013, especially in ailing Southern Europe.[93] Deficit reduction and a weak private economy make an explosive cocktail.

Germany was considered to be responsible for leading the austerity policy, and this suited her.[94] At that time, Germany was embroiled in a general election, the outcome of which had to be waited for in order to solve the mystery about what policy to follow next. Even Draghi delayed decision-taking by the ECB.

It is necessary to bear in mind that it was obvious that any recovery in the Eurozone would have to be led by its largest economy, the one which has benefited most from the common currency area. The Euro prevents the massive overvaluation that the Deutschmark might suffer, yet lends great credibility to Germany, which the markets reward with low cost national debt and low-cost loans to its businesses.

The Bertelsmann Foundation, in a study conducted in April 2013, concluded that a return of Germany to the Deutschmark would mean a loss of 0.5% of GDP annually between 2013 and 2015, i.e., USD 1.6 trillion.[95] However, the markets grant Germany a wide margin of manoeuvre to, if necessary, leave the Euro, believing that it would be the country least damaged by such a negative event. It is without a doubt an undesirable scenario, which is why all member states that are part of the Euro agreed to help those who were on the verge of sovereign default, to avoid the breakup of the Eurozone. Germany is the state that contributes most money to the rescue mechanism, but not the only one.

The authority that Germany imposes on financial markets comes essentially from its constitutionally guaranteed production model. The *Sparpolitik*—a term referring to the austerity policy or budgetary balance—has been in its constitution since 2009. It is also known as *Schuldenbremse* or 'debt brake', which inspired the Fiscal Compact agreed by the Eurogroup in 2011 and which Spain introduced that same year into its own Constitution.

What defines the German model is not only this. It is also based on an export-oriented economy, with large current account surpluses (about 7% of GDP). The very strong German manufacturing industry specializing in equipment and automotive technology makes this possible. Likewise, the small budgetary investment that Germany has made compared to other European countries contributes to this. However, its competitiveness has relied in recent years—and especially since the Schröder government—on very cheap labour and not on productivity (Dullien), where growth is 25% lower than the OECD average, as is the lower ratio of young workers who have completed higher education compared to Canada, France, Japan, Poland, USA, UK or Spain (Posen).[96]

Competitiveness was achieved with the Hartz labour reform laws between 2003 and 2005, which created *minijobs*, while curbing unemployment benefits. It is to this that the high level of employment/underemployment in Germany (6.8% unemployment in 2013) can be attributed.

It is true that, unlike the Spanish labour reform, Schröder respected collective bargaining, the role of trade unions, working hours and job security. However, one of the effects of Agenda 2010 was the drop in income of the working class. For this reason, *Sparpolitik* affects a significant proportion of the elderly population (with a savings culture) and on the other, those on the brink of social exclusion or poverty, with meagre home equity and growing inequalities. It is also a policy of underinvestment in infrastructure—physical and educational—to save at all costs. These savings allow external credit to be granted in abundance. Hence Merkel's overwhelming obsession with defending the German banks that lent to peripheral countries in large quantities.

Germany needs very low inflation as a creditor country (a 40% of GDP creditor position with the rest of the world) and as an economy that favours supply over demand. Its monetary model, contrary to what debtor countries require, is highly protected by the European Central Bank in Frankfurt. Draghi, even if it meant being criticized by the Bundesbank, took great care to maintain inflation at an excessively and unnecessarily low level. German export strength is such that it does not need a weak Euro.

The German economic model enjoys a privileged geographical position, as has always been the case historically since the days of the Hanseatic League, but it clashes with the global economic environment. Germany seeks out foreign demand disregarding its weak domestic demand, which therefore cannot benefit the other countries of the EU to a similar degree.

German exports in 2012 amounted to 43% of GDP, an astronomical amount, which means that there are very strong trade deficits on the other side of the coin; not so much in the EU as in Asia and America. The rapid development of emerging economies, the BRICS, and their transformation into countries with large middle classes, helps to explain the impressive growth of German exports to these regions, above and beyond the 6% surplus, which is considered by the EU to be a destabilizing boundary that should not be crossed (and contrasts, by the way, with the strict 3% deficit, contravention of which incurs a penalty, which however does not exist when the surplus limit is breached).

In short, German economic—not military—power has sat very comfortably with the European post-war architecture. Its savings have been channelled into foreign investment through banks or locally supervised building societies—and so it will continue. It has not had to subsidize less wealthy European countries, or enact an 'income transfer', which the German public rejects. It would, of course, be the country that would suffer most damage from the destruction of the Eurozone.[97]

What has happened is that different facets of the crisis have maximized the extreme imbalance within the Union and in the Eurozone; among other reasons, because of the very pro-production model, so favourable to Germany and the countries of central and northern Europe, Austria, Finland and others. Austerity without any other counterbalances has widened the rift, increasing the German surplus and decreasing work in southern Europe, which has literally moved north. Clear evidence of this is that during the crisis, German exports to Spain, Italy and Greece have collapsed and exports to the USA and China have gone through the roof.[98] There is an almost exact correlation with the economic development of these countries.

The model described has been wearing itself out, has been 'dying of success'. It is not surprising that in the interregnum between the election in September and the agreement with the Social Democrats in December, those affected by the German policy of trade surpluses that 'irritated the neighbours' would be protesting in unison.

The USA did not mind leading the chorus. In late October the US Treasury, in its semi-annual report on international economic and exchange rates, harshly criticized 'the anaemic growth in domestic demand', the production of the leading EU economy and its 'export dependence', generating, according to the Treasury, a strong imbalance favouring 'a deflationary dynamic' in the Eurozone and the global economy.

In early November it was the turn of Barroso and the European Commission, and the no-penalty alert mechanism was activated (13 November) for excessive surpluses.[100] It makes sense. The German surplus thrives on external demand, a demand which is no longer created domestically so, in other words, most products that the German population produce are consumed outside the country. The concomitant effect of this is deflation.[99]

These protests were encouraged by the results of the European economy made public in the third quarter of 2013, demonstrating growth at a paltry 0.1% and a decrease of 0.1% in France and Italy, over the previous quarter. In Germany, growth in annual terms was down. To add to the cold water being thrown over the economy, inflation had fallen to 0.7% in the Eurozone.

Naturally, Germany responded to its critics—especially to those coming from the USA—through statements by opinion formers and public figures.[101] In particular, the position of the German Council of Experts in Economics (the 'five wise men') as government advisors would be highlighted, in their Annual Report 2013–2014 presented on 13 November to Chancellor Angela Merkel. The report exposed fears that the new government might 'dilute' the progress achieved by the reforms of Agenda 2010. That could happen, in its opinion, if a minimum wage were introduced or if restrictions were placed on temporary employment and 'minijobs'. The report is clear in its support for austerity and the export model, and against tax increases that would require the implementation of social policies advocated by the social democrats.[102]

The pact of the Grand Coalition government ignored many of these recommendations and targeted two basic issues. The first: solidarity with other EU countries is not contemplated in terms of income transfer or pooling of debt (Eurobonds), which were explicitly ruled out. Internal solidarity made itself conspicuous by its presence on several points: a minimum wage from 2015 (EUR 8.50 per hour)—higher than that of 'minijobs'—early retirement at age 63 (if contributions have been made for 45 years) for those born before 1952; and increased pensions for the elderly in some cases.

This is where the proposals emanating from the Social Democratic Party can best be appreciated, when they managed to make the law on retirement the first of the legislature. Secondly, the conditionality on aid and fiscal consolidation as European policy—the term 'austerity' is not in the document of 185 pages—were reaffirmed in detail, but offset by an explicit reference to 'future investments in growth and employment 'as objectives of the EU, and the pact of that same name. Therefore, after the elections, it can be said that the debate on austerity in Germany ended in a draw, exactly the same as what had happened at the European Council in June.

The German document sounds lame when it still blames the crisis not on the financial system (mentioned only in passing) but on 'excessive debt', the 'lack of competitiveness' (a word repeated to exhaustion) and 'economic imbalances'. It sounds better when it talks about the EIB and Structural Funds to implement the 'necessary infrastructure', just as when it talks about education and measures to facilitate the access of SMEs to financial resources and to promote exports, 'especially in countries that export little'. It also sounds good in the section on European social policy, in which the possibility of a 'minimum wage' to ensure a 'high level of employment' and 'fair wages' is posited.

The most positive part of the agreement is the injection of consumer spending-power into the German population, which was much demanded from the outside. This increased capacity exists in the minimum wage increase (affecting 17% of workers, especially in the service sector) and higher pensions to certain groups (mothers, the elderly and low-wage workers). In the latter case, the new spending reached EUR 23 billion, including other social measures such as childcare.

The question that hangs over the programme of the German government is how it will be financed, because Merkel rejected increasing taxes in that legislature. The official explanation is that higher spending will be made possible by the increase in economic growth (wishful thinking) or by a fall in interest on the debt (unpredictable). The only step in this direction is the increase in social security contributions.

It is not credible that the new spending, or some infrastructure projects—pushed to one side by Merkel's government—can be addressed without increasing taxes. This is especially unavoidable in an ageing society with a longer lifespan, unless the progressive dismantling of the Welfare State is permitted, this being the ultimate aim of the far right—economic and political—in Europe and America.

Autumn. Swords drawn

In the autumn forecast report for 2013 by the European Commission, the mildly childish euphoria over having come ever so slightly out of recession in the second quarter, turned to disillusionment.[103] Marco Buti, the Director General of Economic and Financial Affairs, had to admit that the crisis was not over. He also admitted that the brakes Ecofin had applied to runaway fiscal consolidation in 2011 and 2012 had had something to do with the positive inflation in the second quarter.

In the second quarter of 2013, the EU GDP rose 0.4% and that of the Eurozone, 0.3%; but in the third quarter lack of growth again took control the situation (0.2% in the EU, 0.1% in the Eurozone). The future was bleak and uncertain in an economy that for four years had been obsessed with the still unfinished deleveraging, and whose credit lines remained inaccessible to SMEs.

The justification offered by the OECD in its Economic Outlook in November 2013 for the sluggish development in the European, world and, surprisingly, emerging economies, is threefold: the slowdown in the purchase of assets by the Federal Reserve, strong capital outflows in these economies, and the problems of the fiscal cliff in the US.[104] The OECD's explanations are very opportunist. They do not acknowledge the underlying problems, with unemployment in the EU firmly installed around the 12% mark and growing, along with strong demographic pressure. The number of Europeans aged between 20 and 35 years is declining by almost 1% each year; the number of those over 60 years of age is growing by 1.5% per year.

Nor is the OECD able to explain the disturbing drift of inflation in the Eurozone. In October 2012 it was 2.5%; in October 2013, 0.7%. An ominous drop, because it showed the impotence of the ECB and its policy of low interest rates in the stimulation of lending, either terms of supply or demand.

The failure in the Eurozone which is, lest we forget, a fifth of the world economy, was even more visible compared to success in America, which had experienced a vibrant and unexpected growth of its economy from 2.8% in annual terms in the third quarter of 2013.[105] Unemployment stood at 7% in November (a year before it was at 7.8%), although some of this is due to the fact that many workers stopped looking for jobs.

The USA maintained this healthy trend until the end of 2013. In the fourth quarter, GDP grew by 2.4% annually, which is an acceptable acceleration from the depressing 1.1% in the first quarter under the impact of rising taxes and federal spending cuts agreed in Congress earlier that year. The best result was in unemployment, which fell further in December 2013 to 6.7%. The causes of this good news were an increase in exports, greater consumption and business investment.[106]

The US created 2.2 million jobs in 2013 and reached the per capita GDP that existed before the Great Recession started. In Europe, only Germany could say the same.

The damage caused by the crisis in Europe—and by the policy mistakenly adopted to combat it—is incalculable. Investment in the EU is still 15 points lower than it was before 2008.

Eurozone GDP in mid-2013 was still 3.1 points below the level it was at the beginning of the crisis; GDP in Spain, 7.5 points below; in Portugal, 7.6 points lower. The Irish was 8.4 points lower, and Italy also lower, at 8.8 points. To round off these figures, Greece's GDP was 23.4 points lower.[107] In all these countries, public and private debt is outrageously high.[108] To this group have been added others in difficulty, such as Holland, which received a reduction in its AAA rating from Standard & Poor's, with only Germany, Austria and Finland now maintaining that rating.

Unemployment is the most egregious of the immovable ills affecting the EU because it tips the scales towards a reduction in production. One figure is worth a thousand words. In mid-2013, 49.6% of the 19 million unemployed in the Eurozone had been out of work more than twelve months, according to the OECD, even worse than the 46% in 2012. Unemployment in the Eurozone in January 2014 stood at 12%, the same figure as October. There was not progress but stagnation, and in some countries like France, an alarming record number of 3,316,200 unemployed was reached.

The hair-raising figure of unemployment amongst young Spaniards, and the not so young, is well known. And it is not falling, because the reform of the labour law is a mechanism for unemployment and underemployment, which explains why our GDP per capita has fallen to 96% of that of the EU, according to Eurostat.

The Eurozone grew by a paltry 0.4% in 2013. The Commission's winter 2012 report warned of the 'serious risk that growth will remain stuck in low gear'.[109] To this lethargy is added the spectre of deflation: 0.2% in Spain and 0.8% in the Eurozone in January 2014, an unequivocal sign of economic downturn,[110] as happened with disastrous effects in Japan in the 1990s.

The results observed in 2013 confirmed the failure of austerity, but European governments had still not learned the lesson, despite the clear difference when compared with the results obtained on the other side of the Atlantic. The USA contrived to combine austerity measures with stimuli for growth and employment in both fiscal and monetary policy, in an unapologetically expansive way. The growth cycle of the USA that began in July 2009 has already lasted 56 months, with the deficit down to 4.1% in 2013, the lowest since the start of the financial crisis, and with corporate profits far superior to Europe: three times more, proportionately, than those achieved after previous recessionary economic cycles. US profits are 20% higher than they were in 2007. Profits in Europe are 26% below those achieved on that date.

This has been irrefutably demonstrated in a recent report by the OECD presented on 5 November 2013.[111] In the report, the degree of comfort or discomfort felt by citizens in developed countries in the context of the crisis was studied. The difference between the USA (positive) and the countries of the Eurozone (negative) is very clear, and according to the OECD is due to the fact that the main response to the crisis in the Eurozone has been the policy of austerity, which has greatly reduced the services and financial means available to citizens.

Consolidation of a Dual Model of Growth: Europe and the United States (2014)

2014—seven years from the start of the crisis—consecrated the strongest division in the Western world when it came to tackling the crisis. The disparate results in the Union and the United States have made clear, more than ever, that policy matters. The Union continued to dominate (with increasing difficulty) the doctrine of creditor countries, consisting in reducing public expenditure as a priority. In the United States, another perspective prevailed: strengthening the economy hit by the recession through stimulus, both fiscal and monetary; two distinct growth models that in this confrontation the second, American one, has won by a landslide.

The data we observe regarding the United States at the end of 2014 are irrefutable. The USA now enjoys virtually full employment (5.6% unemployment). In Europe, however, unemployment remains at around 11%, i.e., a total of 24 million people unemployed.

In the USA there is growth (almost 4% in the last trimester of 2014). In the Union—especially in the South—there is a very slow increase in industrial output after seven years of paralysis, which includes another duality within it: the centre-north of Europe is growing, whilst southern Europe is stuck in chronic stagnation. Together with the above, Europe is also immersed in deflation.

Faced with declining international transfers within the European Union, average investment (public and private) is now 17% lower than it was before 2007. In the 'peripheral countries', the percentage reaches a drop of 47%. In Europe, investment has been two times lower than in the US between 2008 and 2013. The lack of public investment is critical to stagnation.

The general feeling is that if after seven years we have not been able to come out of this pit in Europe, something has to change—a lot—in the politics of austerity. This policy has already become a factor in anti-European sentiment, and the element that explains the most visible forms of the structural nature of the crisis and its duration, which are not simply circumstantial.

The situation is so unacceptable that it has been leaning towards a veiled form of neo-Keynesianism. One example is the Juncker plan, EUR 315 billion of planned investment and the possibility that certain investments are not counted as deficit (Communication from the Commission on 13 January 2015). Although clearly inadequate, the investment proposal is recognition of the failure of the monolithic austerity to date, and the need for flexibility in the rigid principle of budgetary stability, and to expand the explanatory power of the Commission in this regard. This is something beneficial for countries like Italy, France and Spain, that is, three of the largest states of the Union.

Another example of change is the ECB's decision to launch a massive debt purchase programme, breaking with so many years of sterile conservative monetary policy and facilitating the devaluation of the Euro.

The Union went too far in fiscal consolidation, and has now had to backtrack forcibly, without wanting to recognize its error; an error that has led to most EU countries having less GDP than they possessed before the start of the crisis (2% smaller in the Eurozone on average), and higher public debt.

The Union is now the central source of economic activity in the world (Europe, Asia, Latin America) with the disease of stagnation in production and trade. Emerging countries have become infected (in 2014 China had its lowest rate—7.4%—since 1990). The OECD has warned that growth in the world economy for the past 7 years has been at 30%, below the average for the 15 years preceding the crisis. Only in the OECD there are 11 million more unemployed than in 2007. For that reason it seems arbitrary when voices such as the G-20 prophesize global growth for the coming years, when we learn that public and private debt has increased on the planet by 57 trillion dollars since the beginning of the crisis, i.e., 286% of world GDP (McKinsey global Institute 2015); and deflation has spread like wildfire.

The political response must be global, and must include public and private investment. Exogenous stimulus, not austerity as the only medicine until the patient ends up malnourished. Monetary policy alone should also not be the only remedy, which is what it has been in the European Union in recent years.

Without these developments in economic policy for Europe, an irreversible entry into a kind of chronic recession is inevitable—which has continued since 2009, in fact—or what Lagarde has called 'the new poor' and Lawrence Summers 'secular stagnation'. I would call it the 'frozen state' or 'hibernation'. A new kind of Ice Age.

4

The European Central Bank and the Federal Reserve Take on the Crisis

In terms of monetary policy relative to the Great Crisis, there is a before and an after. Prior to this crisis, the central banks had developed their traditional tasks of providing liquidity and monetary stability to the economy without going beyond what was actually needed. From the outbreak of the crisis, they had to face a much bigger challenge: to prevent the collapse of Western capitalism, having failed miserably in preventing the financial bubble that led them to the brink in the first place.

We have seen in Chapter 2 how they acted during the first months after the shock. From that point onwards, the strategies followed by the two most powerful central banks diverged: the US Federal Reserve (FED) and the European Central Bank (ECB). Although the two agreed to lower rates—drastically in the case of Bernanke's FED, and cautiously and hesitantly in the case of Trichet's ECB[1]—and although the ECB allowed banks to ask for all the liquidity that they wanted, intervention in the financial markets through auctions and bond purchasing programmes was much more aggressive and immediate in the case of the USA.[2]

Until then, unconventional action by central banks was focused on the essential problem: the lack of liquidity in a blocked international interbank market. However, there were serious differences as regards the ECB, given the legal restrictions under which it operates together with its more restrained monetary policy culture. Nonetheless, central banks had to somehow replace those international capital markets.

In principle, central banks were responsible for avoiding the sinking of the economic system (particularly the financial sector) while being accompanied in the background by a powerful fiscal policy (Keynesian in nature) led by governments.

Adda correctly called this the 'mass socialization of bank losses'.[3] This policy had some success through joint action by governments and central banks, hence the slight recovery that took place later in 2010 and 2011. However, once Greece had declared itself unable to finance its huge deficit on the financial markets, with the systemic risk (not only for the euro) that this implied, there was a sharp turn towards fiscal minimalism agreed by the EU, or rather, those countries with creditor banks bearing public or private debt.

In fact, in May 2010 all of this changed with the sovereign debt crisis in Europe.[4] This was the starting point for a remarkable transformation in the role of central banks, accentuating also the different nature of the ECB compared to the others.

The new situation upset the roles of fiscal and monetary policy. The first faded, acquiring a deliberately low profile, concealing its voluntary impotence. The second, on the other hand, came out fighting the recession (or depression) and started a 'golden' age of prominence for the central banks, still evident today, giving monetary policy an unreal or superficial face; or, if you prefer, something temporary and transitional.

Proof of this is the excessive growth in the balance sheets of central banks, one result of which is that with interest rates still near zero, the only thing left for these banks was to adopt unconventional measures, as we shall see. Therefore, from the onset of the credit crunch, the FED's balance sheet went from USD 869 billion to nearly USD 3 trillion. The Eurosystem balance increased to about USD 4 trillion (30% of EU GDP) and the Bank of England's quadrupled, to USD 640 billion. Such large numbers could end up affecting these institutions' own liquidity, with them having to print money to restore capital or request it from the government. This, as John Plender notes,[5] calls into question the political independence of the central bank itself, an issue not discussed since the US abandoned the convertibility of the dollar to gold and thus the Bretton Woods system. However, on this issue, the European model has some special features that the crisis has not substantially changed for the moment.

The European Central Bank

The structural constraints of European monetary policy

The European Central Bank is an institution of the Union as are the national central banks of the member states; they constitute the European System of Central Banks (ESCB). But the ECB and the central banks of the states whose currency is the Euro, which constitute the 'Eurosystem'—are those which run European monetary policy (Article 282 of the Treaty on the Functioning of the European Union [TFEU]). In turn, the entity which has legal responsibility is the ECB, which has the 'exclusive' right to authorize the issuing of the Euro, and which is 'independent in the exercising of its powers and in the management of finances' (art. 282.3 TFEU).[6]

Part of that management is the setting of the interest rate for the common currency which, with the outbreak of the sovereign debt crisis, has ceased to be the main instrument of monetary policy, and not even the most effective. Other unconventional measures have appeared, and there has been discussion as to whether the ECB should have fighting inflation as its main objective.

Article 127.1 of the Treaty on the Functioning of the European Union is unequivocal on this point:

> The main objective of the European System of Central Banks [ESCB] shall be to maintain price stability. Without prejudice to that objective, it shall support the general policies of the Union.

Another vaguer conferring of powers to the ECB or ESCB, which appears in Article 127.5 of the Treaty on the Functioning of the European Union, is:

> The ESCB shall contribute to the smooth conducting of policies pursued by the competent authorities relating to the prudential supervision of credit institutions and the stability of the financial system.

The ECB, therefore, unlike other central banks, has price stability almost as its single, primary objective. The monetary policy of the Union is restricted to this, with specific content being decided and implemented exclusively by the ECB. This differs from, for example, the Bank of England (BOE), where the monetary target is set by the Chancellor of the Exchequer, (the Minister of Finance) who, along with Parliament, controls the BOE.

The ECB follows a pattern of fierce independence from political and democratic power. Not by chance, but with an essential objective: to maintain the pre-controlled prices at no more than 2% inflation, according to the rules of the Economic and Monetary Union. What for? So that the owners of capital and creditors, both institutional and private, do not surrender one iota of their wealth to debtors. This is the backbone on which European monetary policy stability is based, and therefore, and is therefore written in stone for the European Central Bank. Under no circumstances must the ECB stray out of this area. If it were to do so, inflation would devalue the assets of the ECB itself and its capital, provided by member countries of the Eurozone.

This explains why the Treaties of the European Union have clearly separated fiscal and monetary policy; however, the course of the crisis at hand has brought them closer, or confused them in some decisions of central banks. For the Maastricht lawmakers, the ECB cannot be governed by short-term political decisions or electioneering that would endanger price control. And what must be remembered is this fact, and all this monetary policy, which sets liquidity in the market, can be a tempting political titbit, because it has much faster and more powerful short-term effects than fiscal policy (budgetary expenses and income) whose effects are only perceived months after any action has been taken.

The walls that the Treaties create between member states (fiscal policy) and the ECB (monetary policy) are completed by the most cited article of the TFEU, number 123.1. This provision prohibits the ECB and the national central banks from granting, in any way, loans to member states or public entities. This clause regarding non-monetization of debt is the exact opposite of the FED's policy.

The ECB is not a lender of last resort. This is a fundamental rule that for some economists like Paul de Grauwe, is the origin of the deep mistrust financial markets display towards those European countries with serious debt difficulties, and the concomitant consequences: certain countries, their governments, and businesses, have been and continue to be subject to discrimination, having to pay higher interest rates than other countries. The effects are lethal in terms of the financial burdens of the state discriminated against and the competitiveness of its companies, and cannot be compensated for with funds for financial stability, like the ESM (European Stability Mechanism), because the latter does not print money. It neither has, nor ever could have, anything like the firepower of a central bank which can monetize all debt (theoretically), giving confidence to buyers of that debt. The Treaties prevent the ECB from buying sovereign debt directly from the member states.

The impotence of an area like the Eurozone to respond unilaterally through its monetary policy to the crisis is one of the main factors that led to sovereign debt being a serious problem from 2010 in the European Union, but not, however, in the USA.

Markets have never regarded the Eurozone as a true common currency area, but rather as a series of unconnected countries, despite sharing the same currency. This is because the treaties do not regulate the Eurozone as a whole, either from the point of view of monetary policy or fiscal policy.

The TFEU Article 123 previously mentioned prohibits aid from the ECB and prevents debt monetization, something which the FED or BOE could do if investors abandoned American or British bonds. In the event that the Treasury in Spain does not sell its debt securities at a reasonable price, it would not be possible to monetize by printing money, whether this is done by the ECB, or, of course, the Bank of Spain, which no longer has the ability to do so autonomously.

The issuance of Spanish, Italian or French debt is not controlled by each country, but it cannot be underwritten by the ECB. The national treasuries do not control this, but neither is there a European Treasury. This is left entirely to the whim of the markets and ratings agencies, something which is decisive for institutional investors.

Furthermore, Article 125.1 of the TFEU, the well-known 'no bail-out' clause, prohibits solidarity via fiscal policy: 'The Union shall not be liable for or assume the commitments of governments [...] Member States shall not be liable for or assume the commitments of governments'.

What this means is that in the Treaty, faced with a situation of debt in a country on the brink of default, there is no provision for any kind of support mechanism in the Eurozone, except the clause of Article 122.2 TFEU, designed for 'natural disasters or exceptional occurrences' that a member state 'could not control'. Only in the face of some extraordinary Act of God is financial assistance from the Union available. This was the lifeline of the first loan to Greece, but the truth is that the Union could have walked away from this desperate situation, leaving the IMF to take over the management of the crisis.

When Portugal and Ireland also suffered the closure of markets to them, the Union reacted, as we know, not using funds drawn from the budgets of the European Union, which did not exist, but through ad hoc fixed-term loans; these had market-level interest rates and strict conditions were set, until the member states were able to return to the markets to finance themselves. The creation of a permanent crisis mechanism (European Stability Mechanism) required the amendment of Article 136 TFEU.

As is repeated again and again from Germany, the Bundesbank and its Constitutional Court, the EU, unlike the USA, is not a 'Union for transferring income'. It is precisely this axiom which hampered the ECB's action in the purchase of bonds from countries having difficulties financing themselves in the markets.

With a European monetary policy built on these fragile foundations, the ECB found itself without the necessary tools to tackle the serious problems that began to call into question the survival of the Euro: the difficulty of public funding of Euro member states, especially in southern Europe, and the underlying issue never resolved and closely linked to the previous one: the banking crisis.

Trichet and the counter-inflationary obsession

There is a crucial difference between the monetary policy applied by the FED, which we shall see, and that which can be put into action by the ECB. This has to do with the complex nature of a common currency area with different governments and different budgets. That is, a single monetary policy, but different fiscal policies. This is what made the reaction to the sovereign debt crisis that erupted in 2010 so dramatic. The exchange rate or the interest rate may be good for Germany, the Netherlands and Finland while not being so for Portugal, Spain or Italy.

The divergence between creditor and debtor countries made a balanced monetary policy impossible. The former preferred restrictive and conservative policies that would not create temptations for governments to relax in terms of the adjustments; the latter, an expansive policy, inflation included, with easy access to cash and liquidity. The Euro also acted like a straitjacket which made devaluation impossible as a way of gaining competitiveness.

These arguments, together with what I have called the 'structural constraints' of the ECB, cast doubt on Trichet's stand about the question of going to the aid of sovereign debt. In the end, the ECB's intervention was part of the agreement made on the night of 10 May 2010. The direct purchase of government bonds by the ECB, prohibited by the Treaty, is also the type of action that has traditionally been considered inflationary. It would have been a casus belli for the German government, as it was for Trichet himself, when the dangers to the Euro were not even visible. But the 'indirect' bond purchase itself was permissible, and necessary. So, on the same 10 May, the ECB launched the Securities Markets Programme, temporary and limited in nature, aimed at buying Greek, Irish and Portuguese government debt to the tune of EUR 77 billion[7] on the secondary markets.

Trichet did not manage to free himself from German criticism, including the president of the Federal Republic, Christian Wulff. In February 2011, Axel Weber, Bundesbank governor, resigned from the ECB Governing Council; and in September, so did Jürgen Stark, the bank's chief economist. The critical view of Weber was based, of course, on the inflationary dangers of the purchasing programmes, to which Trichet replied that the measures were designed to standardize the 'transmission of monetary policy'. It was a mechanical response, which was then reiterated as a mantra by Draghi. But this was not the real reason; rather the galloping debt crisis was.

The bond-buying programme, which was supplemented in October 2010 with a similar one (the Covered Bond Purchase Programme 2), worth EUR 40 billion,[8] allowed the interest of Portuguese and Irish debt to stabilize at less than 6% until the autumn of 2010.[9] Not much, considering the magnitude of contagion to other countries in southern Europe and the unstoppable decline of Greek debt, which would eventually be restructured and affect—supposedly once only—private creditors.

There is a period in the ECB's policy that is puzzling. From April to November 2011, the last stage of Trichet's management, the ECB raised the price of its main refinancing operations. It must be emphasized that then, Mario Draghi enthusiastically supported Trichet in his raising of interest rates to contain inflationary pressures, as well as in policies of fiscal discipline.

The effect of this inconsistent monetary policy, together with other factors, was the increasing pressure on the sovereign debt of Italy and Spain, in the hot summer of 2011. The phenomenon was all the more serious because the sovereign debt crisis—unresolved by neither sovereign governments nor the ECB—was becoming increasingly entangled with banking risks, in a diabolical game of interacting parts. The bonds held by banks lost value, and therefore, bank portfolios lost value too. Faced with this dynamic, market confidence in banks and national debt slumped, especially as regards the bonds of Spain and Italy.

The financial situation was so tense that the debate on Eurobonds or the pooling of Eurozone debt was revived, with the aim of allowing the countries most affected by the flight of investors from their debt (Spain, Italy and others) to be financed at interest rates enjoyed by countries like Germany, France and the UK. As secretary of state, I was at pains to show my position in favour of Eurobonds in the various European forums,[10] even though it was known that this proposal did not have the support of Chancellor Merkel nor that of Jean-Claude Trichet. In a final statement putting an end to his stormy tenure at the head of the ECB,[11] Trichet defended his passive and rigid view of monetary policy, in line with uncompromising anti-inflationary dogma. Unlike Bernanke, he did not know how to use the means at his disposal. For Trichet, interest rates were for fighting inflation, while the purchase of debt (which only worked in certain periods) or one-year loans to banks, and were for giving liquidity.[12] So, as Irwin notes, interest rates could be raised while buying debt. He was unable to separate the main objective, the stability of the Euro, from the secondary one of inflation, which had never been high since the outbreak of the crisis.[13] Nor did he care at all about the weak growth and employment in the Euro area. That, in his view, was the task of 'internal devaluations'—the lowering of wages and pensions—as a form of response from the debtor countries to threats from the markets. It was his way of preserving stability in a currency area with many differences in their short-term economic interests.

Draghi tackles the banking crisis

Mario Draghi took over as president of the ECB on 1 November 2011. That day, the shares of European banks were plummeting. Not so Spanish and Italian government bonds, backed by the ECB's purchases.

This was a symbolic premonition of what has so far been the model developed by the Draghi presidency, in which banks have taken centre stage, as beneficiaries and as agents of European monetary policy.

It has to be reiterated that the ECB is not lender of last resort of the member states, but it can provide unlimited loans to private banks, becoming the lender of last resort for them. This has been Mario Draghi's strategy.

The first thing he did was lower to the official interest rate of 1.5%, which Trichet had bequeathed to him, to 1.25%. A reasonable measure demanded by everyone, when the Union was entering its second recession since the start of the crisis. The IMF supported this step immediately.

The second thing that Draghi decided was to accelerate the purchase of sovereign debt in the secondary markets.[14] With this action, Draghi was responding to complaints from the Italian and Spanish governments. At the meeting of the G-20 in Cannes, the latter criticized the striking difference between the UK and Spain, in favour of the former, in terms of interest rates paid on issuance of national debt, when the percentage of deficit to GDP and the amount of national debt of the UK were far superior to those of Spain. The reason was simple: the Bank of England owned 20% of the British debt, while the ECB had bought less than 1% of the Spanish debt.[15]

The third action undertaken by Draghi was the most important: the injection of limitless liquidity into the economy, not through bond purchases but through three-year loans to banks (previously one year) and more flexible requirements to permit the use of securities as collateral. This is what was technically called LTRO (Longer Term Refinancing Operations). Private banks were in like a shot to participate in such a 'sexy' programme. A programme of three-year loans is simply irresistible to capital. The more than 1,300 banks that opted for the full programme obtained a total of EUR 1 trillion, 18 billion.[16]

This decision had a double effect, Josep M. Bricall notes: improving the situation of the balance sheets of banks and pressure on sovereign debt.[17] Banks bought money at 1%—the percentage to which Draghi had dropped interest rates—to then buy up sovereign debt from their governments at a much higher interest rate.[18] There was another added benefit: the possibility that banks could deposit lesser-backed securities with the ECB for cash, thus encouraging bankers to take on riskier lending, just to have securities as collateral to apply for three-year loans to the ECB.

This is a somewhat contrived process to circumvent the monopoly that banks have on lending to the public sector, and therefore the ban on the ECB buying debt directly from governments. It essentially benefited the banks and not the real economy, because the banks did not transfer this liquidity to individuals in the form of loans. Why would they bother, if they were already making good money in their financial business with the LTRO programme?

The unlimited funding ability for Eurozone banks from the ECB contrasts sharply with the restrictions on the member states. Not even through instruments such as the ESM, to which the creditor countries which were denied a banking license with which they could also have gone to the ECB to request loans at 1%.[20]

It is in this context that the statement in November 2011 by the International Institute of Finance (IIF), which includes four hundred financial institutions, can be explained. The statement claimed that faced with the recession in the Eurozone, the ECB was the only institution capable of providing realistic support in the following weeks.[21]

However, the facts did not seem to coincide with the IIF. The sovereign debt crisis was not fixed.[22] Nor were the deep problems of the toxic assets of the banks, especially the Spanish ones. These were two sides of the same coin: debt and banking, badly interwoven; a problem that does not exist in the USA, where in practice national debt is not in the hands of banks. In Europe it is, and also according to the Basel Accords, zero risk is attributed to that debt. As such, it appears on the books of the banks holding it.

It was this ill-fated situation which made it necessary for the ECB to concede so many facilities to banks. However, the intended results were not achieved, as the exponential growth in the presence of government bonds on the balance sheets of banks was parallel to the growth of this enormous risk exposure;[23] and as such it was understood by the markets.

The risk was perceived as more serious, of course, in countries with more exposure to their own bonds, leading to the structural problems in the Eurozone: the fragmentation of financial markets. The crisis in the financial debt markets had happened before in the Euro currency zone: in May and November 2010 and in July and November 2011. In June 2012, it took on a still more troubling aspect.

The concern of investors about the future of the Euro itself, i.e., its possible breakup, as well as the aversion to risk led to a particularly damaging phenomenon for peripheral countries: growing and significant capital outflows to safe countries such as Germany. The IMF, in its Global Financial Stability Report in October 2012 noted that, between June 2011 and June 2012, capital flight from Spain was around EUR 296 billion (27% of GDP) and EUR 235 billion in the case of Italy (15% of GDP).[24] Another difficulty therefore arose in the financing of these countries and, at the same time, an increased use of the unlimited credit line opened by the ECB. The natural consequence was a rising risk premium, especially in Spain, prompting the Spanish government to seek financial assistance from the Union in June 2012 to recapitalize the most damaged banks, including Bankia. Cyprus also requested assistance from the programme.

This set of circumstances further clouded the atmosphere of distrust in the Euro project.[25] So much so that, at a conference in London on 26 July, Mario Draghi was obliged to react strongly stating that the ECB 'will do whatever it takes to preserve the Euro'. He added, 'Believe me, it will be enough'. That 'whatever it takes' became the phrase of the year, or century, because it had a decisive effect on the markets, which now believed that Mario Draghi—Super Mario—was serious, and that the Euro was not at risk, and that the paralyzed bond purchases would resume.

The perception was correct. On 5 July 2012, the Governing Council of the ECB had lowered by 25 basis points the intervention interest rate, thus placing the rate of the main refinancing operations at 0.75%, leaving at 0% on the interest rates the ECB pays on bank deposits, in order to encourage them towards credit for companies. But he was unsuccessful.

The unprecedented OMT bond-buying programme

The most significant action was still to come based, according to Draghi, on the fact that to the extent that very high interest rates and the associated risk premiums hindered the functioning of the transmission of monetary policy, the more they fell under the mandate of the ECB. In August 2012, the Spanish risk premium was around 480 points. On 6 September, the Governing Council of the ECB met and Mario Draghi announced a new programme to buy sovereign debt in countries with difficulties on the secondary market. Its name was 'Outright Monetary Transactions' (OMT).[26]

The OMT programme was directed towards bonds with maturities of three years or less, and the purchase volume was in principle unlimited. However, to access these programmes, the debtor country must accept the terms set by the European bailout fund, that is, the European Financial Stability Facility (EFSF) and the European Stability Mechanism (ESM) to which the Eurozone governments belong. An essential characteristic of the programme is that conditions are required in terms of adjustments and structural reforms for those committed to the bailout fund.

Draghi countered the inflationary argument with two related concepts that would become part of his everyday vocabulary in public speeches: 'fragmentation of financial markets' and 'transmission of monetary policy', i.e., the process by which changes in the policy rate of the central bank are transmitted through the financial system to the real economy. Something fundamental to an accommodating or even expansive monetary policy, such as that carried out by the ECB.

The fragmented and distorted nature of the financial system in the Eurozone led to fragmentation of monetary policy; in some member states, the ECB cuts in interest rates failed to reach companies (especially SMEs) and households, which pay disproportionate interest rates to finance themselves. Therefore, reductions in interest rates made by the ECB did not benefit the end consumers of credit, if they resided in a country which the markets considered a significant risk. And it is this distortion which the Eurosystem should avoid. Among other things because it affects the single market itself, and 'renationalizes' the banking system.

This is how Mario Draghi explained his reasoning for the OTM to the European Parliament and the Bundestag in October. Draghi assured German MPs that there was no disguised financing of governments, and the sacrosanct independence of the ECB remained, nor was there an unreasonable risk to the European taxpayer due to the safeguards required; and, most importantly, there would not be inflation, because 'for every Euro we inject, we will withdraw another Euro'.[27]

There was no reason for Draghi's rabbit pulled out of the hat in the form of bond purchases from countries in difficulty to scare Germany. In late 2012 the ECB had EUR 218 billion of debt from Eurozone states, of which EUR 44.3 billion (20.3%) was Spanish debt and EUR 102.8 billion (47.2%) Italian debt.[28] This was not expected to rise, because the requirements to do so are a deterrent. If Spain and Italy want the ECB to buy its debt on the markets, they have to subscribe to a programme with the EFSF or ESM, which will force them to sign a Memorandum of Understanding (MOU) with strict conditions on deficit targets and structural reforms.

Since the beginning of his term the discourse of Mario Draghi in response to the crisis has been that monetary policy cannot do everything, and that the austerity policy is correct and that each country has to meet its deficit targets and make the 'orthodox' structural reforms. When talking about fiscal consolidation, Draghi has always known how to choose between tax increases and spending cuts. Without a doubt, he has opted for the latter. In his view, that is the way the adjustment process is perceived by the markets as 'credible, irreversible and structural'.[30]

Draghi's remarks during the summer of 2012 served to calm the capital and debt markets—not the actual, substantial debt—and to lower risk premiums.[31] These were not helpful, however, to restarting lending to companies, or to stopping the recession and unemployment. The structural limits of monetary policy on the one hand, and the impotence of a depressive fiscal policy on the other, made it impossible to achieve the dream of seeing the end of the crisis.

The 'currency war'

To this is added a confusing 'currency war' in early 2013. It began with a statement by Hollande on 5 February, in which he protested against the Euro appreciation experienced in the previous month due to the more expansive policies of the FED,

BOE and BOJ, and further reinforced by the ECB's decision not to lower interest rates.[32]

But if the ECB does not react in any way, the Euro is constantly revalued on the markets, as has happened since July 2012, even more so if the funds buy back Eurozone bonds.[34]

The exchange rate of the Euro was manifestly higher than was desirable for what countries like Italy or Spain needed to be competitive. What was obtained with an internal devaluation of wages was wasted with an overvalued Euro.[35] The fall of the Euro was very slow.[36]

Interest rates again

The largest headache for monetary policy remained the financing of small businesses, those most affected by a strong Euro. The ECB was aware of it, and of what Draghi has called the 'contradictory effects of fiscal consolidation', not to mention the negative results of the austerity policy. Draghi blamed the absence of bank credit to the real economy, especially in peripheral countries, on three reasons: lack of liquidity (the ECB faced with LTRO); lack of capital or, from another perspective, the dubious quality of the assets that banks have on their balance sheets; and increasing risk aversion of investors (which the ECB expressed its inability to deal with).[37] Added to this was the fact that banks were returning to the ECB the money borrowed under the LTRO liquidity programme, so credit to the private sector contracted. The ECB narrowed its balance sheet when the FED and the BOJ did the opposite.

What banks know is that lending to the private sector is more risky than government bond yields, which are much more secure,[38] and for this reason they will not lend, or will only do so at growing interest rates and with more stringent safeguards.

The situation of the financial freeze had not led the ECB to take any unconventional stance as the FED had done, such as buying up mortgage bonds or securities on loans to small businesses. The much publicized OMT programme was unprecedented.[39] The impression was that the ECB's monetary policy was not a 'silver bullet' and had reached a limit. The ECB returned responsibility to the politicians and regained control over conventional monetary policy, as the only solution to what Keynes might have called the 'liquidity trap'.

On Thursday 2 May, Mario Draghi announced in Bratislava that the ECB had decided to cut the official interest rate to 0.5%, the lowest in the Euro era. It had been 10 months since the last cut (to 0.75%). The ECB also extended liquidity to private banks until July 2014; but it decided not to penalize the EUR 210 billion deposited at the ECB by banks, always protected by being the 'instrument needed to transmit monetary policy'. The Governing Council of the ECB, after a difficult internal discussion, gave this response to bad economic data in the Eurozone in the first quarter of 2013 (18 months in a row in recession, and rampant unemployment). It only made vague promises that, in any case, the aggressive purchases of asset-backed securities were now a distant memory.[40]

The ECB maintained the Draghi philosophy: in the conventional sense, reducing interest rates, without completely running out of fuel; and in the unconventional, the preference for banking as an exclusive and unavoidable intermediary between monetary policy and the real economy. This does not solve the endless problem of the lack of liquidity among the biggest job creators, small and medium enterprises which suffer higher interest rates, given that small loans are more expensive than large ones;[41] nor the vulnerability of the Eurozone to political crises.

The most the ECB managed to agree by mid-July (effective from October) was to facilitate the acceptance of financial assets held by the banks as collateral for the unlimited ECB liquidity supplied to private banks at 0.5% interest. The way to do this was to reduce the required quality of these guarantees, which has its side-effects.[42]

Helpless in the face of the credit-crunch

All these measures have not been sufficient to revive the provision of credit to the real economy, because this 'unique' intermediary (Draghi *dixit*) for transmitting monetary policy—the banks—simply did not do so, especially in the countries of southern Europe.[43] Without resolving this Gordian knot, a quick and definitive solution to the chronic lack of sufficient growth to create jobs cannot be found.

Amongst the reasons for which, according to Draghi, credit remains fragmented and paralyzed, the most powerful is the de-capitalization of banks in peripheral countries.

The truth is that this bottleneck arose from the bad practices of corporate management and some governments that did not address the issue at the appropriate time. Stress tests were not conducted with the necessary credibility, enough capital was not injected, and insolvent banks were not wound up.[44]

Inaction prevented the main issue from being tackled in time, and that which is the essential reason for the endless banking crisis, i.e., the huge private debt hanging over the Eurozone financial sector—and the US one—mainly in banks of small or medium size. Their forced deleveraging is one of the most powerful brakes on growth, because it takes away investment and consumer capacity from the economy.

The Royal Bank of Scotland estimates that banks in the Eurozone will have to reduce their financial balance sheets by more than EUR 3 trillion in the next three to five years to meet the standards of capitalization.[45]

Draghi could do something to make sure that the banks give short-term loans with low interest rates to both families and businesses, as well as other banks, and therefore, to properly convey the desired monetary policy. But the ECB president has never seen another way to deal with the crisis apart from through banking, and banks have been very concerned about their debt, which will reach peak maturity in 2015.

The ECB has few tricks left up its sleeve. One is to lower interest rates, given the persistent drought in liquidity and the thus depressed economy of the Eurozone, apart from the stock exchanges. On 7 November 2013 the ECB lowered the interest rate to 0.25%, a record low. This divided the ECB council between positions of north and south; in the outside world it was not like that. Everyone (the European Parliament, the IMF, investors) hailed the measure, which achieved an immediate fall in the Euro and the Spanish and Italian risk premiums, as well as an increase in the stock markets. The reality is that the ECB decision—as indispensable as it is belated—is one more proof of the failure of austerity.

A spectre is haunting Europe: deflation

The main motive, the trigger for the ECB measures, was the danger of deflation on the economy, looming since October 2013. Eurostat published the harmonized index which showed an impressive 0.7%, the lowest level of inflation in the Eurozone since late 2009, when we were in the middle of a price freeze. It reflected a strong Euro but, above all, faltering consumer demand, contracting wages and unacceptable unemployment levels.

Consistently falling prices—inducing the idea that it is better to wait to spend when prices drop even more—ends up adversely affecting the demand for productive activity, corporate profits and jobs; it discourages investment; and causes the well-known increase in the financial burden of the state and individuals, subject to a real interest rate on their higher debt.

A year later, at the time of writing, the spectre of deflation (contrary to the forecasts of Draghi) has not disappeared in the Eurozone, but has reached 0.3%, further and further away from 2%, the supposedly ideal target of a bank whose mandate in reality is to technically avoid deflation.

Christine Lagarde dared to mention deflation on 15 January 2014, at a conference in Washington in which she warned of its dangers. It caused a feeling of unease among the central banks, which were urged not to cancel the unconventional monetary policy until 'robust growth was firmly established'. For Lagarde, it is crucial to 'not prematurely withdraw monetary support' from growth, words that sound like déjà vu when the EU in 2009 conspired to not prematurely withdraw the stimulus for growth.

The EU needs more inflation to reduce the burden of debt, to increase consumption, and to increase the value of assets and tax revenues; to get the economy off the floor. This is the task of the European Central Bank. The ECB can increase the money in circulation, aimed not at financial speculation but for productive investment, so that the potential of the now underperforming and passive real economy are put back into gear, the currency is reactivated, excess capacity is covered, and the Euro's value is not permitted to strengthen.

Now what?

In June 2014, the ECB finally decided to go all out. Draghi announced a reduction in the interest rate to 0.15%; a purchase from banks of 7% of their non-mortgage loans—'targeted' (TLTRO)—at near zero interest, in order to spend EUR 400 billion in the next four years, provided that the receiving banks lend that money to SMEs; a negative interest rate for bank deposits in Frankfurt; and a stop to sterilizing SMP (Securities Market Programme) bonds.

The aim has been to move the once lethargic markets to pursue growth and extend credit for this—or cheapen it—at the same time, and this is probably the real issue, although less admissible: achieving the devaluation of the Euro and facilitating the export competitiveness of the Eurozone.

However, neither has raised the level of inflation or changes in available credit, nor has the Euro moved too much, although it has lost value (USD 1,274).

There has not been the expected and desired reaction, and we have seen an as-yet unknown side of Mario Draghi, puzzled by interest rates unexpectedly down in September, again, to 0.05%, buying ABS securities, crying out in Jackson Hole against austerity and in favour of stimulus as the only measure to end the crisis, saying that the worst thing is to do nothing. It is not surprising that there were equity seizures in late September, to which Draghi replied again spasmodically by announcing the immediate purchase of the famous ABS (private assets or credits for SMEs) and covered bonds (further secured by all assets issued) over two years. All to expand the ECB's balance sheet to a trillion euros, but finding great success in banks.

In 2014 we experienced a long wait for monetary easing by the ECB, always announced by Draghi and never adopted, despite the alarming deflation and strong Euro. Until 22 January 2015, the massive buying-up of debt was agreed upon by the ECB. More than expected by markets: EUR 60 billion each month until September 2016.

The ECB, after years of inaction, took the most necessary and urgent decision due to the issue with deflation (it reached −0.6% in January 2015); in view of the failure of the auction of credit to banks, which the ECB required to lend money to businesses and individuals; and also in view of elections in Greece that would yield a disturbing result for the orthodoxy of Brussels.

It seems that it is impossible to increase the balance sheet by a trillion euros, slimmed down for years and years, but the expansive movement of the ECB is finally right. Insufficient, late, just when the FED does the opposite, but correct.

The Mighty FED of Ben Bernanke

As described in Chapter 2, the FED was always ahead of the ECB in order to avoid, 'with all available instruments' in the words of Bernanke, the recessionary slump in Western economies during the critical period of 2008–2009. He did it by using conventional monetary policy on interest rates, lowering them faster than the exasperating decisions of Trichet. The FED was also ahead in the unconventional nationalization of financial institutions and in the also unconventional policy of buying assets (Term Asset-Backed Securities Loan Facilities), and even of making loans to banks of money (Term Auction Facility) and Treasury bills (Term securities Lending Facility). By doing this, it was following the immortal advice of Walter Bagehot in 1873 to central banks on how to challenge a liquidity crisis: 'Lend freely against good collateral'.[46] The FED, in 2008 and 2009, did not even require 'good collateral' from the banks.

The Federal Reserve launched itself without any hesitation whatsoever into the fight against the main adversary, the recession, also helping to build a newly-minted regulation of the US financial system.

QE1. QE2. QE3

These acronyms which resemble Formula 1 awards are, without doubt, the fastest, most intense and extensive 'unconventional' monetary policy that the Federal Reserve has implemented in its history. This was completely logical, since it was the greatest financial crisis that it had ever faced.

These quantitative easing efforts (QE), as well as the management of the official price of money, are ways of responding to the crisis by injecting liquidity into the economy. With interest rates near zero, there was in the end no scope for conventional monetary policy, with the entirely reasonable objective of increasing aggregate demand.

In Chapter 2 of the first part, I referred to QE1 and QE2 as forms of immediate reaction to the financial shock. QE1 took place between November 2008 and March 2010, a period during which the Federal Reserve bought up massive amounts of Treasury bonds, corporate securities, assets, and commercial paper. The purchases of the Federal Reserve focused on mortgage loan securities, particularly those made by Fannie Mae and Freddie Mac.

Ben Bernanke announced QE2 in November 2010. 'Real interest rates are too low, given the state of the economy, and the risk of deflation is higher than desirable', Bernanke said to justify the measures he was proposing to adopt.[47]

The objective of the FED was to inject USD 600 billion (EUR 425 billion) until June 2011, through the purchase of bonds[48]—and not of private securities—not only to lower the long-term interest rates, but also to boost consumption and improve the employment market. These are the two essential functions of the FED.

While the goals of purchasing and of stopping deflation were achieved, the goal of lowering long term interest rates was not.

On 22 June 2011, the Federal Open Market Committee (FOMC), responsible for discussing and approving major decisions of the Federal Reserve, decided to keep the main interest rate between 0 and 0.25%, 'for a prolonged period of time', said its president, and reported an end to the quantitative stimulus measures through QE2.[49]

However, in September the FED announced what the media dubbed 'Operation Twist': in fact, it returned to exchanging short-term bonds for long-term bonds, to the tune of USD 400 billion.[50]

The agreed-upon policy of debt monetization, followed faithfully by the Federal Reserve in 2010 and 2011 had a positive impact on growth and inflation, as well as on the restructuring of the financial system, both private (the greater beneficiary) and public, thus making possible the financing of the soaring US deficit at a very low interest rate, crucial to getting the economy out of the pit of depression. Because of this, the monetary policy of the FED achieved more than the fiscal policy of the Obama administration.

The FED, in complicity with the government, maintained the line on monetary stimulus in 2013 and linked Operation Twist, which ended in December 2011, with a new programme of buying long-term bonds: QE3. Its volume—USD 85 billion per month—was enormous, demonstrating the determination of Bernanke to put all the effort of the Federal Reserve into helping the weak economic recovery and making unemployment drop sharply. In each month of 2013, the FED purchased USD 45 billion in bonds, in addition to the USD 400 billion which from September 2012 the FED spent buying mortgage assets.[51]

Coinciding with the announcement of QE3, the Federal Reserve introduced in late 2012 what for some has been a historic change in monetary policy and the policy of the central bank. It undertook to keep the official interest rate of short-term money close to 0%, as long as unemployment did not fall below 6.5%. The FED had no doubts when it came to linking monetary policy with the situation of the economy and not to inflation, as has been the case in Europe. Somehow, the FED managed to break down the artificial walls built over many years between fiscal and monetary policy, and between conventional and unconventional monetary policy. It acted, in truth, concerned about the pointless, never-ending political debate on the 'fiscal cliff' between Democrats and Republicans. The FED acted in any case with the assurance that their stratospheric purchases, made by printing money, would not produce inflation. At the same time, it helped both to cover the budget deficit (7% of GDP) and to enable households to pay their mortgages after a surprising resurgence in the housing market and housing prices in the USA.

In his appearance before the Senate on 26 February 2013, Bernanke showed great faith in their actions, which had helped economic recovery, not only in real estate but also in the production of automobiles and consumer durables.[52]

Communicating the exit strategy

Ben Bernanke, in a speech he gave in Chicago in early May, warned about some worrying signs according to which banks seemed to be developing speculative activities to compensate for low interest rates. It was an admission that the policy of monetary stimulus was in danger of creating new bubbles in asset prices. Investors rushed to go anywhere in the world to find consistent returns on their money.

Although Bernanke said that withdrawing stimulus prematurely was not good, he continued to use ambiguous language on the phasing out of QE3. The message was: we have to think of a roadmap for the exit.[53] From there, Bernanke changed the course of financial behaviour. His statements along with other events helped introduce more confusion: injections of money from the Bank of Japan ('Abenomics') and, simultaneously, the marked slowdown in the economies of the emerging markets of China, Brazil, India, South Africa, Thailand, Philippines, Indonesia, South Korea, Turkey and Israel.[54] The central banks of some countries reacted by lowering interest rates. Investors began their flight to other latitudes.

This explains the drop in bonds and shares on international markets, particularly abrupt on 11 June. Volatility settled into the markets and changed the direction of the investment dynamic. If in the first half of 2013 the problem was the creation of bubbles, in the summer it was the uncertainty and risk aversion of the markets, faced with the loss of credibility of central banks—starting with the FED—in the maintenance of expansionary monetary policies.

Good news, bad news

What was happening was that good economic news, paradoxically, was bad for markets accustomed to cheap money because this brought ever closer the FED's bringing to an end of its expansionary policy. The data coming from the United States, despite sequestration (tax increases and spending cuts), was getting better, especially the jobs market.[55] Bernanke recognized this in the eagerly awaited press conference on 19 June. The FED would keep interest rates low in the short term until 2015, and in any case, not before the unemployment rate dropped below 6.5%, as long as inflation was not being fuelled, which did not seem likely.

The Wall Street press immediately expressed its opposition to the maintenance of the monetary policy, which it considered to have a similar bent towards the neo-Keynesian or progressive policy reforms for health care or tax increases on the rich advocated by Obama.[56]

From across the political spectrum, the evolution and attitude of the FED was criticized, attributing it to the pressure from the political right and their constant accusations towards Bernanke that he was weakening the dollar and jeopardizing prices. Once the FED had conceded that QE3 could be ended, and that the effect would be a rise in interest rates in the long term, it would be very difficult to return to those low interest rates.[57]

The most significant thing, obviously, was the market response to Bernanke's statement; i.e., the reaction to the communication policy of the FED. Communication had become an embodiment of the unconventional monetary policy of the US central bank. It has the disadvantage that it cannot prevent a nuanced suggestion from being followed by a lurch in the markets which right away, to protect themselves, anticipate what they think the central bank will do.

Markets around the world reacted with strong bond sales, raising long-term interest rates—which the FED does not control directly—and, therefore, the costs of mortgage holders.[58]

All this was a risk for the economic recovery which had come about sustained by the housing market, thanks to low interest rates, not because household income had increased. Uncertainty had taken hold in the financial markets[59] and also in government; because if the FED stopped buying bonds—the great privilege of the

USA—the budget deficit would require the shortfall to be found from revenue in the private sector. This would mean an increase in taxation.

Farewell to Bernanke and QE3

The second half of 2013 had become that of 'waiting for Godot'. Each month was agony for the markets, journalists, analysts, legislators and even the White House. That was on the inside. Outside, it was the same story. Stock markets, investors and governments around the world were glued to the news to see when Bernanke would decide to taper the dollars injected every 30 days into international financial circuits. Data that could encourage the FED to put a cap on QE3 was scanned furiously. Employment and unemployment. GDP. Industrial demand. Inflation, and so forth.

What mattered to the FED was the jobs market. Not only the figure of 7% unemployment, from which the FED would begin to inject less money (it was at 11.0% in 2009), but the employment rate, i.e., the number of people with a job. The percentage of those who were employed in 2013 was 58.5% of the US workforce, considerably lower than the 63% it had been before the recession. Bernanke stressed the relevance of this approach at the hearing conducted on 17 July 2013 in Congress. It was necessary that the number of unemployed should not increase, as it was necessary that the number in work should not decrease.

The employment rate is a telling figure because by expressing the relationship between adults of working age and those effectively employed it therefore quantifies those who, discouraged, have stopped looking for work. There are also two other important qualitative figures attached to this with reference to those who leave employment: those who do so voluntarily, and those who are dismissed. In a normal situation—like now in the USA—the latter now outnumber the former. In a dire situation, there are more dismissals.

Bernanke always surprised and confounded the supposedly clever markets. Until on 18 December 2013 the FOMC (Federal Open Market Committee), by nine votes to one, finally decided to drop the monthly purchases by the FED (USD 5 billion in T-Bills and USD 5 billion in mortgage backed securities) by USD 10 billion, and on 29 January by another USD 10 billion, and on 20 March the same, leaving bond purchases and mortgages at USD 55 billion a month, which in any case is still a huge amount of money. The total opposite to the drip-by-drip ECB purchases. The idea was that QE3 would fade gradually until the end of 2014.

The patience of Bernanke in reducing the power QE3 was influenced by the uncertainty that Congress caused to the US economy, thanks to the threat—carried out—of a 'government shutdown', and the debt ceiling. In October when all doubt evaporated, the FED felt more empowered to activate the tapering, in addition to the above reasons.

The other deciding factor was the unemployment rate, which reached 7% in November 2013 and 6.7% in December, because the labour force decreased. Other indicators were positive: low inflation, a rising real estate market, and wages rising slowly with further growth expected in the third quarter of 2013. Enough for the FED to take the steps awaited for many months. That did not stop Bernanke, in his last speech as president of the FED in Philadelphia, talking about a 'clearly incomplete' recovery in the USA.

For the period in the FED beginning under the command of Yellen (1 February 2014), it has been essential to convince employers and consumers that they will continue to have low interest rates because the FED will be relentless in maintaining low official interest on short-term money. They are, ultimately, those who condition or influence the long-term interest rates (set freely by the markets) to also be kept down. Yellen predicts 1% in 2015.

But she will have to consider carefully when to start increasing interest rates to avoid asset bubbles and excessive appreciation of the dollar at the same time—not a simple task, to maintain this balance.

The takeover of Yellen coincided with a change in the policy of communication from the FED, which changed from focussing not so much on the specifics (numbers of unemployed) as on various factors (production capacity, debt, abandonment of the search for employment) and other economic variables, such as salary, to go to a 'qualitative' evaluation to determine monetary policy towards more or less stimulus, that is, quantitative easing.

QE has not been a bad deal for the bank, which makes intermediation (i.e., commissions) for almost all operations of the FED. They have paved the way for loans (another difference with the impotence of the ECB) and banks have fattened their asset balances. Bernanke saved Wall Street; he did not let it sink.

Expansionary US monetary policy, which ended in October 2014, has been good, it is true, modestly shoring up the slow but steady US recovery, in which it is not easy to discern which part corresponds to Bernanke and which to Obama. Monetary policy creates few jobs directly, but does create them indirectly by providing liquidity to the economy; and, above all, it helps prevent them from being destroyed. This was the success of the Bernanke era.

In conclusion, the two significant models among central banks are undoubtedly the FED and the ECB. These represented, and represent, two ways of responding to the crisis via monetary policy, although with clear leadership on the part of the Federal Reserve, which has been followed in the recent evolution of the other most important central bank of the Western economy: the Bank of England, the lender of last resort for the British economy.

The arrival in June 2013 of a new governor, Mark Carney—former governor of the Bank of Canada—has meant a shift towards more intensive economic stimuli and in particular, to a monetary philosophy detached from the priority of the fight against inflation at all costs.

The New Role of Central Banks

The Great Crisis has changed the form and substance of the action of central banks in Europe and the USA. Nothing will be the same after a period in which the classical fiscal policy of the banks was stripped bare and exposed, helpless against the might of the financial markets.

Central banks have a fearsome power as a result of their independence: the fixing of the interest rate at which they will buy (or sell) assets, which partially determine the currency in circulation. The FED also has another string to pull in times of turbulence: the money-making machine to lend directly to the government. The ECB can only buy debt on the secondary market—and with limitations—as ruled on 7 February 2014 by the Constitutional Court of Germany. The ECB is therefore less powerful than the FED, as we have seen.

However, what has really changed since 2007 is the political objective of the use of weapons held by central banks. Until the Great Crisis, and virtually since the end of Keynesianism, central banks had been sticking to a routine and boring function: keeping inflation low, around 2%, and stable. As Bhidé and Phelps rightly point out—the latter Nobel Prizewinner in economics in 2006—the FED, in the last two decades, had fallen asleep at the wheel in monitoring the solvency of banks and in preventing uncontrolled monetary growth, without orientating itself towards productive credit.[60]

When it all blew up and governments prematurely withdrew stimuli slowing their borrowing, central banks, with the initiative of the FED, had to leave the arena and use their conventional monetary instruments (interest rates near zero) and unconventional (buying bonds, QE) with such force that the quantitative became the qualitative. The form and content—non-conventional monetary policy, avoiding the collapse of banks and credit, and saving the economy have converted the central banks into competitors to the ministries of finance, but without the democratic legitimacy of the latter. They will legitimize themselves if they act correctly to defend general interests over and above those of a single country.

It was therefore no surprise that the FED and the ECB acquired a decisive surgical intervention, the monitoring—and healing, where necessary—of financial institutions through asset analysis and stress tests; a 'macro-prudential' oversight of the financial system as a whole to prevent risk. All this, of course, with the convenient separation between this function and monetary policy; and knowing that it cannot supplant the policy that governments have an obligation to apply; especially in situations where growth—in the case of Europe—has continued to be almost non-existent for years and requires consumption and investment to be stimulated.

It was also no surprise that the FED—always in the forefront of these things—should have opened up a new era by converting public doctrine into a goal that was already part—although barely—of its legal remit: the fight against unemployment. The Bank of England (BOE) has followed it since the arrival of Carney. Even the Bank of Japan followed. But the ECB, subject to a political straitjacket, has not done so. The most Draghi has been able to do has been to force the purchase of bonds—with the Bundesbank always complaining—using the pretext that it is the only way that monetary policy can be transmitted to markets, which, as we know, has not been achieved so far in the countries of southern Europe. No one is going to argue with the FED over its activism in achieving economic ends—stability of the financial system—and social ends—employment. This is not the case for the ECB, and this is an obstacle to ending the crisis and for the productive development of the Union, because full employment is not attainable only from decisions taken whimsically by the private sector, in the productive or financial economy, as prescribed by the monetarism of Milton Friedman. Employment is promoted by public authorities, and one of them is the Central Bank, which should work in coordination with other authorities, national and supranational.

There are several ways to overcome the obstacles experienced by the ECB either by changing the treaties, or reforming the German Constitution, or by having them interpreted in a different way by the Court of Justice in Luxembourg and the Constitutional Court in Karlsruhe.

One thing is clear. Central banks which cannot go beyond their traditional functions to achieve financial stability in the broader economic and political sense, will be out of the game—and socially delegitimized—in the crisis scenario in which we live. Central banks have to deal with financial and economic stability, which in turn depend on multiple macroeconomic indicators. Today, employment is the main one. If, as happens to the ECB, there is a restriction that puts you at a disadvantage as compared to the Federal Reserve, what will be damaged will be European society itself, defenceless against the hegemony of the financial markets.

Unlike the British model, where the Bank of England is controlled by (and accountable to) the government and Westminster Parliament—which set the monetary objective—the ECB has become an organ only monitored by the Bundestag and the Court in Karlsruhe. The time has come for the European Parliament to deal with this. It will be one of the tasks that have to be carried out once the new term starts after the 25 May elections, and with a vision that goes beyond the borders of the Union.

Central banks are not islands in globalization. Their decisions immediately affect the interrelated body of the world economy. We can find no better example than the collapse of financial markets in many emerging countries, at least immediately because of the phasing out of stimulus by the FED announced in May 2013, and started from January 2014.

The responsibilities of central banks are also global. They cannot limit themselves to protecting short-term interest rates, as if that were the only way to achieve stability of the economy. Their horizons are much broader and their functions should be, too. In a democratic society, greater representation implies greater democratic control. That is one of the challenges of the Great Crisis.

Part III

THE LEGACY OF A CRISIS

5

The Assault on the Welfare State

The European Social Model Hit Hard

Although it may be hard to believe, the profusion of negative macroeconomic data which the policy of austerity has furnished us with does not represent the worst aspect of the crisis. Rather, it is the impact on the greatest achievement of democratic Europe: its social model, known as the Welfare State.

During the second half of the 1980s, the European Commission, presided over at that time by Jacques Delors, came up with the concept of the 'European social model', which became part of the framework of the emerging Economic and Monetary Union. The thinking was to go beyond simple economic integration and to give the European structure its own social identity, its own character, which would differentiate it from the American capitalist model.

By 'European social model' I mean one with its own characteristics: a high level of social protection, aid targeted at the most vulnerable sectors of society, an uncompromising attitude towards unemployment from government agencies, leading to the latter adopting a dominant position regarding the definition and application of a genuine social policy, which would not be left to the whims of the market. To this should be added the crucial role of 'social partners'.

The European social model has been one of the victims of the crisis and of the policies applied to counter it. This has had a particularly doleful effect on the southern European countries: Greece, Italy, Portugal and Spain.

The fragmentation of the European political arena has been accompanied by the fragmentation of the economic arena—through the breach between creditor and debtor countries—and by social fragmentation between the countries of the north and the south, and between the centre and the periphery. This division has been accentuated by the Union's inability to control social policy, which is exclusively controlled by individual States.

The policy of economic adjustment is based on the loss of competitiveness in the above-mentioned peripheral countries leading to a demand for greater flexibility in the labour market and lower production costs.

Germany and the reforms implemented during Schröder's mandate are usually held up as an example to follow. However, maintaining employment levels in Germany has been carried out at the cost of an increase in impoverished workers. The Hartz law led to a widespread increase in *minijobs* in the service sector, jobs which are exempt from welfare costs.

Nonetheless, Schröder's reforms affected neither the collective bargaining system nor the working time directive. Nor did they make it easier to make staff redundant in the brutal way brought about by the reform of Spanish labour law (Law 372012 6 July).

The policy of austerity and its impact in depressing demand are the factors which have deepened the wound in one of the bases of the European social model, namely the pursuit of full employment, a vital component of which is the negotiating ability of workers and trade unions, which has been weakened by the undermining of free collective bargaining.

Another field of experimentation has been old age pensions, judged by the champions of adjustment to be too generous, both in terms of cost and retirement age. There are basically two systems: one based on distribution and Bismarckian contribution, i.e., systems financed by contributions (the United Kingdom, Ireland, central and southern Europe) where those currently in employment pay the pensioners; and the other system financed by taxation (Scandinavia and the Netherlands) based on the Beveridge Report of 1942.

The effects of a falling birth rate and an increase in life expectancy call these systems into question. The crisis has aggravated this situation. The European Commission has calculated that old age pensions as a proportion of the GDP of the EU (of 27 member states) will rise from 11.3% to 12.9% in 2026, hence the recommendation to raise the retirement age, lengthen the working life and to deindex pensions from inflation.

The European Commission deems this reform absolutely necessary. This is exactly what was done in Greece and Italy between 2010 and 2012, and in 22 other countries since 2008, raising retirement age, almost always without the agreement of social stakeholders.

The challenging personal situation which pensioners face is cushioned to a certain extent for those who own their own houses (80% of homes in Spain, Greece and Italy). Nevertheless, the probability of high unemployment in the future, and of an unpredictable job market, presents subsequent generations of pensioners who may not have been able to contribute to private pension plans with a dramatic panorama.

As for utilities such as energy and water tied to public ownership, they have undergone a structural change in Greece and Portugal due to the extensive programme of privatization demanded in return for European Stability Mechanism loan agreements designed to promote fiscal consolidation. This has brought in its wake more unemployment and, of course, higher prices and tariffs.

In the European Union, 16 member states reduced their spending on education between 2008 and 2011, an act which had a bearing on the reduction in youth employment. Education enables social mobility. A study was published on the Eurostat website (on 11 December 2013) on the 'Intergenerational transmission of disadvantage', defined as the probability of inheriting a poverty ranking on account of various factors, one of which is the educational level of one's parents. The results for 2011 are as follows: in the EU (of 28 member states) 34% of people between 25 and 59 years of age whose parents had a low level of educational attainment (Compulsory Secondary Education or less) remained themselves at the same level, while this proportion fell to 8% if their parents had a middle-range educational level, and to 3% if their parents were in the higher education bracket. The conclusion is undeniable. The level of education of a person in Europe determines to a large extent that which their children will have, although not perhaps in absolute terms. Someone who is highly-educated will find it difficult to see their children with a poor level of educational achievement. And the opposite will be the case, if the parental education level is low.

The decrease in healthcare expenditure (for purely budgetary reasons) has been especially severe in Greece, Ireland, Portugal and Spain, according to the IMF. The European Commission has specifically stated that these savings were impromptu and had nothing to do with efficiency or quality. On the contrary, they could lead to higher expenditure in future.

The Council of Europe, in a report made public on 29 January 2014, categorically concluded that austerity in Europe had caused profound violations in those human rights in Europe guaranteed by the European Social Chapter (employment rights, child protection, unemployment insurance, etc.). The Human Rights Watch 2014 world report goes along the same lines.

The attack on the Welfare State has infected the structure of Europe itself, largely depriving it of its social dimension and along the way damaging political and trade union bodies, although this has not prevented an upsurge in industrial action during these years of crisis, as has been previously noted. It has grown in pace with galloping inequality, both between countries and within each country, as another by-product of a policy of austerity which has gone on too long, thus turning an economic problem into a profound social and political problem. Over the coming years, political confrontation will revolve around the sustainability of the Welfare State, or European social model. It will constitute the battleground of the right-left axis. Neo-Conservatives are already suggesting that it will be impossible to maintain social security payments. Those of us who do not share this viewpoint are obliged to find arguments which will help strengthen social and economic rights, because this is the essential basis on which we can overcome the Great Crisis.

The Four Horsemen of the Apocalypse

The Council of Europe's Commissioner for Human Rights, during the visit he made to Spain in October 2012, was very clear: austerity measures 'have a particularly negative impact on the human rights of children and the disabled', and the cuts in the education budget over the last three years are 'undermining equality of opportunity for children and making it more and more difficult to access quality education'.

In 2010, European healthcare expenditure fell for the first time in many years, as was previously pointed out. In a paper presented to the European Congress on Cancer, which took place in Amsterdam in September 2013, its authors establish a strong link between public health expenditure per capita in 27 EU countries and the rate of survival after a diagnosis of cancer. The higher the expenditure, the lower the rate of mortality, because it is possible to offer early diagnosis and more accessible and effective treatments. Therefore the greater the cutbacks, the greater the forecasts of mortality.

These examples of the effects of the policy of austerity on two major areas of public policy, health and education, demonstrate the socially destructive results produced by injuring the Welfare State.

The Welfare State, which is better situated in the European arena than in any other part of the world, is neither a luxury, nor a semi-detached part of Western political systems, nor an optional extra. It is a vital part, the spinal column, of European societies. Thus, if it shrinks, in quality and quantity, it deeply affects the social body, destroys its cohesiveness and conjures up 'the Four Horsemen of the Apocalypse' scenario: unemployment, underemployment, poverty and inequality.

Unemployment

Prior to 2008, the average unemployment rate in the Eurozone was below 8%. In December 2014, the unemployment rate was 11%, reaching 23% for youth unemployment (before the crisis, it was 15%).

Since 2010, the Eurozone has lost a million and a half jobs, as against the seven million which have been created in the USA. However, only one in five workers who became long-term unemployed in the USA during the crisis has gone back into work, either temporary or permanent, despite the fact that unemployment in the USA has fallen to 5.9%.

When a person is unemployed his dignity is damaged. Pope Francis put it well: 'Lack of work weakens the spirit and causes fear and mistrust of the future', to which he added: 'The current economic system is leading us to tragedy'.

This tragedy is particularly apparent among the long-term unemployed, who end up abandoning the search for work. They are assiduous clients of social support programmes, their last—and only—resource. According to various economic studies, the longer a person remains out of the labour market the less likely it is that they will go back into work, even if the economy starts to improve. The view taken by Burtless, an economist at the Brookings Institute, is that although the crisis affected the whole of society equally, recovery will be skewed, and for the long-term unemployed it will in any case be too late.

In Europe the panorama is devastating, with 'structural' unemployment constantly on the increase. The crisis has brought about the highest long-term unemployment rate in a decade, which has been particularly damaging to the young, with enormous difference among the countries of the Eurozone (from 6 to 60% of young people out of work). More than half of the long-term unemployed have been in this position for over two years. For those who find themselves in this predicament, the dismantling of the Welfare State is even more dramatic. Because it is precisely at the moment that they most need economic support from government bodies that fewer are receiving it.

The other side of the unemployment coin is the level of unemployment. The objective of Strategy 2020—approved by the Union in 2010—is that, by that date, the employment rate among people aged 20 to 64 will be 75%. The crisis years have slowed and reduced employment levels to 68.5% in the Eurozone and 65.3% in the OECD, even lower than pre-2008 figures, which is yet another argument in favour of a stimulus package. But the European summit on unemployment on 8 October 2014, faced with persistent, chronic unemployment, was a disaster.

Underemployment

There is, moreover, the case of those who, although not actually unemployed, are employed in such adverse conditions—in terms of wages, working hours and bargaining ability—that it really can be termed 'underemployment'. During the crisis years, salaries in the EU and the Eurozone have fallen abruptly in real terms, with Spain at the forefront.[14] Also in the US, as the price to be paid for a return to employment. The market has proved itself incapable of rewarding work appropriately. 'Internal devaluation' (since there is no question of any other type of devaluation) has formed a part of the anti-crisis strategy, i.e., making products more competitive via salaries so that exports increase. For external, not internal, consumption.

The situation is so alarming that the governments of two large European countries, Germany and the United Kingdom, have decided to establish—or increase—the minimum wage. For his part, Obama proposed raising the minimum federal wage by 40% in two years, so that it will reach 20.10 dollars in 2016.

In its July 2013 report, the ECB, going above and beyond its natural remit, urged those countries with high unemployment rates to continue with internal devaluation through 'the reduction of employment protection legislation, the abolition of indexation of wages, a reduction in the minimum wage, and granting permission for wage negotiation at company level'. The IMF went so far as to suggest lowering the minimum wage to encourage youth employment (the OECD said the opposite). The reality is that wage devaluation has not led to job creation, but rather to more unemployment. This is because demand is lower and the fall in salaries, which should have resulted in more competitive prices, has not occurred because business profits have remained the same or increased, i.e., the sacrifices demanded of the workers have only served to increase profits and return on capital.

This takes us on to a study carried out by the ILO in 16 developed and developing countries analyzing whether aggregate demand is led by wages or profits. The study concludes that there has been an ongoing decline in the proportion of GDP allotted to salaries since the end of the 1970s and beginning of the 1980s.

Nevertheless, it turns out that this devaluation is lopsided. According to an FEDEA (Fundación de Estudios de Economía Aplicada) report issued in December 2013, only the lowest paid workers—up to 17%—have experienced the loss of purchasing power. The purchasing power of the higher paid has increased.

The ILO study shows that a decrease in the workers' slice of the cake leads to countries as significant as Germany, France, Italy, the United Kingdom, Japan, Turkey and South Korea finding it harder to return to growth. In other countries such as Canada, Argentina, South Africa, Australia, Mexico, China and India this has not happened. However, this academic study claims that a one-point fall in employee contribution to GDP reduces GDP overall by 0.36 points. This would lead to a world without growth where workers' capacity for consumption was constantly decreasing. Building up financial resources would be pointless. This only goes to show that the chronic underemployment model is not only antisocial but also anti-economic. It demonstrates that recovery from the crisis is not what it seems and that the new model is structurally unstable in terms of jobs.

Poverty

It is no longer necessary to be jobless to live in poverty in a European country. The dismantling of the Welfare State has made it possible for someone who is in employment/underemployment to actually be poor.

The Oxfam report *The Austerity Trap* warns that at present almost one in 10 families in which someone is working are living in poverty. This is what is known as 'active poverty'. In Cyprus, Ireland and Italy, figures for this type of poverty have reached record levels.

According to Eurostat, in 2011 a fourth of the population of the EU, 119.8 million people, were at risk of poverty or social exclusion: four million more than the previous year; very far off EU projections for that year in Strategy 2020 (95.7 million). In 2013, the figure rose to 122.7 million people at risk of poverty through level of income, or severely deprived of access to accommodation and material goods, or in homes with very low levels of employment. This situation is worse on the periphery of the EU, and is clearly better in central and northern countries.

The constant increase in these figures is directly linked to the policy of austerity and the measures demanded by this policy: a reduction in benefits and access to essential services for specific social groups; a fall in unemployment protection; the freezing of the minimum wage; wage devaluation. In Europe it is becoming increasingly difficult to escape poverty.

According to the 2013 *Cáritas Memorandum*, severe poverty now affects three million people in Spain. This is the highest percentage in Europe, along with Romania and Lithuania. The number of people living on less than 307 euros per month is double that of those who found themselves in the same situation in 2008. In 2012, 600,000 homes had no income whatsoever. The same year, Spanish households enjoyed an average income of 23,123 euros, 3.5% less than the previous year, the fourth successive year of decline.

Both reports, Oxfam's and that of Cáritas, agree on the breakdown in family support and the explosion in poverty among minors (26.7% of the under-sixteens). If poverty becomes chronic, it will not be long before life expectancy also dips.

Poverty in the USA has also worsened during the crisis, especially in the Afro-American and Hispanic communities. Nearly 46 million people live in poverty today, more than in the past 50 years, since President Lyndon B. Johnson launched his doomed 'war on poverty'. The percentage of poor people now stands at 14.5%. American families now earn 8% less than 2007 levels.

It is paradoxical that poverty is spreading in Europe at the same time as it is falling in developing countries, although this should not be taken as drawing comparisons between completely different realities.

What is clear is that the phenomenon of poverty has returned, that its effects on social cohesion are lethal, and that the outlook for the entire world is geared towards further deterioration, as indicated by the United Nations Index on Human Development. The effort to return to the situation we enjoyed before the crisis may take years, if the policies which inflicted this paralysis are not changed.

Inequality, the challenge of our times

As authorized studies have made known, inequality has been increasing in developed countries since the 1990s. This has been instrumental in curbing social mobility, which is intrinsically linked to economic equality. The former was already in evidence during the period of economic growth at the end of the 20th century. However, this tendency became more pronounced when it made a 180 degree turn at the beginning of the 21st century. In this way, what signalled an increase in inequality between countries (north–south) in the last century, became a much greater inequality within each country, characteristic of a crisis which has brought together the worst things we could possibly imagine. One of the paradoxes of the Great Crisis in Europe has been that the richest have increased their share of national income while the poor have seen theirs diminish. This situation is reflected in an even greater imbalance between business profits and unit labour costs. Piketty puts it simply: capital enjoys greater profitability than an increase in productivity, especially at a time of low growth. This phenomenon is simply unsustainable.

President Obama, in a speech delivered on 4 December 2013 on the banks of the Anacostia, in one of the poorest districts of Washington, cited inequality as 'the most important challenge of our time', condemning the fact that 'most economic growth in the past few years has ended up in the hands of a fortunate few'. Social mobility has been curbed. A child born into the poorest 20% of the population has one chance in 20 of moving up into the wealthier top 20%. However, the chances increase to between two and three in 20 if the child is born into the richest 20%.

According to the UBS 2013 report on the wealthiest 211,000 in society, the 'ultra-rich'—by which is understood those with net assets in excess of USD 30 million—their wealth is equivalent to 40% of world GDP, despite the fact that those in possession of it account for 0.004% of the adult population. In 12 months, this wealth has increased to the level of India's GDP. In 2014, the number of 'ultra-rich' people increased by 6%, and their assets by 7%.

The wealthiest in the USA and Europe 'recovered' during the crisis. The powerful financial markets increased their capital despite high unemployment, the recession and slow growth in Europe. Only in the Middle East did this wealth grow more quickly than in the USA and Europe. In Europe the number of multimillionaires dipped slightly, but their collective wealth increased by 3.7% in 2013 to 2.12 trillion dollars. According to Oxfam (January 2015), the assets of the top 1% in the world in 2016 will be greater than the remaining 99%.

According to the 2011 Eurostat data, the poorest 10% in the EU account for 3% of income while the richest 10% account for 24%. The income of the 10 richest people in Europe exceeds the total costs of the stimulus package rolled out in the EU in the 2008–2010 period (EUR 217 billion, as opposed to the 200 billion in the package). According to the IMF and the OECD, Spain is the industrialized country which has seen the greatest growth in differences between rich and poor. At the same time, in the past decade the social divergence has become more and more accentuated between the North and the South in terms of salaries and the working population.

There are various reasons behind this disparity, but there are essentially three which should be mentioned: the multiplying effect of huge unemployment which, additionally, weakens the position of the worker in company negotiations; globalization and technological advances which favour an economy linked to finance; and the political decision which has accorded debt, particularly new income niches, a privileged position compared with progressive taxation. This is what has happened above all in the USA, whose level of inequality is similar to the European one before taxes are taken into account, but greater after tax and credits to social programmes. Moreover, the USA does not have VAT.

In a survey carried out by the newspaper *USA Today* and the Pew Research Centre in the third week of January 2014, 61% of Republican voters, 68% of Democrats and 67% of floating voters responded that the gap between the rich and other citizens had grown in the past 10 years. A conclusive result reflecting reality: the wealth of the richest is seven times that of middle class families and 70 times that of the poorest families, that is to say, the biggest gap in three decades (Report from the Pew Research Centre, 2015).

The inequality produced by the crisis is complex. It has chipped away at the social stratum which had been the axis of the European model for decades, a broad middle class, affected by all four Horsemen of the Apocalypse, including inequality. The middle class has shrunk in the face of the emergence of a job market which offers either higher salaries in the financial sector or seriously unreliable junk wages (a thousand euros or fewer) intended to be snapped up by young people in search of their first jobs. The generation gap can now clearly be seen.

Growing inequality increases exponentially when it starts from a basis of previous chronic inequality. This is what has happened to women, who have always suffered salary discrimination, and consequently, end up with unfair pensions.

The inequality brought about by the crisis is in itself a trap from which it is difficult to escape. It has been created by the sudden paralysis in economic growth, fuelled by the policy of adjustment, spread by the cracks in the columns of the temple of the Welfare State (the decline in social security payments), and overridden for a long time by unemployment and underemployment, both of which lead to poverty. To close the circle, inequality itself can only lead to the death of growth.

Nobel Prizewinner Joseph Stiglitz has repeatedly pointed out that if the economic model favours wealth creation in the most powerful social strata to the detriment of the poorer ones, the tendency towards downturn is unavoidable. The better-off classes are naturally apt to spend less, except on luxury goods. Money goes to the place which is least likely to help the recovery of the consumption/growth cycle. The International Monetary Fund has calculated that a cut of 1% in the national budget can reduce GDP by 2% (not 0.5%, as previously thought). The same conclusion was reached in the OECD in its December 2014 report.

So it is that, apart from ideological and moral considerations, more economists are beginning to believe that, when the inequality threshold is crossed, what is actually then attacked is financial stability and economic growth. This is the view of Raghuram Rajan, for whom the credit bubble of the early years of the previous decade was caused by inequality. In Chapter 2 of this book it has already been pointed out that the US government brought about an increase in 'easy' mortgages for the American middle and working-classes, as a way of compensating for their limited family income and raising their standard of living artificially. In the same way, this was the root of the unrestrained growth in business profits, which owe a great deal to the decreasing minimum wage.

Unemployment, poverty and inequality always lead to xenophobia and racism, and especially to ruthless treatment of economic migrants and asylum seekers.

Cuts in the Welfare State hit immigrants, who are the most vulnerable. The European social model is inclusive, but its intrinsic pluralism and protective nature are betrayed when people are excluded on the basis of their nationality or skin colour. In these cases, the model has also been stricken to its core.

In the European Union, xenophobia has emerged in politics through the rapid growth of populist, anti-European parties which have attained high levels of support in the establishment.

The Washington Non-Consensus

Upstairs, downstairs

A short time ago, John Ruggie, professor of International Relations at Harvard University, stated that, 'in the USA inequality in wealth distribution has never been as wide since the twenties as it is now. It is scandalous and unacceptable'.

Warren Buffet, one of the richest men in the world, the standard-bearer of American capitalists, pointed out, at an event in new York organized by *The New York Times* (during the last week of November 2012), that the wealth of the 400 richest Americans had increased five-fold during the last 20 years. He summed this up in the apt sentence, 'My gang has been leaving the middle class in the dust'.

In the USA, the executives of major companies earn up to 273 times more than their workers, something which represents both an ethical and economic risk. The income of the richest 1% rose from 9% of national income, in 1980, to 23% in 2007, and today is even higher. That 1%, the richest, possesses 34% of the country's wealth.

The highest incomes in the USA, after taking an initial hit during the recession, have come back strongly. Ninety-five per cent of income from the economic recovery since 2009 has ended up in the hands of the richest 1%; of the total, 60% went to the wealthiest 0.1%, those people whose annual incomes exceeded 1.9 million dollars. This social sector continues to advance without let or hindrance, to the point that it is now in better shape than before the crisis. One per cent of the US population, the richest, increased their income by 31% between 2009 and 2012. Ten per cent, the super-rich, account for half of all income and 75% of total US assets. The gap between the better- and the worse-off has widened during the years of crisis, as far as income and assets are concerned. The former (3%) won and the latter lost. These are figures from the FED, which is clearly worried about the threat to growth implicit in inequality, along with what Yellen has called 'sources of political opportunity': the education of the young, ownership of small businesses and inheritance.

This affects the lowest echelon in terms of income. The food assistance programme (SNAP, its acronym in English), which had 28 million users in 2007, and whose budget the Republicans voted to cut, is currently serving 48 million people.

For the poorest, although the recession is over, the crisis is not. Quite the opposite. The poorest sector of the population, 40%, saw their income fall by 6% during the crisis years in the USA. In my opinion, this is an indicator that the crisis has profoundly damaged the social structure, the strongest constituent of basic political legitimacy in the Western democracies, those most severely hit by it. Programmes like SNAP, aimed particularly at children, have prevented the gigantic crisis from being even more predatory.

This profound inequality is, in turn, a factor which, as has been noted, conspires against growth and development. These enormous social divisions prove a barrier to consumption in economies whose vitality depends so much on it—as is the case in the USA—especially in times of high unemployment during a recession.

This is exactly the opposite of what liberal economists in the USA have always maintained, claiming that a disproportionate hoarding of wealth is an incentive to investment and spending. The crisis in Europe has disproved these arguments.

In the USA, the other axis of the Western world, the crisis in the Welfare State has been experienced in its own way. To start with, a social model like the European one has never taken root there. The United States has a highly regionalized anti-government culture, which has proved a stumbling block in the development of social programmes and public services.

Current political debate has become polarized in an extreme way between the leader of the Democrats, President Obama, and the Republican Party, precisely because the former has seen, in combating the crisis, the opportunity to reintroduce the New Deal philosophy. From the outset of his first administration, the president has tried to introduce an agenda based on two fundamental points: as far as expenditure is concerned, reform of healthcare; and as far as income is concerned, an increase in taxation on the wealthiest. The Republicans have based their most uncompromising attacks on these two themes.

As well as these two highly significant issues, there has been a third since early 2013: wages. In his State of the Nation addresses, Obama has tossed a hike in the minimum wage of USD 7.25 to USD 9 (from EUR 5.6 to EUR 6.9) into the thick of the political debate—and has repeated it several times. This means an increase of 25% when indexed with inflation.

The federal minimum wage is not binding on the States, which have their own, but the enhancement of salaries—the exact opposite to the dominant discourse in Europe—already forms part of the reforms which they have managed to include in the political agenda (legislation is required) and the business sphere. This seems only fair given that productivity in the USA has grown by more than 90% in the past 30 years while average family income has grown by less than 8%. But, above all, it is a sound economic proposition which will help kick-start growth. It is important to remember that in the USA 70% of GDP is accounted for by consumption, so the latter is, by definition, decisive.

The message is clear: we need to increase consumption in order to feed into the production process the fuel which it requires to return it to its normal pace.

In any case, in the USA the political debate on Welfare has revolved around healthcare and the social security budget, and consequently, around the finances required to handle them. This is what we are going to examine next.

Obamacare

At the end of the first half of his first administration (2010), the president managed to get agreement on healthcare reform. Later on it would have been impossible, because in the 2010 *mid-term* elections the Republicans, or, to be more precise, the most reactionary and fundamentalist faction of the GOP, the so-called Tea Party, gained control of the House of Representatives.

This step forward was transcendental: 50 million Americans did not have health insurance in a country which spends 18% of its GDP on health, double that of the European Union, and which in exchange has double the infant mortality rate of Europe and Canada and lower life expectancy.

The public contribution to American healthcare is Medicare, a federal programme for the elderly, and Medicaid, a programme for the poor, run by the States, both of which have been highly valued by the population since their foundation in 1969, the period during which Lyndon B. Johnson was president.

Obama's reforms (Patient Protection and Affordable Care Act) did not envisage transforming the predominantly private healthcare sector into a public one. The transformation essentially involved compelling every adult citizen, with State help, to take out health insurance or face a fine. It would no longer be necessary to depend on workplace insurance; in any case, all companies with over 50 employees would be obliged to provide medical insurance.

This would also mean an end to the arbitrary ability of insurance companies to choose those they wish to insure, who will obviously be the healthiest and youngest. Now, the government can demand that medical history should not be taken into consideration for insurance purposes. At the same time, healthcare reform has an economic objective.

The Republicans and conservative groupings do not see things this way and have ended up waging an unceasing war of attrition on healthcare reform, including an attempt to block the expansion of Medicaid, by rejecting it in some states. They have used the same strategy as that used in the case of the budget.

Financing welfare

Obama, elected in 2008, encountered no political obstacles until the Democrats lost their majority in the lower House in the 2010 elections. The economic and fiscal debate which unfolded during 2011 became an ordeal, with the larger number of Republicans planning to use the budget as a battering-ram against more progressive policies. Despite Obama's well-meaning, and perhaps somewhat naïve, attempts the Republican machine applied a policy of no to everything.

Obama's strategy was to accept sharp budgetary cuts in exchange for higher income from taxation, a long-term strategy which many Democrats did not share; nor did the euphoric Republicans, at the opposite end of the spectrum, as they had no wish to accept even a single dollar rise in taxes. They demanded unconditional surrender.

The unceasing fiscal battle left the Republicans politically divided and wounded in the court of public opinion. From this they learned that they should try to avoid another confrontation of this type. Especially approaching the onset of the 2014 *mid-term* elections. This was why they accepted budgetary negotiations with the Democrats on the 2014 and 2015 budgets. But after the Mid-Terms of 2014, the negotiations were dead.

Obama's dream is of a *grand bargain* in expenditure and taxes, which would make it possible to reduce the deficit and to finance, in the short term, infrastructure, education and technological projects, which the president again expressed in his State of the Union 2015 address and subsequent budget proposal. The message is clear: to favour the battered American middle class. His political reach goes beyond this and is projected in the election campaign for the presidency and Congress in 2016; because there is a reality, which is that most Americans are worse off than at the beginning of this century and the middle class has been receding during the past 50 years.

At the moment when the final chapter of this book is being written (November 2014), it is not possible to know what will happen next in the political battle over healthcare reform and the budget. What is certain is that this two-sided tension will have an influence on the two truly political decisions: debt and taxation. This explains why the political differences are so unyielding and bitter. Underlying this controversial issue are the differing stances of the Democrats and the Republicans on the Welfare State, and thus, on how it should be financed.

Social costs are going to grow, even if only in tandem with unavoidable legal obligations (Social Security, pensions, important healthcare programmes like Medicare), reaching 14% of GDP in the next quarter-century, although the average for the last few decades has been 7%. Alongside this, if taxation rates do not change, the deficit will grow by up to 6% in the same period, according to the Budgetary Office of the Congress of the United States (CBO). And with the deficit, its consequence: debt.

This is the root of the vicious circle in the fiscal argument in the United States, or, what is actually the same thing, the dialogue of the deaf into which American political argument has degenerated. The Democrats want to finance a Welfare State.

The Republicans, led until recently by the Tea Party, are diametrically opposed. They seek total privatization of the economy, with no holds barred, as the only way to ensure growth. They do not want a Welfare State which demands taxes from the wealthy.

The crisis in the Welfare State plays a key part in what I have dubbed the 'Ice Age'. It is the great political decision which Europe and the United States must now take. It is unacceptable to use the Great Crisis to dismantle solidarity in Western culture. There are two basic elements on which the latter depends: taxes to fund the Welfare State and the financial system which can prevent it.

6

Debt, Tax Crisis and Tax Evasion

A Culture of Debt

In recent decades, the Western welfare state and the capacity of private spending—that is, public consumption and private consumption—have become increasingly based on a mechanism which is by definition both vulnerable and variable: debt, or, from another perspective, a 'culture' of debt.

Debt has been taken up by all social classes. A debt culture has taken root, and has been popularized, as a way placating virtual protests or complaints against constant and growing income inequality. This, as we saw, has been polluting the social structures of the West since the second half of the last century. It was the true 'opium of the middle classes', which have formed the backbone of modernity and the post-industrial revolution.

The current emergence of Asian countries was brought about by investments in US and European debt which countries with capital surpluses (China, Japan and others) have made in recent decades. The Asians loaned money to the West at low interest rates and, with this money, the latter bought from them all those different 'Made in China' or 'Made in Japan' products, thereby off-shoring manufacturing as a precursor to the loss of manual labour in Europe and the US.

Remember what happened to Spain with its discovery of America, whose treasures blinded the economy of the metropolis and hastened the fall in productivity and competitiveness that were the basis of the decline of the Spanish Empire. In this dynamic, whether in the sixteenth century or in the twentieth century, only the bankers and creditors benefited, and to extremes.

Debt expresses the thirst for public and private consumption, which have different origins and causes.

National debt

In the Western world, inventor of the coin, credit and debt, the loans that nation states have issued for bank credit have been the traditional, and the financial institution par excellence. However, globalization and financial deregulation in the 1980s expanded the spectrum of creditors to all of the various financial actors, central banks, private banks, insurance companies, private equity funds, sovereign funds from emerging countries, investors of all types in stock, and so on. This quantitative and qualitative expansion of the capabilities of borrowing—what is termed 'disintermediation'—largely explains how states have become appendages of financial creditors, the famous 'markets'. This was foreseen by Adolph Wagner in the nineteenth century, namely, that public expenditure grows in line with the increasing economic development of a country, and with it therefore, its reliance on debt.

Reliance has been greater as government spending has turned to places providing money in return for payment of interest. Credit grew considerably, boosted by interest rates that central banks—mainly the FED—kept low. The flow of credit was helped by the absence of inflation. This was possible because the relocation of industries to other countries also helped consumer prices go down.

The welfare state, with rising costs, especially those produced by the demographic effect (health, pensions) or economic (unemployment) has been financed this way. It has been done this way because of a growing aversion to the political use of taxation, and an appeal to the 'generous' markets has been preferred.

In any case, the power of a state to impose a tax burden on citizens, without time limits, provides a particular attraction to savers hungry for profit and investment security. Thus, the financial 'sex appeal' of the state's business is at the same time the trap that makes it fall into the pit of debt. It is not surprising that the book by Biasatti and Braquet on government debt starts with: 'Since the 1990s, the economies of the rich countries have become true economies of debt'.[1]

With the outbreak of the financial crisis, the two debts, public and private, in practice have focused on the first one, since the State has to respond to the second one—as a systemic risk—and in particular the banking debt.

When this happens to a state that is part of the Eurozone, it cannot resort to the monetization of the debt, i.e., the central bank printing money and buying bonds. It is other banks—some of them the central banks of Asian countries—who buy debt directly issued by member states of the Union. The ECB can only, as we know, indirectly buy back debt on the secondary markets, or accept it as collateral from banks coming to Frankfurt in search of liquidity.

The legal limitation against the ECB buying debt directly—or, in other words, acting as a real central bank with its own national currency—has harmed the countries of southern Europe, who are the quintessential debtors (Italy, Spain, Portugal, Greece and Ireland). In contrast, it has benefited the countries of Northern and Central Europe (Germany, Finland, Benelux, Austria) the creditors, which have become havens for investors, thus usurping the natural guarantor role that should be played by the European Central Bank.

The national debt to GDP indicator is always the focus of financial markets, which look very closely at the ability of southern European states to repay their debt; more precisely, to pay interest on the debt. The states involved in the endless snowballing of the refinancing of debt merely pay attention to the interest payments required and issue new bonds when the previous ones expire.[2]

This dynamic is projected onto the interest rates which States must pay investors so that the latter will purchase their debt. Central states, with Germany at the forefront, manage to place their issues of bonds at near-zero interest. The peripheral countries are forced to pay higher interest rates, as are their companies.

Financial markets are in the best of all worlds. They know that the ECB will not let Spain or Italy fail if they cannot be financed. They know this even more clearly after Draghi's famous remark. Consequently, in 2013, from the third quarter, the big investors returned to Spain and Italy—not so much to Portugal or Greece—because the return on public bonds was high compared with that of Germany, whose bonds are still highly prized by the markets.[3] The interest offered on Italian or Spanish at 10 year securities went down in 2013. Their appeal was that they were better business than investing in German and French bonds, and also Spain and Italy are 'too big to fail'.

However, that does not mean that financial risks have disappeared, because national debt (later we will touch on private debt) is increasingly high, to the extent that it is possible to raise the inevitable question about their sustainability, and about the sacrifices required of a society to pay them back.

Despite the austerity and adjustment policy ordered by European creditor countries—with the objective, presumably, of ensuring repayment of the debt—this has been breaking negative records every year of the crisis.

At the end of the second quarter of 2013, according to Eurostat, the national debt of the 17 countries of the Euro—in nominal and relative terms—increased to 93.4% of GDP.

Compared to the second quarter of 2012, debt increased EUR 450 billion in the Eurozone (89.9% to 93.4%) and also in the entire Union (84.7% to 86.8%).[4] The debt of Eurozone countries grew by EUR 450 billion in one year. Meanwhile, the annual output increased by EUR 30 billion. This is without doubt an untenable situation.

Figures for EU debt may be surprising if we look at the fact that in 2012, the deficit declined in absolute terms compared to 2011. In the Eurozone, it went from 4.2% to 3.7% of GDP, and in the EU (of 28 member states) from 4.4% to 3.9%.

All this data is dangerous for countries with no devaluation capacity, or the capacity to go to a central bank to print money.

This picture of the situation becomes even more worrying when we turn our eyes towards another matter no less sinister: private debt.

Private debt

Economists such as Ben Bernanke and Michael Clark have said that the volume of private debt does not matter and it is not even worth quantifying; it is the high level of national debt which causes depressions. It suits them to think like that, because private debt in the USA amounted to 310% of GDP in 2008, an even higher level than the 240% of the 1929 Great Depression.

Other economists, like Keen and Taylor, have dissociated themselves from this view, noting that excess debt in the private sector is the fastest route to deep recessions.

One or other of them may be right, but the truth is that the presence of high levels of private debt does not do anything to provide governments with additional weapons with which to revitalize the economy in situations of depression.

In the European Union it was much worse, because the overblown and bad private debt caused the sovereign debt crisis. For example, in Spain, Ireland and Portugal, with their real estate bubbles, the astronomical private debt was crucial to triggering the catastrophe.

Private debt was mostly (not now) in the hands of mortgaged home owners, companies (corporate debt) and the financial sector, now in a slow process of debt reduction.

Before the crisis, joint private debt in Spain, Ireland and Portugal in the hands of families and corporations accounted for 200% of GDP, more than in the USA (175%).

With the crisis, private debt, basically put on the books by limitless leveraging, became guaranteed by the state—or became national debt—and was even the subject of the EU bailout in the case of Spanish savings banks.

The big problem with private debt in the EU and in the USA was their toxicity, which contaminated an already polluted financial system. According to the International Monetary Fund, this toxicity has not disappeared. It is still held in part of the banking debt in the Eurozone, the corporate debt of Italy, Spain or Portugal,[5] and the debt held by households in Ireland and the Netherlands.

So with private debt we ended up in the same boat as that of national debt: its short and medium term unsustainability for the debtor countries of southern Europe. The short term is already here, and it is called 'internal devaluation'.

Internal devaluation

In order for the productive economy to finance its development—and hence its debts—it is necessary to create a surplus in public and private accounts which, in turn, reward their agents (capital and labour), as well as the creditor financial sector from which it has borrowed. According to experts at Natixis Asset Management, Spain would need an annual budget surplus of 4% of GDP to stabilize its debt; 7% in Italy; 11% in Portugal, and 24% in Greece. Mission impossible.[6]

When, as has happened in the crisis in the peripheral countries, this excess starts to slow or becomes negative, the debt grows even more. This—in the hands of the banks—can then only be tackled through decapitalization of the real economy both internally—internal devaluation—at a cost to companies of shareholder value and to workers in the form of layoffs and wage cuts, which immediately leads to an increase in the much-vaunted 'productivity'. What Marx called 'added value'.

Similarly, in the public arena, the state has to take money out of social services, i.e., the welfare state which, in various political systems, means infringing the Constitution. Some constitutional courts have found this to be the case, erecting a bulwark to protect fundamental rights (Portugal, for example).

The result is that debtors—people and countries—in a growing crisis like the present one, have to suffer huge restrictions on their ability to consume and in their social and physical capital, in order to transfer these to the creditors: countries, financial institutions and the shareholders and executives of the latter. And this despite the fact that it was the financial sector which was to blame for triggering the crisis and such a hellish dynamic.

This massive devaluation process is what has been having such a violent effect on institutions and the rights that the welfare state established decades ago, the most valuable aspect of the democracies of Europe. But there is another private dimension that is coming apart at the seams: the hitherto strong social contract between employers and employees.

Indeed, combating the weight of public or private debt by lowering wages, thereby giving more benefits and liquidity to companies, involves shifting the debt, in turn, onto the workers. Directly, through the loss of purchasing power, and indirectly, as difficulties in paying individual credits are increasingly felt. This is what has been happening in the Western economy since before the appearance of the crisis, and very rapidly thereafter.

In parallel, there is a constant 'redistribution' of income from the so-called 'real economy' to the financial sector, i.e., to the owners of capital assets. To be precise, this reallocation takes the shape of 'servicing the debt'—the paying back of capital and interest—or 'debt burden' if we only count the interest.[7]

Exit options

The pressure that the crisis has created for the maintenance—or the abandonment—of the social welfare model, which the issue of debt highlights so clearly, has forced people to consider what to do about it. Politicians, economists and sociologists have expressed many different positions in recent months.

Growth

Some of the ways out of the crisis are quite obvious. I am referring to GDP growth, which is the denominator in the ratio of national debt/GDP. If there is more growth, the debt burden decreases for purely arithmetical reasons, and because the state can reduce its borrowing from the markets. The numerator of this ratio is the debt itself, which can only descend in quantitative terms if there are primary fiscal surpluses (the budget balance before accounting for the payment of interest on the debt).

Both growth and the level of debt of a country are objective facts of economic policy, but not policy instruments thereof. They are subject to inherent uncertainties, and they cannot be thought of as levers available to governments. They are more a result of policy than the policy itself.

In this sense, the austerity policy has proven to be an inadequate solution. Trying to reduce the debt by simply forcing increased savings—and the decline of consumption—is a mistake, because the result is recession, which plunges us deeper into the abyss of debt.

Eurobonds

Until the outbreak of the sovereign debt crisis, the markets considered all bonds in the Eurozone to be reliable, and did not demand especially disparate interest rates. The Greek episode completely changed the game. The Eurozone was no longer regarded as a currency area. The image of togetherness was shattered. Markets, seeing that neither the ECB nor the other Euro countries would come to the defence of their fellow members, began to discriminate against states according to their economic power and their hypothetical ability to guarantee the repayment of the loans. Funding for the peripheral countries became much more expensive, sometimes impossible. A true common currency area would mutualise debt, but this did not happen.

The most talked-about option (since it was put on the table years ago by the secretary general of the European Socialist Party, the Dane Paul Nyrus Rasmussen) to replace national debt and obtain low interest rates, was indeed that of 'Eurobonds'. The mutualization of debt has been considered the only way in which financing of member states' debts in the market could be done so as not to favour one (central Europe) over others (Southern Europe).

What started as a social democratic approach has ended up being welcomed by peripheral states, regardless of political beliefs, because the benefits are obvious. The power of a single, secured debt across the Eurozone would be enormous, and the consequent reduction in interest rates requested by investors would be immediate.

One of the economists who has been most in favour of and fought for Eurobonds has been the Belgian Paul de Grauwe, professor at the London School of Economics. In his opinion, it is the best way to protect the weaker Eurozone countries from the panic that may be triggered in the markets fearful that their investment will not be returned. Eurobonds are a message of the continuity of the Euro.[8]

On every occasion that the issue of Eurobonds has arisen—or the topic of a Eurozone budget—it has come up against the brick wall of the government of Chancellor Merkel and some Nordic countries, either because of 'moral hazard'—the possibility that some countries might go into deficit without sufficient responsibility and prudence—or because Eurobonds would somewhat push up the cost of German debt. Germany—its government, its society—has refused to approve Eurobonds. And it has convinced European authorities, as is clear from the document *Towards a genuine EMU*, signed by Van Rompuy, Mario Draghi, José Manuel Barroso and Jean-Claude Juncker, which was presented to the European Council in December 2012. In addition, as if anything else were needed, the coalition arrangements between German Social Democrats and Christian Democrats, in December 2013, in which Eurobonds were ruled out, have ended up giving unmistakable signs that it will be a long time before Eurobonds see the light of day.

Inflation and debt monetization

There are other solutions that share some characteristics with the above. They offer partial solutions and at the same time, are particularly complex to implement. I am referring here to two types of measures: a) an inflationary policy that eats away at the debt—possible, though difficult in the current structure of European monetary policy; and b) debt monetization by the ECB, consisting of a massive purchase of debt from the debtor countries.[9] This idea is not viable if we take into account the strict prohibition under the various treaties regarding the monetization of debt.

Debt restructuring

This involves partial debt default or, in more euphemistic terminology, the restructuring of the debt of countries that, with many difficulties and in time, have to repay billions of euros to creditors. This is what happened with Greece and Cyprus, and what could happen to Portugal.

Recently, various studies by economists have been published taking the drama factor out of debt restructuring and proposing automatic reductions in interest rates if the debt of a country rises to a certain level, extending the maturity date if GDP falls beyond a certain level. They are forms of bail-in, which require the commitment of investors, and are still somewhat futuristic in their outlook.[10]

Debt restructuring in the Eurozone is at least no longer a taboo. However it is not on the agenda, because the mere acceptance of this hypothesis would have great effects on financial markets and, therefore, the risk premium of the Euro countries.

If posited as an actual solution, it has some side effects, as it is a political decision that would involve far too many actors: governments, investors, debtors, European political institutions, financial institutions, the International Monetary Fund and other multilateral organizations.

On the other hand, we are considering an interim solution. At this point, the defence of the welfare state requires a paradigm shift in national economic policies because, lest we forget, the welfare state is based on income and expenditure that are essentially national.

What is at stake here is whether the European social model is to be maintained or if it is to be definitively broken. Whether, as is increasingly heard in conservative political circles[11]—and some supposedly progressives ones—the welfare state is not sustainable and must be trimmed or directly abandoned, as stated by the Dutch centre-left (sic) government. It did so in the opening speech of the parliamentary year delivered on 17 September 2013 by King William, who pointed out that Social Security and dependency are unsustainable. The British Tories are a perfect example of the policy of restricting benefits payments.[12]

The future of the European social model has already been aired, and one must wonder about the policies that both preserve it and transform it at the same time, in terms of its approach to economic growth and tackling inequality. This brings us to the main player: taxes.

Taxing Times

Benjamin Franklin said that the only inevitable things in life for humans were death and taxes. It is no by chance that one of the Framers or Founding Fathers of a state should have made that reflection. He wanted the state to be born strong and have the constitutional attributes that every state should possess. Firstly, sovereignty; and, as the highest expression of it, the power of demanding some economic means from all its citizens, without coercion and individual compensation. This is what is called 'taxation'.

Almost two centuries later, Franklin would not have been able to say the same thing. The conservative revolution of his compatriot Ronald Reagan, described above, was essentially the dismantling of taxation power in the USA, benefitting only those on higher incomes and to the detriment of social expenditure. This Anglo-Saxon model has determined the fiscal policies of the West and driven regression in its social model.

The 'neoliberalism' of the 1980s declared war on direct taxes with the invaluable help of the Laffer curve. The academic and political influence of a school of thought proposing nothing less than dismantling the whole taxation structure was unstoppable. Even Sweden, the country ranked second in the Gini index of equality, approved a reform in 1991 that reduced the top rate of income tax from 87% to 57% and corporate tax from 58% to 30%. The outcome in Western countries was fiscal crisis in some states that wanted to spend more at the same time as rapidly cutting taxes.

The crisis that began in 2007 is also the expression of that unsustainable tax-exempting model. Until now, austerity has been the policy that has allowed progressive taxes to be lowered. However, today we are on the road to a dilemma as to whether fiscal consolidation must be conducted with larger spending cuts than tax increases, or vice versa.

Thus, tax reform as a central tool to provide a solution to the dire budgetary strains caused by the crisis has entered the political agenda of developed countries. No one has been able to isolate any other efficient and equitable mechanism to stop the constant and unstoppable rise in debt, in a context of slow or no growth.

In fact, countries that have been able to face the crisis with lower fiscal strains, like the Nordic countries, are those with a stronger and broader tax system, and those where taxes account for the largest percentage of GDP of the OECD.

Between 2000 and 2009, the tax burden on families without children in OECD countries decreased by between 1.4% and 2.1%; even more so in the case of families with children; and somewhat less in the case of individual taxpayers.[13] In the EU, the tax burden since the start of the crisis fell from 40.5% of GDP in 2007 to 39.4% in 2012. There have been significant discussions in the political-theoretical sphere about this. However, from 2009 in the geopolitical context of Europe and the USA, the taboo regarding taxes began to be broken, to the amazement and fear of economists of the stature of the previously cited

Arthur Laffer. In a book published at the time (the End of Prosperity), he railed against tax increases, arguing that these would put an end to an era of prosperity that had lasted half a century.

Not coincidentally, in October 2013, the IMF published an interesting and well-documented work, significantly called Taxing Times. Its starting point is the realization that national debt in advanced economies in 2014 will reach a historic peak of 110% of GDP, 35 points above its 2007 level figures. These are very high-risk figures.[14] The IMF poses three questions: whether the country can squeeze out more taxes; whether they can tax better and more efficiently; and what they can do to increase the legitimacy and sustainability of their tax systems. We will now look in more detail at those questions and try to answer them.

The debate about income taxes

Since the crisis, income tax on individuals has divided American politics. On 15 August 2011, the billionaire Warren Buffett said in an article in the New York Times that he had paid 17% of his income in taxes, far less than his secretary and any employee of his office. Buffett advocated abolishing the Bush Jr. tax cuts for those making over a million dollars in capital gains and dividends.

Bush also enabled hedge fund executives to pay tax at a lower rate. Hence tax rates in the USA fell to their lowest level since Harry Truman was president. In 1950, the highest marginal income tax rate was 91%. In 2011, it had fallen to 35%. But the very wealthy (incomes over USD 500,000) paid 24.5% and even the super-rich (over 10 million dollars) paid 20.4% (!) because the dividend tax fell under Bush from 39.6% to 15%. On assets, taxes were simply eliminated.

Obama represents the beginning of a phase of strengthening taxes on higher incomes. The same wave then spread out around the European Union. In France, Sarkozy proposed a tax on large fortunes. In Italy there was talk about it, without actually achieving anything.

The exception to the rule, as always, has been the United Kingdom: the Conservative government has lowered direct taxes, on both income and corporations. It was one of the few EU governments—along with Greece and Latvia—to lower the highest marginal income tax rate from 50% to 45% in 2013. With this, the UK goes from fifth place in the EU ranking of this tax to occupying the eleventh place, together with France and Germany. The reason, as always, so that senior executives will be attracted to the United Kingdom.

Nine EU countries increased their tax rates on income, contributing to a rise in the global average of 0.3% in 2013, the second consecutive year of increase, according to KPMG.[15]

The most significant change has occurred in the USA. After the expiry of cuts to the wealthiest decided and implemented by Bush, the maximum marginal rate increased from 35% to 39.5%.

The increase in value-added tax

In 2010, tax revenues—including social security contributions—in the Eurozone stood at 39% of GDP. In 2011 they went up to 39.5%. The increase in revenue was based on the increase in indirect taxes and coincides with a time of some economic recovery, which then evaporated in 2012.[16] Indirect taxes are preferred by governments for their immediacy, albeit being the most unfair means of taxation. The USA does not have VAT, but in the EU it is a key source of tax for the single market. Between 2008 and 2014, the standard rate of VAT has risen two points on average in the EU, and about 1.8 points in the Euro area. Spain led the way with a hike of 5 points, just behind Hungary (7 points), and tied with Romania. The increase in VAT has been the favourite tactic of the Troika in bailouts in countries such as Greece, whose current government rejects this measure.

The reduction in corporate income tax: fiscal devaluation

After years of steady decline, corporate tax in the OECD accounts for about 10% of tax revenues. It is the most elastic tax in the face of economic growth. Between 1986 and 2009, corporate tax in the OECD was lowered an average of 10 points.

In the USA, the big debate of the moment is about the comprehensive reform of the tax system, which is very difficult given the degree of confrontation between the two major parties on this subject, and which will not slow down after the Republican victory in the elections of November 2014. There has been a long war of attrition between big companies and small businesses and the self-employed because, in general terms, the big ones pay corporation tax, while the small ones, since the 1980s, have not paid it (so-called 'pass-through companies'). The owners only pay tax on personal income. The latter companies are the majority in the US, which for the Treasury represents a fiscal bloodbath.

The contrast is enormous. The largest companies have long complained that their profits pay the same tax twice. Firstly, at the corporate level; and then, when dividends are distributed and tax returns are done. However, the pass-through companies can distribute profits directly to their owners, without paying a dollar in corporation tax.[17]

The number of these companies grew after the tax reform of 1986, which placed personal tax at a lower level than that of corporations. Now that once again income tax has exceeded company tax (39.6% versus 35%, marginal), the pass-through companies have never been more appealing as a means of avoiding 'double' taxation, since tax avoidance schemes have allowed profits to be delivered directly to the owners, treated as capital gains, which are taxed at only 20%.

The ongoing trend in recent decades in the EU has been to lower direct taxes, particularly favouring bigger taxpayers. Corporate tax has been reduced with the clear objective of fiscal dumping, to attract capital.

In the Eurozone it fell, thanks to the crisis, on average 9% (from 34.4% to 25.4%). This is the case in Germany, the Nordic and Eastern European countries and the countries of southern Europe, Spain, Italy and Greece. France intends to lower the corporation tax rate from 33.3% today to 28% in 2020. Portugal hopes to place the maximum rate of corporate tax at 19% in 2018. Ireland maintains its ridiculously low level of 12.5%.

Tax rates also fell outside the Eurozone. Cameron's government found itself in power with a corporate tax rate of 28%; it has been reduced to 26% in 2011 and to 21% in 2014, and it has already been announced that this year it will be 20%, the lowest rate in the G-20. Cameron has completed the drastic reduction in income tax on patents (10%), as have Ireland and the Netherlands, to attract multinationals highly dependent on their intellectual property. Despite broadening the tax base, the ability to collect corporate tax in the European Union has been weakened (down 0.6%).

Looking briefly at Germany, Oliver Passet explained the situation very well in a recent study. Germany, even without its 10-point decrease in corporation tax in 2008, has a very favourable 'hinterland' of countries to which it can outsource certain production activities (Central & Eastern Europe) with low tax rates. There is a whole system of industrial assembly which finishes in Germany, after importing industrial components from neighbouring areas.

Thus, within the EU—except for France, Belgium, Estonia and Slovakia—there has been what Oliver Passet has described as 'fiscal devaluation' with corporate taxes; something that must be added to the other devaluations caused by the crisis. The reason lies in the 'agonizing search for competitiveness', another magic word.

Fiscal devaluation has become the weapon of competitiveness left to European states shaken to a greater or lesser extent by the recession. The means of doing this has been via the previously mentioned corporation tax, which has sparked a race to the bottom to lower interest rates and attract capital, because companies' mobility (unlike labour) makes them increasingly immune from taxation. How is this offset? With rises in the most unfair taxes: indirect taxes, VAT and surcharges on electricity tariffs (in Spain) and other essential services.

Unlike the tax privileges (secrecy and zero taxation), which some 'tax havens' offer unlawfully to non-resident companies or individuals in order to attract assets, dodging national law that requires them to pay taxes, in the case of fiscal devaluation it is a question of giving privileges to 'resident' companies. Some are seduced by lower and lower corporation tax rates. Thus production costs are reduced and they can compete in international markets on better terms. In exchange, treasuries earn less in respect of corporation tax, as a whole, because they are unable to harmonize the tax.

Between 2006 and 2014, the biggest fiscal devaluations have occurred, in this order, in Bulgaria, Hungary, Slovenia, Romania, Finland, Sweden, the UK, Czech Republic and Spain—predominately countries with a trade surplus. The negative result produced represents a new European divergence. Instead of tax harmonization, there is discrimination.

Let us say that in the EU, SMEs (which predominate in Spain and Italy) are discriminated against with respect to large companies (which predominate in central Europe) in terms of taxation—because the interest paid for external finance is deductible from corporation tax. SMEs have more difficult access to credit and therefore finance themselves to a greater extent than larger companies.[18]

Since the 1980s, the narrow stratum of the very rich has made off with an increasingly spectacular part of the national income through the tax system. There is already extensive literature that proves this point.[19] The strength of taxation on income contrasts with the weakness of capital gains taxation, which has lower rates: only one fifth of the revenues of the states comes from them, according to Eurostat. This undoubtedly contributes to social inequality.

Wealth tax, M.I.A.

Inequality is alarmingly high if from the income families receive, part is regularly moved to the more static investments of property or assets. In advanced economies, 10% of landowners own more than half of the wealth (75% in the USA). However, taxes on capital-in the past, something very important—now represent barely 2% of GDP on average in the OECD. In central and northern Europe it has been abolished.

An investigation carried out by the Luxembourg Wealth Study shows that a 1% wealth tax on the 10% richest landowners could raise around 1% of GDP each year. Similar results have been obtained in very recent calculations made by 15 Eurozone countries.[20]

As for taxes on the transfer of assets—inheritances—they have virtually disappeared. This circumstance is quite incomprehensible. The purpose of this tax is precisely to avoid the automatic and mechanical transmission of inequality at the expense of wealth obtained through effort and labour.

In the IMF study cited above, it is concluded that, if the tax revenue that could be gained by taxes on the rich were maximized, there would be ample scope to raise the highest marginal rate, without suffering declines in tax revenue.[21]

Naturally, these conclusions, valid in general for the most developed capitalist countries, are not rigidly applicable to all of them. France boasts one of the highest tax levels in Europe and perhaps the highest in the world,[22] while Spain suffers a tax burden nine points lower than the Eurozone average, and has a much bigger margin for tax growth.[23]

Germany, with an intermediate level of tax burden (38.7% in 2011), has ruled out a tax increase for the moment, according to the agreement between CDU and SPD government in November 2013.

The Social Democrats proposed increasing the tax on capital gains to 32%; increasing marginal income tax from 45% to 49%; and reintroducing a property tax. Perhaps in the future due to increases in social spending, it will be necessary to raise taxes despite these government agreements.

Looking beyond Europe, the differences, current and future, are even greater. Thus, Japan is considering lowering corporate tax. Japan had a VAT rate of 5% and Abe's government had a hard time increasing it (up to 8%), under pressure not to do so.[24]

In India, the government decided to increase social spending in the budget that took effect in April 2013 and, in turn, sharply increased taxes on the very wealthy and societies in order to maintain the deficit target of 4.8% of GDP. The government increased taxes by 10% for nearly 43,000 taxpayers who had declared income of more than 10 million rupees a year. It also doubled the tax on companies with taxable income of over 100 million rupees and on foreign companies.[25]

To conclude this section, we have to conclude that there is ample room for modifying tax policy in Europe, to balance what the citizens, businesses and corporations pay in taxes. As for the richest—in income and assets—there is room to raise taxes. Regarding the less wealthy, there is the option of decreasing the tax burden on this group.

This policy is one that can address the problem of the lack of demand that grips our economy, and rescue the welfare state from purgatory.

On the other hand, assuming the position of a progressive taxation policy would be the best strategic decision that the Western world could make: a drastic reduction in debt and increased contribution through the natural and democratic pathway of taxation.

The Tax Avoidance Industry. The Pieces of the Plot

All over the world, tax evasion, defined as tax fraud, that is, as punishable criminal wrongdoing, is now a serious economic, social and moral problem. What is taken by those who cheat on their taxes then falls on those who honestly pay what they owe under the law. This problem assumes extraordinary proportions when governments face a liquidity crisis that is transferred to budgets in the form of cuts to the welfare state.

Perhaps the most comprehensive estimate of tax evasion that has been done so far in terms of the wealth hidden in offshore jurisdictions—commonly known as tax havens—has been conducted by the Tax Justice Network, a rigorous institution, and published on 22 July 2012. It emerged that the private financial assets deposited in such jurisdictions vary between USD 21 and 32 trillion. We should remember that USD 21 trillion represents total US and Japanese GDP, i.e., 10% of global wealth or approximately half of global debt.[26]

This only includes assets that are financial in nature, without adding real estate, yachts, gold bars, etc., also in offshore territory.

According to the European Commission, tax evasion in the European Union means a loss of EUR 1 trillion for tax administrations. VAT fraud—a tax through which member states provide revenue to the Union—amounts to EUR 193 billion per year, which is 1.5% of European GDP. These figures are higher than those offered by other studies, such as the Tax Justice Network (TJN).

France is probably the European country most concerned with the problem of tax evasion. On 9 October 2013, after 10 months' work, the MPs Dupont-Aignan and Bocquet presented a report on tax havens approved by the Committee on Foreign Affairs of the National Assembly. One of its conclusions was that tax fraud is costing France between EUR 60 and 80 billion a year (to get an idea of the amounts involved, corporate tax raises only EUR 53 billion).

The Tax Justice Network numbers are more moderate than those of the European Commission and the French National Assembly. If the USD 21 billion evaded, according to TJN, produced a return of 3% per annum, and to this profit a tax of 30% were applied, tax revenues of USD 190 billion would be raised each year; this amount is, of course, what governments are therefore losing. USD 77.5 billion, according to Oxfam (May 2013), which would be due to the European Union; USD 100 billion in losses would suffered by the USA, according to Congress.

Whatever the source, the capital hidden in out-of-reach jurisdictions is of such magnitude that it goes beyond being morally reprehensible. Actually, it represents an entire 'system', i.e., the offshore economy. As opacity is also obtainable in more serious and reputable jurisdictions, some in the USA and the EU—that is, on-shore—I prefer to call all of this the 'tax avoidance industry', which has been built up in recent decades in the wake of the complete liberalization of capital.

Its purpose, the reason for its existence, is to not pay taxes; either in their home countries, or anywhere else. The success of this industry is unquestionable. It has increased with the crisis—of financial origin—which has brought more funds and companies to tax havens, just when they were most needed for productive investment and tax revenues.

Evidence of that success is revealed by the following fact: there were 20,000 offshore companies in the Seychelles five years ago, when the financial crisis was just beginning. Today, there are 120,000. It could be said that the tax avoidance industry is the pathological part of the system; another structural component of the Ice Age; organized crime. It is starting to look more and more like an enduring conspiracy to carry out a continuing offense.

Like any criminal plan, it can only succeed if it has the three elements of the plot: the perpetrators, the necessary collaborators, and the accomplices. There are also victims: the taxpayers.

The perpetrators: runaway capitalists

The stars of all these tax crimes are the tax evaders, the capitalists —not the capital—who break the social contract, and instead of being taxed and shedding a part of their capital, they dedicate themselves to making a profit from it in the form of interest. Instead of paying the state, they prefer to lend. Perhaps even to the state itself to which it unlawfully denied the tax.

That strategy, multiplied by a huge flight of capital—which has gone to investments in national debt—has contributed to the way that states have been flooded by debt to the point of being embroiled in a global crisis from 2010. This reaffirms the idea to which I subscribe whereby increasing Western debt has a high political correlation with the decline in tax revenues, a decline due to lower rates and to increased tax evasion. Avoidance is its most intensely pathological manifestation. It is the epiphenomenon within this trend over recent decades.

The action of the capitalist evader has a supranational dimension. He seeks to circumvent tax laws by surreptitiously leaving the state in which the disappearing wealth was created, in order to escape with his foreign capital to a kinder and more understanding territory which does not ask any awkward questions or mention anything to anyone else.

The international tax avoidance industry differs from 'internal' evasion in that, in the latter case, monetary or physical capital that does not wish to or cannot leave the country, dodges the tax authorities by disappearing from its sight and becoming invisible, both the money itself along with its corporate profits. This is what is known as the 'black economy', something extraordinarily strong on the southern flank of the European Union.

Some studies estimate that the Spanish black economy has now reached a quarter of GDP. The report drawn up by Friedrich Schneider (2013) estimated that the black economy in Spain, including undeclared employment and inadequate records of revenue from sales and service providers, could amount to around 18.6% of GDP. This would mean that Spain collects between EUR 60 and 80 billion less, when total tax revenues and social contributions in 2012 were EUR 347 billion. The recent report by Gestha (2014) reduces the amount that would be collected by the Spanish State to EUR 50 billion.

The average European black economy accounts for around 18.5%. Germany would have a 13% black economy; France and the UK, 10%.[27] In Italy, it is estimated that 'internal' tax evasion is EUR 120 billion per year.[28] According to the Financial Crimes Unit of the Greek police force, such tax evasion adds up to EUR 45 billion per year.[29]

In Europe as a whole, the amount not collected by the public treasury through being undeclared income is EUR 1 trillion. We are not talking now about the black economy, the evasion practised inside national boundaries, but rather the vast capital flight triggered by the crisis, whose owners wriggle out of contributing to the public purse of their own countries by migrating to external tax havens. A type of capitalist who hides his capital when his country is borrowing up to the hilt.

The necessary collaborators: the opaque tax havens

To carry out massive tax evasion it has been necessary for the 'escapee capital' to find a suitable safe haven to hide out in; headquarters from which to launch their similarly opaque investment decisions.

Since the 1970s, an increased demand for these shelters has been created. The media has dubbed them 'tax havens' or 'Treasure Islands' (Shaxson), on account of the fact that a large number of these jurisdictions are island states which will reveal nothing about foreign capital. A country is considered to be a tax haven or an offshore jurisdiction when it satisfies some of the following criteria: banking secrecy; low or almost zero taxation on capital coming from abroad, i.e., for non-residents; absence of regulation and, therefore, freedom of internal organization through shell companies; and lack of international cooperation in reporting these fraudulent activities. Half of global transactions pass through tax havens—a third of all global financial resources.

The information which can be gleaned from the IMF—the Coordinated Direct Investment Survey (CDIS)—is undoubtedly spectacular. From it can be deduced, for example, that in 2010, Barbados, Bermuda and the British Virgin Islands jointly received more direct foreign investment (5.11% of such global investments in the world) than Germany (4.77%) and Japan (3.76%). During the same year, these three jurisdictions made more investments in the world (4.5% of total) than

Germany (4.2%). There is more: in 2010, the Virgin Islands were the second largest investor in China (14%), after Hong Kong (45%) and ahead of the US (4%).

Bermuda is listed as the third largest investor in Chile. Similar percentages can be seen for Mauritius, as the maximum investor country in India (24%). Cyprus, the Virgin Islands, Bermuda and the Bahamas are among the five largest investors in Russia. Jersey is the leading exporter of bananas in the world. Words fail me.

Where does this capital come from? From developed Western countries, of course. From the USA (EUR 110.7 billion in 2011). In Europe the figure soared even higher: according to Eurostat, the flow from EU countries to 'Offshore Financial Centres' rose in 2011 to EUR 58.9 billion, 11 times more than in 2010. Most of the direct investment in such financial havens came from Luxembourg (EUR 44.3 billion), followed by the UK (EUR 10 billion).

The OECD provides us with other highly interesting data, concerning investments that are made from tax havens through the so-called 'special purpose entities' (SPEs). These are a necessary part of the tax evasion industry, since their fraudulent practices are based on anonymity, i.e., the inability to establish a connection between the owner of the capital and the account in which it is deposited. It is therefore essential to use interposed companies or entities which are essentially 'dead', but ready to be revived in a matter of hours in response to the anonymous call of whomever may need them. It is necessary to be willing to conduct business opaquely and unscrupulously.

SPEs are firms with few employees, if any; they require almost no physical or productive presence in the economy of the host tax haven, and their assets or liabilities consist of investments in or from other countries. Their core business is the financing of groups or being a holding company, usually dependent on a multinational that has its headquarters in another country. SPEs are used to attract and handle capital of dubious origin, and are controlled by a non-resident company in the tax haven. The SPEs, then, are underground channels connecting non-residents' capital in the country/island tax haven with other non-residents.

Among the corporate instruments shrouding the true ownership of the capital are the trusts. The off-shore trusts are the most important, because they allow the owner to retain ultimate control. As is cogently explained by JL Escario, the owner hires someone by proxy to be an administrator, theoretically independent (a trustee), to deal with the management of assets, on whose returns they do not have to pay tax because the assets are not the personal assets of the administrator.[30]

Some striking examples are given by the OECD of SPE investments in respectable countries, which in practice act as tax havens. The total investment in shares within the Netherlands in 2011 was USD 3 billion, 207 million. Of this amount, investments by SPEs were worth USD 2 billion, 625 million. The same is true if we look at investments heading out of the Netherlands. Three-quarters were made by SPEs, i.e., by shell companies.

In Luxembourg it is the same story; and also in Austria and Hungary.[31] The latter, like Cyprus, are EU member countries, but have so far continued to serve as tax shelters, where opacity and banking secrecy is the rule. The same thing happens in Switzerland and in the US onshore havens (Delaware, Alaska, Nevada, Wyoming, South Dakota), where legal firms offer confidential services, armour-plated against creditors or taxes. However, use can also be made of ersatz states such as Monaco and Liechtenstein, the Seychelles, the Channel Islands, the Caymans, Nauru, St. Kitts, Antigua, Tortola and Singapore.[32] There is a wide variety of models to choose from.

The most outrageous and unsustainable situation has been that of Austria and Luxembourg, which have resisted calls to get rid of their beloved banking secrecy for years: it provides obvious benefits. The Luxembourg financial centre alone represents 36% of the country's GDP, and tens of thousands of direct and indirect jobs. In May 2013, both requested time from their EU partners, and they did not lift the veto on the reform of the savings tax directive, to the obvious disappointment of the EU, led by Commissioner Semeta Argidas. Austria and Luxembourg demanded the same regulation for their European 'competitors': Switzerland, Liechtenstein, Monaco, San Marino and Andorra. All this despite the fact that on 10 April the then Prime Minister of Luxembourg, Jean-Claude Juncker, had presented to the House of Representatives his favourable position regarding the automatic exchange of information, under pressure from the USA, on residents from outside the country, although he upheld secrecy for residents.

The savings tax directive, which came into force in 2005, organizes an exchange of information on the interest produced on accounts existing in any EU country held by taxpayers resident in another EU country. Since then, there has been an exception for Austria and Luxembourg, who wanted to remain offshore jurisdictions. Brussels always tried to ensure the disappearance of this exception, as well as the extension of this directive to other life insurance products and certain front companies. They ended up getting it. On 11 March 2014, Luxembourg and Austria surrendered, announcing they would accept the directive and accepting the automatic exchange of banking information, which is intended to combat tax evasion.

Luxembourg has always been regarded as a comfortable place for US companies that go from country to country—doing 'treaty shopping'—looking for more attractive tax treatment on the part of the authorities. In Luxembourg, huge deductions in corporate tax are made and allow companies to pay very little tax, which in effect becomes a kind of state aid.

The European Commission opened an investigation against Luxembourg in October 2014, for giving illicit tax advantages to Amazon, joining those already granted to Fiat. But the scandal came on 5 November, when the International Consortium of Investigative Journalists and forty mass media outlets revealed what constitutes the core of the Luxembourg tax system: 340 multinational beneficiaries of tax agreements with the Juncker's Government in order to avoid paying billions of euros. They are called 'tax rulings' and occurred between 2002 and 2010. The companies that benefited from these shady deals paid 2% on profits instead of the official rate of corporation tax in Luxembourg, which stood at 28.6%.

The issue is already known as 'LuxLeaks' due to being exposed by nearly 28,000 pages of confidential documents taken from the archives of Price Waterhouse, one of the auditors who had come up with these agreements, together with the other 'big four': Deloitte, Ernst & Young and KPMG. These audits were not limited to providing technical assistance but, as stated in the House of Commons, to promote 'tax avoidance' on an industrial scale (Report published on 6 February 2015).

The Luxembourg Government has been forced to suspend agreements on tax exemption, and Juncker to announce a very significant shift in European taxation. But this move will not give back to the other states the billions of euros which should have been taken in taxes, and which vanished into thin air in Luxembourg.

Holland is another example of a jurisdiction which facilitates tax exemption, and therefore, the country that has received most money from US companies, and several well known rock bands. It shares this dubious position with Bermuda, Ireland and the Cayman Islands.

In Cyprus, its role as an off-shore jurisdiction—favoured by wealthy Russians as a refuge to avoid paying taxes—disappeared at the demand of the EU, in exchange for the rescue package of EUR 10 billion agreed on 24 March 2013. Cyprus had an astronomical banking industry seven times the size of its real economy, largely devoted to money laundering and to investing in Russia, whose depositors have suffered a significant reverse from this decision.[33]

Switzerland deserves special attention because it is the quintessential classic tax sanctuary, and also because it acts as a financial intermediary in other economic activities and is the main trading centre for commodities. According to data from the NGO Christian Aid, Switzerland is the hub for 25% of world trade in raw materials. Geneva is the largest exporter of oil in the world, and 60% of the coffee trade is controlled from Switzerland.[34]

The Swiss Confederation arrived quite late to the banking business. Its central bank was founded in 1907 and, until the late nineteenth century, each of the 26 cantons minted its own currency. However, World War I completely changed the future of banking in Switzerland, whose lack of regulation made it the world's financial centre by definition. Above all for the welcome which, since the establishment by law in 1934 of banking secrecy, has been extended to capitalist tax evaders. With its subtle distinction between 'tax avoidance' and 'tax evasion' and its EUR 2 trillion in opaque deposits, Switzerland has been without a doubt—right up to the present day—the headquarters of the offshore tax evasion industry.[35] This factor accounts for its banks representing 10.3% of Swiss GDP.

This age-old Swiss tradition of 'flying under the radar', based only on the alleged right to defend against invasions of privacy by the State, began to weaken in 2009 in the midst of the crisis of Western treasuries—and not by chance. The United States Department of Justice issued arrest warrants against Swiss bankers who had travelled there. In 2009 the same department reached an agreement with the largest Swiss bank, UBS, resulting in the handover of the names of 4,450 clients, wealthy Americans with checking accounts in that entity. UBS was fined EUR 780 million, admitting aiding and abetting tax evasion.

The Justice Department correctly understood that those who had fled UBS had moved to other Swiss banks, which obligingly offered their services to maintain secrecy. In January 2012, Switzerland's oldest bank, Wegelin, pleaded guilty to tax evasion on account of helping conceal assets worth USD 1.2 billion in the first decade of the new millennium. Simultaneously, it announced the closure of all its activities, after 272 years. Credit Suisse has been fined (in May 2014) USD 2.6 billion.

There are 13 other Swiss banks, or Swiss branches of international banks, which are subject to criminal investigation by the US authorities: Credit Suisse, Bank Julius Baer, Pictet Bank Frey, Zürcher Kantonalbank, Basler Kantonalbank, among others. The other banks that have enabled tax evasion since 2008 will end up paying millions in fines of between 20% and 50% of the value of the amounts not declared.

The decisive action by the USA, very different from European passivity, convinced the Swiss Federal Council—despite opposition from the conservative Swiss People's Party—that an agreement with the world's greatest power was inevitable if Switzerland did not want see their access to the huge US financial market closed down. It also convinced the association of Swiss banks. Since 2009, it has urged its members to refuse to open current accounts for US residents who have not paid tax in the USA.

Final agreement was reached, between governments, after stubborn resistance in the lower house of the Swiss parliament, which in June 2013 had refused for a second time to approve the reform of banking secrecy. Banking secrecy was lifted for the USA. Its attorney general, Eric H. Holder, announced emphatically on Tuesday 27 August: 'This programme will significantly enhance the efforts of the

Justice Department to aggressively pursue those who attempt to evade the law by hiding their assets outside the United States'. Holder was referring to the FATCA (Foreign Account Tax Compliance Act) programme, which requires institutions to report foreign assets of US citizens and green card holders to prevent tax evasion through offshore investment. So far, the US authorities have recovered USD 5.5 billion in unpaid taxes and fines, and estimate that they may recover another USD 5 billion from banks in Switzerland, India, Nepal, Hong Kong, Singapore and other countries. The US Senate believes that Credit Suisse alone, which is currently under investigation, could be helping some 22,000 Americans avoid taxes, with accounts which are estimated to hold up to an USD 10 billion.

The small commercial bank Valiant Bank was the first to declare that it will be part of the agreement signed in August by authorities in Switzerland and the USA. Of its 40,000 customers, 400 are American. It was followed by a large number of the 300 Swiss banks that are not under investigation and which had until late 2013 to sign the agreement.

Following the agreement with Switzerland, banks were required to report the current accounts of US taxpayers with balances exceeding USD 50,000, as well as those operating across borders; they also had to close the accounts of those who had evaded taxes. This was the price of bringing some peace to the Swiss banks, and restoring something of their good financial reputation.[36] It will now no longer be illegal for a Swiss bank to provide information about US Customers residing there. Switzerland's perspective is that of an inexorable decline in funds deposited in their banks, in the absence of security and legal stability. Many US citizens with black money in Switzerland renounced their nationality. First things first.

It was not only the atmosphere that changed dramatically with the financial crisis; Switzerland had become very isolated in its banking secrecy from the time its supposed allies Austria and Luxembourg used it as a defensive argument used against the harsh criticism within the EU.

Other elements to consider are the political scandals which arose in France and Spain involving Swiss banks (Hervé Falciani).[37] The latter was one more case of an avalanche of personal information leaked to the media by employees of the financial entities, which brought out into the open the use of opaque Swiss accounts to bribe, break tax laws and hide money. The so-called 'Swiss Leaks' was very hard to accept in an era of budget cuts.

The debate over the demise of banking secrecy, the end of tax privileges for wealthy non-residents and the rooting-out of fraud has already been launched in Switzerland, in the cantons of Valais, Ticino, Geneva and Vaud, leading haunts of tax evaders. It has sharpened the normally half-hearted fight between right and left, with the prospect of a referendum to 'normalize' the Confederacy in financial matters.

Europe has been slower than the USA regarding the need for transparency in Switzerland. In this respect, it has tended to lag behind, and the Union has also admitted that within its borders, there are some bad examples. But the crisis, which has been a tax revenue crisis, coupled with the aggressive US policy and Austria and Luxembourg's demand for an end to be put to Swiss banking secrecy to make this palatable to themselves, has forced the EU to finally take Switzerland seriously.

At the moment, there have been two significant developments in this regard. The first, Swiss agreement to adopt the 'Multilateral Convention on Mutual Administrative Assistance' to fight tax evasion-promoted by the OECD—joining 60 other countries including Austria and Luxembourg. A convention supported by the G-20, which opens the way from bilateralism to multilateralism, and replaces requests for information with its automatic exchange. However, the legislative process in Switzerland is very long and uncertain. They have to go to Parliament and then have the usual referendum.

The second fact is that Switzerland has accepted the demands of the OECD to revise its double tax treaties and to enhance transparency in the ownership of shares along with stricter reporting rules. In this case a referendum is also needed, and at this point no one knows what will happen in view of the result of the one which abolished the free movement of persons with the EU. This is a very graphic illustration of Swiss tradition. Maximum freedom for capital; minimum for people.

Switzerland therefore has advanced relative to the USA by accepting the implementation of FACTA in combating tax evasion; but compared to Europe or other countries it has continued to be a tax shelter, an offshore jurisdiction.

Switzerland is not the only major country that is considered a tax haven. There are authors, like the previously quoted Nicholas Shaxson, who bestow this rather dishonourable name on the City of London, as the top spot for the international financial market. As such, in London capital converges with that traded in the Channel Islands and the Caribbean, as explained in detail in the French National Assembly report of 9 October 2013 to which reference was made earlier.

The accomplices: the banks and financial institutions

The best example of complicity in tax evasion is that which is carried out all the time by financial institutions that provide financial and technical support. It is estimated that tax havens are home to 4,000 offshore banks and two million 'front companies'.

The financial system, which is now finally supranational—or 'metanational—'provides the evader with a technical platform which makes their illegal action profitable, and to this end, discreet. In late 2010, the 50 largest private banks managed USD 12.1 trillion in escaping assets invested by private clients across borders. This is approximately half the volume of offshore assets in the world, as calculated in the report by the Tax Justice Network. The other half is the offshore equity managed by hedge funds, money managers, insurance companies and, in general, non-banking intermediaries and small banks.

The group at the summit has managed, directly or indirectly, nearly three-quarters of private wealth offshore, in constant growth. Their names are known. The Tax Justice Network mentions a large number of very prominent world banking organizations, experts in creating corrupt accounts and accused by the prosecutors in Brussels of being a criminal organization.

These larger banks, which boast an oligopoly in managing the proceeds of capital flight, are precisely those who staged the massive financial crisis that began in 2007. They are the ones who later benefited from generous zero interest rate loans guaranteed by taxpayers,[39] which these banks have been defrauding by assisting tax evasion.[40]

It is well known that the taxes which evaders do not pay have to be offset by other taxes paid by honest taxpayers. When taxes are not enough, then States resort to the increasingly galloping issuance of debt. The megabanks—too big to fail—which are real highways to evasion are at the same time those who seize the opportunity to buy Southern European government debt, which offers a good return on investment. So, instead of helping taxes to be paid, they underwrite debt which has been issued because of a lack of tax revenue among other reasons. It is clearly better to lend (with interest) than to pay taxes to the state.

The entry of international banks into the tax evasion industry makes these tax havens difficult entities to locate geographically. The banks managing this capital move the money when needed; it is awarded to an intermediary finance company, nameless and faceless, and then moved from here to there and divided into many pieces, all with one supreme purpose: to hide it from the eyes of the bewildered and powerless national treasuries, sometimes rendered complicit through their own inaction.

This is why there has been talk of a 'pirate banking system'. This kind of behaviour reminds people a lot of the legendary buccaneer, also outside the law and beyond its borders, taking refuge in the 'South Seas', under no flag and on lawless islands.[41] A banking system just inviting tax fraud to it.

Another party that cannot be omitted when talking of accomplices to the plot are the lawyers. Amongst these some Swiss lawyers are particularly prominent. Their complicity with the tax evasion industry has been evident in the off-shore leaks operation, by means of which thousands of documents on the implementation of massive tax evasion reached the European media in the spring of 2013.

Through hundreds of real cases, this leak has allowed us to understand how lawyers—from Geneva to Saint-Gallen—have advised and cooperated in assembling offshore companies that rich clients need to avoid annoying Treasury checks in their own countries.[42]

Thus, the loop of the tax avoidance industry closes. Each of the sectors fulfils a function; the capitalist's evaders contribute the capital itself, which drip-feeds funds to the benefit of other sectors: political (the offshore jurisdictions) and financial, aided by the mercenaries of the pseudo-Right.

The desperate politics of step-by-step

The difficulties of states and international organizations in curbing financial and tax crime have made history in recent decades, and above all in recent years.

The outbreak of the crisis, and its immediate effect on faltering tax revenues, resulted in the ambitious London G-20 summit, on 1 and 2 April 2009.

The bombastic phrase registered at its conclusion has been quoted ad nauseam: 'The era of banking secrecy is over'. The G-20 launched a verbal crusade against tax havens, threatening sanctions and focusing on creating 'lists' of such jurisdictions. At the Pittsburgh meeting (on 24 and 25 September), this commitment was reconfirmed.

After Pittsburgh, these good intentions faltered until the meeting in St. Petersburg (on 5 and 6 September 2013); here the G-20 used assertive and convincing language when in paragraph 51 of the conclusions they 'absolutely' endorsed the OECD strategy on a 'multilateral and bilateral' model of automatic exchange of information.

For the G-20, the automatic exchange (not request) of information should be the new overall standard, compatible with confidentiality and the appropriate use of the information exchanged. The G-20 set a timetable and said they really expected the start of the exchange of financial information between the members of the G-20 in late 2015; and they called on all countries to sign the Multilateral Convention on Mutual Administrative Assistance in Tax Matters.

The EU has led the exchange of information since we established the Directive on taxation of savings in 2005. On 22 July 2013 the Council adopted two directives against so-called VAT 'carousel' fraud, which refers to rapid dealing in certain products to avoid payment of VAT, particularly in cross-border transactions.

Since 2008, the European Commission has been proposing to plug the obvious gaps in the savings directive, which only refers to individuals. It is intended to make the policy apply to mutual funds, pensions and payments through trusts and foundations.

In 2013 there came a shift in government attitudes. One reason, of course, is the crisis itself. However, what triggered the decisions that were embodied in the European Council in May 2013 was a series of scandals involving massive tax evasion of European capital via tax havens.

The most important is what is known as *off-shore leaks*, sponsored by the International Consortium of Investigative Journalists, in partnership with Le Monde, *The Guardian* and The Washington Post. This leaking of more than 2,500 documents revealed the existence of tens of thousands of secret accounts belonging to 130,000 individuals of 170 nationalities, including 4,000 Americans; 120,000 related to hidden offshore companies in tax havens, among which several islands under British jurisdiction stood out. Other cases such as the French former minister Cahuzac, or the billionaire Bethencourt, rubbed salt into the wound.

The other important fact which has driven the Union to begin to take action on this matter was the adoption of the FATCA programme imposed by the USA on all other countries.

A first hint of movement was the letter that the governments of the five largest countries, Germany, the UK, France, Italy and Spain, sent on 9 April 2013 to Commissioner Semeta, committing themselves to an automatic, binding and complete exchange of information about interest generated by bank accounts opened outside a citizen's country of origin. This is the beginning of a European FATCA, which requires an automatic exchange of information on interest earned on savings accounts opened by European citizens, irrespective of their place of residence.

The letter of the five was sent one week after the off-shore leaks. The day after the declaration of the five, Luxembourg formally admitted its willingness to provide banking information to its European partners.

On 9 May, a month after the revelation of off-shore leaks, the USA, UK and Australia jointly announced having managed to obtain a list of companies in the Cayman Islands, Virgin Islands, Cook Islands and Singapore; a case of tax evasion larger than off-shore leaks, involving a hundred of the richest British citizens. London, Washington and Canberra hinted that other countries may be given access to the files.

This revelation coincided with the announcement by George Osborne of the achievement of an agreement with the British Overseas Territories, financial centres, to achieve complete fiscal transparency. They had agreed to an automatic exchange of information, bilateral with the UK and multilateral with the G-5, the UK, France, Germany, Italy and Spain. The agreement would affect all data on the account holders, their accounts and the payments and movements of the same.

The European Parliament approved a *report on the fight against tax fraud, tax evasion and tax havens*, led by the MP Mojca Kleva (21 May 2013), and the text is worth summarizing.

The report stresses the failure, sometimes the awkwardness, of multilateral national actions, and calls for a coordinated EU strategy, to the point of regretting that the agreements with the USA under FATCA law (Foreign Account Tax Compliance) are being developed on a bilateral basis between states with no common EU negotiating position.

The European Parliament is clear and direct in its proposals. It believes that it is necessary to revoke the banking licenses of institutions that encourage tax fraud or which are established in tax havens. These should be identified with specific criteria in order to create a 'European public blacklist' before 31 December 2014. It would thus be possible to prohibit contracts and public aid to companies based in these offshore areas, with which member states should suspend any double taxation agreements in force.

When the report was adopted, there was still not a single tax haven on the (empty) OECD list. This gives an idea of how far there is still to go in effectively combating tax havens.

To make this fight more effective, as well as the member states—which are sovereign in levying taxes—joining the fight, it is important to create a 'European tax authority' to coordinate the exchange of information among states and to collaborate on prosecuting tax fraud. This is one of the proposals that the Council of European Affairs of the Fundación Alternativas made to the European Council in May 2013. The centre of the proposed Alternatives Foundation is to harden sanctions on financial institutions and non-cooperative jurisdictions that do not implement minimum European standards.

The European Council, as always, was disappointing in its conclusions on the fight against tax fraud. However, we should not disregard the fact that there has been some progress, unimaginable only a few months earlier. It strengthens the commitment to an end to banking secrecy and the 'automatic' exchange of information, and in the context of the EU, the Commission was tasked with presenting in June (which it did) some modifications to the policy of 15 February 2011 on administrative cooperation, to enable the exchange of information covering all types of income generated in connection with assets held in financial accounts (dividends, capital gains, balances, interest). It has boosted negotiations with Switzerland, Liechtenstein, Monaco, Andorra and San Marino. It has called for revisions of the Directive on taxation of savings. It has given instructions on combating VAT fraud. And it has reiterated the need to combat money laundering, by reviewing the 3rd Money Laundering Directive.

However, at the European Council there have been no more specific commitments in relation to fraud. A blacklist of tax havens has not been adopted. Banks are not prohibited from trading with them. It has not compelled member states to open a register of off-shore companies, without which tax inspection is effectively toothless.

The conclusion about the current state of tax fraud is that it has finally appeared on the agenda of 'world government', the start of the realisation of just what a staggering quantity of non-tax-paying fugitive capital is in the balance. Even the increasing conviction of some investors (not enough yet) that investing in companies that evade tax damages their reputation. However, the tax avoidance industry remains intact.

Again, there are some distinguishing nuances between the USA and Europe. There, they have already got a powerful weapon: the FATCA Act, which is applied and works. Here, not yet.

Multinationals and Their Sophisticated Tax Avoidance Schemes

In the Internet era, the transformation of global economies and trade from a national basis to an international basis has subverted the relationship between the new, great, productive processes—the multinational companies and their tax obligations. More precisely, the quintessential tax, corporation tax.

We referred earlier to the dwindling marginal rate of corporation tax by almost 20 points between 1980 and 2007 due to competition among states to attract capital, in contrast to the steady rise in indirect taxes in the EU. The mutation of corporate tax has not stopped there. During the crisis, it has also affected the tax base, which is corporate profits, through a contraction in the amount on which they have to pay tax.

In countries such as Ireland, the Netherlands and Luxembourg, foreign companies are granted low or no taxation on all kinds of internal transfers like loans, in order to artificially reduce earnings. The possibility of such manipulation is granted by the ban in the EU on obstructing the flow or trans-border movement of capital. The immediate beneficiaries are, as we all know, the multinational companies.

There are many changes that are too easily attributable to globalization. With regard to the erosion of the tax base of companies, this is absolutely true. The unrestricted movement of capital and goods, the service economy, together with the universal development of digital technology have altered the functioning of large companies, which have inevitably become multinational; above all, to optimize profits.

It is not surprising that multinationals have not hesitated for a minute to take steps to circumvent their tax burdens as far as they possibly can. They have used all the legal loopholes: they have notionally devalued their intellectual property assets, such as patents and trademarks; they have shifted them to low-tax countries (the most popular destinations were Ireland, Switzerland and Singapore).

Multinationals never acted as decisively—organized in a network of different companies—as when they try to evade taxes. The fiscal strategy has been increasingly aggressive. It is about competition, the drive to reduce production costs, the payment of taxes very clearly amongst them. One way of carrying it out has been the relocation of profits to the highest bidder, taking advantage of the complacent attitude of some states, which have not shown very much loyalty to their European partners.

The rotten apples

Apple has won pole position in the race to avoid paying millions in tax. One fact explains it better than a thousand words: at the end of March 2013 Apple had USD 145 billion in liquid cash and bonds on its balance sheet. But right then, it went to the markets to borrow money to the tune of USD 17 billion in bonds, the largest private corporate bond transaction in history.

Why would a company like Apple, with no cash problems or heavy investment plans, launch a deal committing itself to such astronomical borrowing? Very simple: because it did not want to distribute profits in cash to its shareholders via European money, on which it would have been forced to 'import' the profits obtained in Europe to the USA, and therefore pay American company tax at the rate of 35%.

The debt issued by Apple was at a very low interest rate, and was also tax deductible. So Apple repurchased the shares, paying for them with USD 17 billion and thus avoided paying any tax to Uncle Sam, something that it has always been reluctant to do. Totally legal.[43]

What lies beneath—or above—Apple's decision is the concealment of profits, just as it does when it pretends to hold them all in Cork (Ireland).

The US Senate estimates that Apple, despite having most of its management and organization in the USA, has found a way to keep 70% of their profits overseas[44] and avoid paying USD 74 billion in taxes between 2009 and 2012.

Carl Levin, chairman of the Research Subcommittee of the US Senate on the tax avoidance practices of multinationals, accused Apple of using 'shell companies' to escape taxation in the USA and Ireland. Apple seems to have found the Holy Grail of tax avoidance: it does not pay taxes in the USA on profits made in the rest of the world in its strongest subsidiary companies based in Ireland, and pays virtually none in Ireland in accordance with the law, because Apple is controlled from the USA. The most important multinational company outside America—the holding company, Apple Operations International—has not paid corporate tax in any country in the last five years, despite having taken in USD 30 billion—unbelievable.[44] Ireland has been a tax haven for Apple.

In view of the figures, it was ludicrous for Apple CEO Tim Cook to claim before the Senate that he 'had paid all taxes owed to the Internal Revenue Service', which is the US tax agency.

The number one at Apple fiercely criticized American tax collection, according to which no taxes are paid on profits from overseas, but if you take them to the USA then you pay 35%, with no rebate. Cook suggested, on the offensive, that if corporate tax had a lower marginal rate, US multinationals would repatriate their profits from overseas to the USA, and pay corporate tax on them.

As Floyd Norris, chief financial correspondent of The New York Times, rightly points out, Tim Cook's opinion is like saying that multinationals can freely choose whether to pay or not pay taxes.[45] This is what gives them the power to blackmail the State and force it to sharply lower rates of corporate tax, on pain of not repatriating profits to the metropolis. Apple and other companies are clear on their policy: given the choice between paying 35% in the US or 2% in Ireland, they will choose the latter.

The Apple case is also the case for other US multinationals that hold more than a trillion and a half dollars under the control of other jurisdictions. Control in theory, because much of that money is invested in US bonds.

Google's case is similar. There was also an inquiry by the British Parliament (2012), where the transfer of their huge profits to Ireland and other paradise islands was explained, avoiding payment of more than USD 1.5 billion in taxes that year. In 2012 it paid the UK only 1% of its income. Between 2006 and 2011, it had USD 18 billion in sales, and had paid USD 16 million in taxes.

Google itself declared EUR 1.4 million in losses in 2012 in Spain, and during the previous year, EUR 75,000.[46] The technique was the same: Google shifted profits to Ireland, through improbable billings to Google Ireland.

Starbucks paid less than nine million pounds tax in the UK between 1998 and 2012, during which period it recorded sales of GDP 3 billion. On 14 November 2014, the Commission filed a complaint in the Netherlands about illegal state aid for Starbucks via 'tax fuelling'.

Amazon works the same way. The only difference is that the shifting of their profits takes place to Luxembourg, in exchange for very low fees. This explains why such a small country receives more than one-tenth of the world's foreign investment (IMF data).

Cadbury is another company that follows an aggressive strategy to avoid taxes, which contrasts with the sweetness of their products. Their billion-pound turnover and a hundred million in profit in the UK in 2012 became a Lilliputian tax payment of GDP 6.4 million. Like many other British companies, Cadbury chose Ireland to establish its financial headquarters, and thus obtain an increase in profits.[47]

Vodafone did not pay a penny to the UK in 2011 by way of corporate tax, but has 19 million customers there. The trick in this case was not only offshoring subsidiaries to Luxembourg, but also greatly reducing its tax liability by deducting interest on debt on total profits, a tax technicality legally available to companies, which makes no sense whatsoever. What Vodafone did was create debt in its subsidiaries that it had to 'pay', and upon which interest is also paid. This interest is then deducted from corporate tax.

Finally, we can turn to Facebook, also enveloped in imaginative tax-avoidance schemes. Facebook Ireland Limited turned their huge profits into losses, using the pretext that they had had to pay the parent company based in Ireland for the use of intellectual property. The parent company has as its shareholders, in turn, subsidiaries of Facebook based in the Cayman Islands, which does not levy income tax.

Facebook uses a mechanism known as the Double Irish, also used by Google and other multinationals with interests in intellectual property. It is called the Double Irish because it uses two companies officially registered in Ireland but of different types. The first, resident in Ireland for tax purposes, pays royalties to companies that hold and use the most valuable and essential intellectual property for their products, which reduces profits and therefore the tax payable in Ireland. The other company, not resident in Ireland for tax purposes but in a tax haven, receives royalties for intellectual property that it owns, avoiding Irish taxes. In this way, the profits are channelled to off-shore jurisdictions.[48] All of this is possible because Irish law has hitherto entertained the possibility that companies may be registered in Ireland without being resident in Ireland for tax purposes.

The empire strikes back

It is easy to see that Ireland is in the eye of the hurricane. The US Senate resolutely called it a 'tax haven', which was obviously rejected by the Irish government. For the Senate, Ireland is at the heart of Apple's strategy and those of other multinationals to avoid taxes by hiding taxable income; and it has begun fighting back against tax avoidance by multinationals, starting there.

Companies registered in Ireland operate throughout the EU single market, but they can prove that sales were generated by the headquarters in Ireland. So their corporate tax is paid there, i.e., 12.5%, the lowest in the EU except Slovakia. In reality, according to the government's own data, the effective rate is half of this.

This is not what is valued most by multinationals and Internet companies, but rather it is the ease with which Irish law—and the loopholes in US law—permit opaque transactions with offshore jurisdictions, making Ireland an international haven for evading corporation tax, particularly for companies with high use of patents, such as pharmaceuticals or those in the field of information technology. Google has its industrial and intellectual property assets—its patents—in the hands of an Irish company based in Bermuda, which has zero corporate tax. LinkedIn, likewise, is located on the Isle of Man. Adobe has not even revealed which tax haven it uses.[49]

Ireland, as we have said, can register a company as non-resident for tax purposes, which enables it to evade taxes in Ireland and beyond. That is, under current Irish law, when the company is controlled and directed from outside Ireland by non-residents, and is related to trade in Ireland.

However, this legal loophole has become impossible for the Irish government to maintain, under international pressure, particularly from the USA. It has become irresistible since the Senate found that Apple had avoided paying taxes on the USD 44 billion in profits obtained outside the USA. On 5 October 2013, Michael Noonan, the finance minister, agreed that companies registered in Ireland could not act as stateless companies for purposes of tax residency, which is what had allowed Apple pay 2% corporate tax in Ireland. This quantum leap in Ireland in adjusting its tax code takes effect from 1 January 2015, which gives the thousand multinationals registered in that EU country a year to restructure their tax avoidance strategies.

Nevertheless, groups actively campaigning against tax evasion such as Citizens for Tax Justice continue to criticize the fact that the so-called Double Irish mechanism has not disappeared, making it feasible to move capital from Ireland to Bermuda and other countries that do not require the payment of corporate tax. Like Google, who effect the transfer to Bermuda through the Netherlands using what is known as a Dutch Sandwich.

The Irish government is saying that the solution is in the hands of the USA, which could tax the profits that their companies earn abroad but do not repatriate to US territory, and it has expanded the Double Irish until 2020.

The quarrel with Ireland is only one aspect of what is an already unstoppable movement in the USA of taxing the record profits made by American companies abroad (40% of annual profits are not taxed, a percentage which corresponds to the two trillion dollars which US corporations are estimated to hold outside the USA).

This dossier has become a huge part of US policy, because the dynamic of large companies moving to Europe, countries with less taxation (Ireland, Netherlands, United Kingdom), is unstoppable. It has been pointless to try and reproach them for their lack of 'patriotism'. Capital has no homeland. Some Democratic senators like Carl Levin are at the forefront of the solution to this outrageous problem. In addition, strategic UK tax movements favour this trend, leading to a decision to transfer the headquarters of a company as important as Pfizer, which is using the technique of purchasing at least 20% of a foreign company to achieve this migration. It means savings each year of EUR 1 billion in taxes. For the USA, migrations of headquarters—called 'inversions'—will mean the loss of 20 billion dollars in the next decade. Hence, the objective is to avoid such a disaster.

This goal can be achieved using various formulas. One is that corporate tax should be paid in the country that has generated the highest economic profit. Another is that all profits are taxed in the USA (there were supposedly USD 42 billion in 2013).

What is beyond doubt is that tax havens, low-tax jurisdictions, unjustifiably absorb—thanks to their privileged position—proportionately greater profits than when the company in question makes its profits in other countries with rates of corporation tax within international standards. A study by the Congressional Research Service found that subsidiaries of US corporations in the five major tax havens (Netherlands, Ireland, Bermuda, Switzerland and Luxembourg) generated 43% of profits outside the USA in 2008; but only 4% of its workers and 7% of its foreign investments were located in such countries. For them, being tax havens, their main source of profit is precisely tax avoidance.

On 21 July 2014, the US Senate made public an investigation which revealed that between 1998 and 2013, more than a dozen hedge funds made billions of dollars of transactions using mechanisms—known as 'basket options'—to evade taxes.

These mechanisms were created by Barclays and Deutsche Bank. One hedge fund alone, Renaissance Technologies, saved itself 6 billion dollars in tax.

Europe: eppur si muove

The only mention that the European Council of 22 May 2013 made in its conclusions on tax avoidance was: 'The work will continue with regard to the recommendations of the Commission on aggressive tax planning and relocation of profits.

The Commission intends to present a proposal for a directive on the transfer of parent companies and subsidiaries by the end of the year and is considering provisions against abuse documented in the relevant EU legislation. The European Council looks forward to the next report from the OECD on tax evasion and tax bases of off shoring benefits'.[50]

The EU has linked up with the OECD in its work in this field to remove most of what can now be called without any reservation 'double non-taxation', something that is achieved with the 'aggressive tax planning' of multinationals.

On 19 July 2013, the OECD presented the Plan of Action on Erosion of tax bases and Relocation Benefits (BEPS). BEPS arises when there are legal gaps or friction in the interaction of national tax systems, which lead to double non-taxation in corporation tax.[51] For the OECD, with the consensus of the G-20, 'the benefits should be taxed where the activity takes place and the added value is created' (St. Petersburg Declaration, paragraph 50).

The Plan of Action is well conceived, and easily and accurately diagnoses the fact that the digital economy gives large corporations the facility with which to commit tax abuses, from the use of interest on alleged debt with its subsidiaries to deduct taxes, to aggressive transactions, all through the artificial division of ownership of tangible and intangible assets (intellectual property) between entities of the same group or the transfer of profits to other companies in the group, not corresponding to the creation of proportional economic value. The OECD proposes targeted measures with implementation dates during the years 2014–2015. The idea is to control such practices by multinationals, forcing them to give information by country of all relevant economic data.

However, up until now the control or prohibition of such abusive behaviour by large companies has not been achieved.

There is no prospect, for the moment, that the Commission will request information on the operations of business groups in all sectors, as required by the European Parliament.[52]

In another area, on 25 November 2013 the Commission presented a proposal for a directive on parent companies and subsidiaries. It does not apply to cases where the residence of the parent or the subsidiary is outside the EU. Its purpose is to deter subsidiaries whose sole purpose is to be the recipient of the most profitable business by establishing themselves in jurisdictions with low or no taxation for foreign companies, producing the 'tax gap' that has been growing throughout the length and breadth of the crisis in corporation tax.

The proposed amendment to the policy is to avoid 'double non-taxation'. The reform includes a general anti-abuse clause to combat aggressive tax plans by the multinationals.[53]

However, this directive will not avoid practices by multinationals in circumventing corporation tax in their home countries. In the EU there is plenty of hypocrisy on tax avoidance. Some EU member states, while solemnly advocating combating irregularities or abuses of large corporations, provide low corporate tax to attract them to their territory. This is, without a doubt, the root of the practices that enable companies to avoid paying taxes by quietly fleeing to those jurisdictions. That is, Luxembourg, the UK and, of course, Ireland. Here it is worth giving an example of unfair tax competition among European partners to attract investment: FIAT Industry decided in May 2013 to transfer their tax residence to the UK to take advantage of lighter taxation. It is going to be hard to convince the UK to change its tax policy, or Ireland, when it means the arrival of foreign capital investment. Let us recall that Ireland did not give up its corporate tax rate of 12.5%, not even in exchange for being rescued to the tune of EUR 85 billion that it received as bailout money from the EU.

Hence the fundamental solution to tax avoidance, at least within the EU, is to achieve two things: a common tax base of corporate tax, and harmonized rates. The first is in the proposed OECD information exchange since 2014, and ratified by 54 countries at the Berlin Conference (October 2014).[54] The second—harmonization—is another thing altogether, as it means securing unanimity in the Council of Ministers of the EU and the reform of the tax codes of member countries, not at all a simple task since the current trend is to attract capital by running down the rates of corporation tax. Governments as different as Portugal and the UK are moving in that direction. Osborne was very clear: 'In this global race we cannot sit still'. Even Obama has proposed lowering the rate of 35%, in a broader strategy of pursuit/seduction of American multinationals.

There is another possibility in the hands of the Commission to 'harmonize'—although this is not what they call it—corporation tax rates, and avoid tax dumping in various European countries. We are of course referring to the request for information on 12 September 2013 that the Commission (Competition Division) sent some countries (Luxembourg, Netherlands, Ireland) on the possible tax agreements of their governments with some multinational companies, assuring substantial reductions in corporate tax if they set up in those countries. We saw how the US Senate concluded that Ireland had allowed Apple to pay 2% tax on profits off-shored on the island, far below what is supposed to be the statutory rate (12.5%). We also saw the 'special relationship' of Starbucks with the Netherlands. Let us add one more item. Netherlands and Luxembourg recorded foreign direct investment (FDI) amounting to EUR 5.8 trillion at the end of 2012: more than the USA, UK and Germany combined. The Netherlands had FDI worth EUR 3.5 trillion, but only EUR 573 billion of this came into the 'real' Dutch economy. The rest of the money was mostly tied to brassplate companies, created only for tax evasion or avoidance. Luxembourg recorded EUR 2.28 trillion in FDI, but only EUR 122 billion reached their real economy.[55]

This move by the Commission was the precursor to the possible opening of a formal investigation, it has been confirmed, and is in any case, a precedent which weighs heavily in the fight against tax evasion. This is because, in reality, a too-low tax rate that embodies unfair competition with other members of the Union has an 'equivalent effect'—that of direct state aid and intervention. What else is it, if not that? It is an amount that the state does not receive in order to favour some companies that compete on better terms with each other in the single market. This is a line to be followed in the future by the Commission, because fiscal dumping is incompatible with the relations of good faith that must exist between countries belonging to the European Union.

That good faith should ultimately lead to abolishing the unanimity currently required for decisions in the field of taxation in the EU.

Progressive Taxes Make a Comeback

The mantra of fiscal consolidation and the impenetrable wall of debt have led the Western crisis to the dilemma of Hamlet, omnipresent in all governments' choices: cut spending or increase revenues. That's the question.

This has always been the budget dilemma. In the last decades of the twentieth century and the first of this century, more or less steady growth allowed taxes to decrease—especially direct ones—and debt issuance to accumulate in capital markets eager to lend. This was how the demand for maintenance of social programmes and infrastructure spending was resolved. That dynamic imploded in 2007 and 2008, when the social model came into conflict with an economic model thoroughly infected by this culture of financing. Then, we were at a crossroads: less spending or more taxes? The US and European paths diverged. Obama chose to raise taxes on the rich and develop a stimulus policy while Bernanke helped in terms of monetary policy. The European Union opted, with the results that we know all too well, of the prescription of austerity in spending, plunging consumption rates without sharing out the responsibility in the form of taxation. It ultimately opted for the financial model over the welfare state. The proof of this is that, despite emphatic appeals to lower debt, public and private, European governments have been encouraging it through corporation tax. This is the only way to explain the tax deductibility of corporate debt, i.e., full deduction of their interests in corporate tax as previously explained. By contrast, stock dividends are taxed. That is, capitalization through debt is favoured over capitalization via corporate shares (by capital itself). The first is deducted in corporation tax; the second pays taxes.

For some time now, I have been publicly advocating the need for a 'tax about-turn' in Europe. That is, the need for a break with what I have called 'the era of debt' ad infinitum. The debt crisis has brutally revealed that we can no longer replace tax with debt. We therefore have to make an about-turn, more urgent than ever following the failure of two attempts to respond to the crisis with more debt (2008–2009) and through more austerity (2010–2013).[57]

There is no *tertium genus*, to continue with Latin. We either have to borrow money from those who have it, or will we have to demand it from those who have a duty to contribute it through taxes.

If we want the European social model not to fall apart, we have to choose the difficult path of equitable distribution of effort, which is what progressive taxation consists of, without prejudicing the ability to consume and therefore, productive activity.

Naturally, this is not a black-or-white choice. The debt will continue. The policy must ensure that expenditure is prudent and controlled. That is right: what it is about is moving forwards in a new political and strategic direction. The era of debt should be replaced by the era of fair taxation. The state economy should rely more on taxes than on debt. Taxes have to go back to being the natural source of public revenues in developed democratic countries. In Europe and America.

It is ultimately a question of power and democracy. As professor at Columbia University Katharina Pistor says, government funding has been determined less and less by electoral cycles and increasingly by debt repayment schedules.[58]

There are not sufficient legal commitments to a balanced budget like the 'golden rule'. If there is not a parallel legal guarantee ensuring fiscal sustainability in social spending, the rule about keeping a balanced budget could become worthless or worse, a straitjacket for the welfare state;[59] the straitjacket will be tighter, the heavier the burden of government debt, and/or the lower the rate of growth, a variable which it is impossible to predict.

The commitment to the return of taxes to the centre of economic policy is not an ideological occurrence. Two institutions, the International Monetary Fund and the World Bank, have had to yield to the evidence of the changing times that the crisis has brought us. In the 2014 Report on World Development (published on 6 October 2013), the World Bank states: 'Most individuals are fundamentally unprepared to overcome big shocks (parental illness), systemic shocks (financial crisis) [...] risk management requires an assumption of collective responsibility and the pursuit of concerted actions [...] the authorities have a key role to play'.

For the IMF, this role means increasing the global tax burden. The Fund encourages a more equitable taxation, focusing on 'higher levels of income distribution'. This measure could yield 0.25% of GDP. Christine Lagarde offers a pragmatic reason: fair taxation is needed 'to find a balance in public finances'.[61] The context in which we place this IMF position lies in the fact that, in advanced economies, public debt will continue to grow uncontrollably in the coming years. This eventuality raises for the Fund itself the option of debt restructuring in some countries, or an inflationary monetary policy. Both would certainly be unorthodox routes. The alternative is, then, either increasing equitable tax collection, or strong and rapid fiscal consolidation. The Union has opted for the latter.

Europe, which has the most developed Welfare State (although the one most in decline), does not currently have a powerful political proposal centred on taxation as an essential part of public policy.

The USA, coming from a much lower starting point than Europe, does have one. Obama has just formulated one in the Budget project for 2015–2016, with a clearly redistributive bent. It proposes, among other things, a tax of 19% on profits that US companies obtain abroad and which are not 'repatriated' to the USA; increases in capital gains tax (28%), including the inheritances of the richest as well as a new tax on big banks. In parallel, Obama proposes to lower taxes on middle-class families, facilitating the rights of children and also educational rights.

The European Commission or, more accurately, a report by the Directorate General for Economic and Financial Affairs which reports to Commissioner Olli Rehn, a few months ago came to two common-sense conclusions: first, that fiscal consolidation has depressed economic activity, and second, that the adjustments weigh down the economy more when based on cutting spending than when they focus on increasing public revenues.[62] It is quite obvious. Budget expenditure activates the economy by increasing aggregate demand and contributes to competitiveness when investing in infrastructure. However, expenses have to be financed, and this can only come from the debt or taxes.

It should be noted that kick-starting consumption does not automatically lead to an increase in GDP. This happens if there is underutilized capacity and if there is labour available, which is unfortunately what this Ice Age has left us.

It is usually said in the business world that tax breaks encourage investment and hiring. Not so. No entrepreneur invests if he cannot see the demand, the prospect of increased consumption. And in a stagnant economy such as we have, consumption can only be stimulated by public action, e.g., through social spending and job stability. Not where legislation undermines employment, makes it more precarious, and introduces total uncertainty for workers, who are, moreover, the social group with most marginal propensity to consume.

Debt has an adverse effect because it lowers private investment, besides sending a message: having to introduce higher taxes in the future to repay the debt.

Debt is sustainable if its growth corresponds to an increase in the productive economy sufficient to provide means to repay the debt and its associated interest, another difficult variable to predict.[63]

Without Taxes, There's No Paradise

Taxes, and not debt, are what have ensured the enjoyment of social and individual rights that Western democracies have built up with great sacrifice in the twentieth century.

It is no coincidence that the states of the European Union in 2000 had revenue equivalent to more than 40% of GDP, on average. Nor is it accidental that countries with the high percentage of tax revenue to GDP were Sweden (51.5%), Denmark (49.4%) and Finland (47.2%). These are the countries that best ensure the enjoyment of the rights which are needed by the most vulnerable, and which protect the most prized public services, such as education and health. They are the countries which most strongly guarantee universal coverage of such rights.[64] Jim Yong Kim, President of the World Bank, has a memorable phrase, when referring to Latin America: 'We must break the vicious circle of low taxes and bad services'.

In their wonderful book *The Cost of Rights*, Stephen Holmes and Cass R. Sunstein give a persuasive argument that freedom and rights depend on taxes.[65] The social and individual rights we hold most dear, and that in Europe we do not want to let go of, require the State to spend, and therefore, it must collect taxes. They are essential to be able to carry out social transformations and to run institutions, courts, police, public administration and essential public services. It seems obvious to say so, but the quality of a democracy is in direct proportion to the taxes paid by its citizens.

Holmes and Sunstein demolish this idea so deeply ingrained in the American right that the state is the enemy of freedom, and therefore should not give money in order to function. The reality is the opposite. For that reason it is so important that the State is legitimate and has full of authority to impose taxes. A state without money cannot protect rights, even the right to own property. A state without money cannot maintain programmes to lift millions of children out of poverty, in the first world and other worlds.

Private freedoms and rights have a public nature, in terms of having a public 'cost' (budget expenditures) and a public 'price' (tax), which are not the same as the ethical and intangible 'values' attributed to them.

The fact that rights—all rights—have a price to pay in terms of taxes to the State, means that their protection involves a redistribution of fiscal, social and economic efforts.

We went into detail in the above pages regarding regressive evolution of the tax burden in Europe and the USA. It is not necessary, therefore, to repeat this. However, it is necessary to note that 'structural' reforms such as those affecting taxes, have to concentrate on increasing direct taxes and decreasing indirect ones, such as VAT, paid alike by millionaires and the most disadvantaged; despite which, the IMF and the big European banks recommend that it be raised.[66] The tax reform which I consider correct in these times of impoverishment is to make large fortunes, inheritances and those with large assets pay more.[67] Such reform should lower taxes on the middle class, and exempt those with least purchasing power.

Nothing will be achieved without going in the opposite direction to the socially destructive and discriminatory dynamic that the crisis has accentuated in the tax system. Post-crisis fiscal reform must fight inequality, poverty, underemployment, and unemployment—the Four Horsemen of the Apocalypse which the policy of fiscal consolidation has merely strengthened.

In particular, the fiscal reform that Europe and the USA today need to be implemented is taxing activities that contribute less added value to the real economy. I am referring, of course, to purely speculative financial activity that only creates virtual wealth, and that dominates to such an extent in the financial world. Therefore, it is quite reasonable to establish once and for all the tax on international financial transactions (see the next chapter).

It is in such transactions that we find large-scale tax evasion, which does immeasurable systemic damage to the state, and consequently to the rights that ought to be protected through the collection of taxes. It damages the citizens, businesses and other entities that do pay tax.

The present Governor of the Bank of England, Mark Carney, says: 'If tax is permanently evaded, on a personal or business level, the result is that the burden of fiscal adjustment carried out in virtually all advanced economies falls hardest on those who pay their fair share. And, as a result, they end up paying more than their fair share'.[68]

One of the components of the Great Crisis has been the internationalization of tax fraud, sometimes in gigantic proportions. But it is not fought with the political will that the scale of the problem demands.

The tax avoidance and evasion industry is already a structural element of the capitalist economy in the new century. It is not easy to convince people of the power of the democratic state to protect your rights if you lack the power to crack down on tax havens, to publish blacklists, and to imprison fraudsters.

This is a fundamental challenge we face to free ourselves from the shackles that still restrain us after seven years of deep economic and social decline. It is a challenge for the state, and the international community. It is a challenge we must win to enable a key weapon against the Ice Age: the return of progressive taxation.

7

The Hegemony of Financial Power

At the Heart of the Crisis and of the Fraud

By this point it is abundantly clear that financial power is the undisputed cause of the Great Crisis. We have run into it in every chapter of this book.

The free movement of capital—but not of people—decreed by the Anglo-Saxon alliance in the 1980s and 1990s aspired, and managed, to elevate investment banking to the very top of politics and economics, over and above classic commercial banking. Albert summed it up in three words: innovation, internationalization and deregulation. This philosophy was the 'Trojan horse' which infiltrated Europe through mechanisms as determining as interest rates, tax and monetary policy.[1] Above everything else the money supply stands out, i.e., credit/debt, which, for Durant, constitutes the rudder of economic growth over the past few decades in the USA, to the point of several times exceeding the increase in GDP, especially in the years immediately prior to the shock.[2] The crisis has also stripped the big banks naked in terms of being the subject of administrative and criminal offences.

When banks stopped being banks

Banking enjoyed the best of all possible worlds. The supposed regulators did not require any of the organizations to keep a proportion of capital to guarantee their loans (assets) or current accounts (liabilities). The international procedures of the Central Banks Committee and their regulators, created in 1988 and based in Basel, were fairly lax in their definition of capital, which allowed the entities a wide margin to constantly increase their balance sheets.

The banks were directly responsible—those indirectly responsible were the liberalizing, permissive governments—for the way the West stuffed itself with money, put into the current accounts of countries with deficits by those with surpluses, which was what led to property inflation.

However, it was not only those entities with a banking licence who contributed to the financial tsunami. Shadow banking, with neither rules nor regulation, took the greatest number of transactions away from traditional banking circles. In unlimited quantities. And above all, using products as sophisticated as 'derivatives', which took on a life of their own vis-à-vis the operations and risks which they were supposedly going to mitigate against (those from which they themselves were derived).

By the end of 2010, the total number of derivatives contracts in the world had reached USD 669 trillion. Ninety per cent of them were over-the-counter (OTC) transactions in the public markets. This figure equates to USD 100,000 for each person on the planet, i.e., the value of everything produced in the world in the past 20 years.[3]

The financial economy has become detached from the real economy but dominates it through credit. US financial sector profits in 2007 accounted for 40% of total business profits, as opposed to 10% in the 1980s.[4] The Great Crisis has served to underscore the power which the opaque banking industry now exerts over the entire economy.

Constant accumulation of private debt, supplied for years with 'irrational exuberance' in the USA and the European Union by banks and financial entities, was the origin of stagflation in 2007–2008. It was short-term debt, vulnerable to any breakdown in the informal credit chain which had been constructed like a house of cards.

Short-termism became the lubricant of the financial system and of derivatives. To the extent of actually functioning on a day-to-day basis (the 'repo' market) and speculating on a fall. This was its Achilles' heel. Lenders (basically investment funds, pension funds, etcetera) lend money and assets in the short term to financial agents in banks and hedge funds, who in turn invest them or use them to guarantee other credit operations and thus turn a profit. In the years prior to the crisis, these operations—approved by Moody's and Standard & Poor's—became increasingly short term. Banks and agents obtained good returns, at a time when official interest rates remained stable and inevitably lower given the massive injection of funds from China and other emerging economies. Nevertheless, there was a risk that, if one link in the chain snapped, the whole building would crumble. When Wall Street no longer receives short-term money, the flow of liquidity to Main Street businesses falters.[5]

This is what happened from 2007 onwards and in a violent way in 2008 with the collapse of Lehman Brothers, which carried away with it the most valued possession of the financial world: confidence. No one trusted anyone with a loan either short- or long-term. The major banks, simultaneously borrowers and lenders, were left without enough capital of their own (around 3% of their total indebtedness) to deal with their depositors and creditors. This is what we saw in the first part of this book.

Financial irregularities

Some of the biggest banks, deemed 'Systemically Important Financial Institutions' went beyond disastrous management into the murky hinterland of administrative irregularities and lawbreaking. This is the case of Crédit Suisse, facing a fine of USD 1 billion.

In the USA, the most striking case was that of J.P. Morgan Chase—the biggest bank in the country—and its CEO Jamie Dimon, who in 2008 seemed to dazzle everyone with his purchases of other banks. Today people view him very differently, but this has not affected his grossly excessive salary.

In July 2013, J.P. Morgan paid USD 450 million after federal regulators accused them of fixing the energy markets in New York and Michigan. The heaviest fine came later, precisely in response to the purchase at the end of 2008 of Washington Mutual and Bear Stearns, teetering on the brink of bankruptcy. J.P. Morgan knew that both of these banks had, in their day, sold mortgage derivatives to investors and public bodies such as Fannie Mae and Freddie Mac, without informing them of the high levels of risk which such products entailed.

They were also involved in long-running litigation with the Justice Department and other American authorities, which ended in a fine and with compensation to the value of USD 13 billion for the stricken investors.

J.P. Morgan, like other banks, parcelled up toxic loans in deeds guaranteed by mortgages and sold them to investors who were unaware of this fact.[6]

On 7 January 2014, they had to agree to pay USD 2.6 billion for not having warned the government about Bernard L. Madoff's multi-million dollar fraud.[7] J.P. Morgan had acted as Madoff's reference banker for two decades. His victims lost USD 17 billion which they have still not recovered.

In Europe, the best-known cases of banks being legally challenged for illegal conduct, before and during the crisis, are related to the fixing of interest rates for financial operations. This affects millions of savers, house purchasers and businesses.

The European Commission has imposed fines for contravention of competition legislation between 2005 and 2010.

The firms penalized were Deutsche Bank, Société Générale and RBS for colluding in falsifying information about the Euribor and the strategies of the derivatives market.[8] RBS, Deutsche Bank, Citigroup, RP Martin and—not surprisingly—J.P. Morgan have also been penalized for indulging in similar practices regarding the Libor in London and the Tibor in Tokyo.[9]

Sanctions on European banking have been slow to arrive, although better late than never. They are based on competency regulations, i.e., they do not apply to the irresponsible conduct (which is limited by the Penal Code) of the international banking system which unleashed the crisis, but rather to lateral or peripheral activities which involve secret accords to distort competition in the markets.

There is still no regulatory authority, either national or international, with the profile of the Securities and Exchange Commission (SBC) in the USA, or the Financial Conduct Authority in Great Britain; nor do the sanctions have the same cohesion as previously seen in the USA. This is proof of the supervisory and regulatory vacuum which has overseen the Union's financial market.

The American and British authorities took action a year and half earlier against the manipulation of the Libor by UBS, Barclays, the Royal Bank of Scotland and other banks. The companies involved paid more than USD 3 billion in fines. It is simpler in the Anglo-Saxon arena than in the EU. In the USA and in the United Kingdom, it is easier to impose individual sanctions.[10]

In November 2014, in the USA, the United Kingdom and Switzerland, the regulatory bodies imposed a fine of EUR 3.4 billion on a number of investment banks such as the Royal Bank of Scotland, Bank of America, UBS, HSBC, Citigroup and, inevitably, J.P. Morgan, for manipulating exchange rates in the currency markets (Forex). Four trillion euros are traded in the currency market every day.[11]

Suspicions of financial fraud have existed since the beginning of the crisis. Even the Vatican has been affected and had to accept an internal investigation at the end of 2013 to uncover possible money laundering and tax fraud through the use of tax havens. A mission given new impetus by the arrival of Pope Francis.[12]

It is only now, seven years later, that we have started to notice supervisory bodies stir, something which is not yet reflected in criminal convictions, the only thing which has a truly preventive effect on white collar crime.

The USA has taken the lead in this awakening of oversight.[13] The investigation has been widened to include the ratings agencies. In early 2013, Standard & Poor's was sued by the Department of Justice, for overvaluing, from 2004 to 2007, debt 'parcelled' with toxic assets, and being aware of the deceit being practiced upon clients. Everyone knows that it was this practice, by Standard and other agencies, which had an enormous influence on the unleashing of the financial shock.

Irving H. Pickard is the representative of the collective which is seeking to claw back thousands of millions of dollars owed to the victims of Madoff's 'Ponzi scheme'. Picard took their case to the Supreme Court in October 2013, asking for permission to sue the big banks, which, according to him, are behind the fraud. It is helpful to cite the arguments used by Picard in his appeal writ, 'Bernard L. Madoff did not act alone. The fraudulent plan could not have persisted so long or defrauded so many of so much, without a network of financial institutions, feeder funds and individuals who participated in his fraud or acquiesced in it—just like any large-scale financial fraud'.[14]

In reality, Picard's reasoning was behind the initiatives put into action since 2013 by the Justice Department, by the SEC and by the inspector general of the Troubled Asset Relief Programme. The investigations have an ambitious objective, which is to find out if a series of Wall Street banks defrauded the subscribers of mortgage deeds in the years following the financial crisis, by devaluing them or deliberately artificially inflating their value to buy them or sell them to other entities, some of which were rescued with public money.

At the same time, the investigation is looking into the falsification of the value of assets which the banks had on their books, amounting to a total of thousands of millions of dollars. We once again come across old acquaintances: J.P. Morgan, Barclays, Citigroup, Deutsche Bank, Goldman Sachs, Morgan Stanley, Royal Bank of Scotland and UBS.[15]

Bailing out the Banks

In 2008, amidst the chaos, a cynical political consensus was born: to protect the banks from probably going under. The villain of the piece, the one responsible for the overwhelming debt which swallowed up millions of people and businesses, and for the subsequent depressive de-leveraging,[15] guilty of causing the recession along with massive unemployment, the credit crunch, fraud on a grand scale, and the sudden freezing of the economy, had to be saved from itself. If it were not refloated, there would be no hope at all of economic recovery.

Since 2008, financial institutions all over the world have received public support to the tune of several trillion dollars. The numbers are mind-boggling. Many of the guarantees provided by governments will never be demanded from them; some others will possibly be honoured. However, a large amount will not be restored, because of banking losses, which in the USA and Europe amounted to a trillion and a half dollars between 2007 and 2010.[17]

The banks were on the brink of disaster between 2009 and 2011. Their stock market value fell dramatically, with particular intensity in 2011, to the point that the BCE, the FED, the BOE, the BOJ and the National Bank of Switzerland agreed a coordinated action plan to inject three tranches of liquidity into the financial system in the form of three-month dollar loans.

The banks would have crashed but for the existence of the agreement adopted by the finance ministers of the G-7, the richest countries, on 10 October 2008 in Washington. They declared that they would undertake decisive action and use all means at their disposal to 'support the systemically important financial institutions and 'prevent their collapse'. As a result, the whole international financial system, or at least its most important nucleus, ended up in a privileged position.

As we have seen, in the USA the financial crisis led to the creation of TARF (Troubled Asset Relief Programme), which in practice injected USD 421 billion into the banks (among which AIG stood out with USD 140 billion) and which, at this moment in time, have been completely repaid.

In the European Union, according to the Commission, the financial sector was granted public moneys, between 2008 and 2011, to the tune of EUR 1.6 trillion (12.8% of EU GDP). More than a trillion of these euros were earmarked for guarantees, EUR 320 billion for recapitalization measures, EUR 120 billion for devalued assets and EUR 90 billion for liquidity measures.[18] The most costly rescues, in terms of percentage of GDP, were those of the Netherlands (12.5%) and the United Kingdom (9%), and, outside the EU, Iceland (13%). The USA spent approximately 5% of its GDP.[19]

None of this included the monetary policy applied by the central banks, who adopted a very clear philosophy: the protection of the financial system. This was especially true of the European Union, whose Central Bank, it is important to remember, in December 2011 put unlimited liquidity at the disposal of the banks for a period of three years, at an interest rate of 1%. Nonetheless, it did not lend anything to the financially-drained public bodies.

Given that European governments opted to withdraw their stimulus packages early, without allowing time for growth to return, the entire effort to recapitalize the banking sector could only fall on the State. From 2008, the European Commission made an exception for the banking sector: it authorized the use of public funds, which is expressly forbidden by the Treaties. In the last analysis, the burden of providing this aid was shouldered by the taxpayer, in the form of astronomically high public debt, and a clear and present threat to the member states, which accepted responsibility for the shameless decapitalization of the banking sector brought on by the high-risk strategies into which it had launched itself.

This transfer of wealth was like Robin Hood, only in reverse. The emerging 'moral risk' is clear. The big banking institutions know that the ratings agencies are going to put a higher value on their assets than on those of smaller enterprises, because their systemic nature protects them from bankruptcy. The State will always come to their aid for fear of an even greater cataclysm. Mervyn King, the Governor of the Bank of England, put it well: 'Global banks are international in life, but national in death'.

The Dodd-Frank Act and the Volcker Rule, the New Regulation of the American Financial System

The American financial system does not depend, like the European one, on the banking sector. The latter accounts for only 30% of it. What worried the Obama Administration (Tim Geithner), Congress and the FED was how to handle, with the maximum political consensus possible, true regulation of financial institutions, especially the non-banking ones (the banks fall under the supervisory remit of the Federal Deposit Insurance Corporation, FDIC).

A large number of problematical aspects have arisen following on from the regulatory disaster which prevented the prediction and avoidance of the financial crisis.[20] The first aspect faced by the government related to powerful financial corporations. For example, the possibility of allowing entities with systemic risk to fail (like Lehman Brothers), along with the demands for capital and liquidity which would make it difficult in the future. In addition to this was the question of whether or not to re-establish or abandon the link between commercial banking and investment banking enshrined in the Glass-Steagal Act, which had been abolished in 1999 by the Gramm-Leach-Billey Act, all of which strengthened Wall Street's freedom to speculate.

The second key question was who should oversee the whole of the financial system and the regulatory authorities (FED; Securities and Exchange Commission; SEC; FDIC; Commodity Futures Trading Commission; CFTC) and what powers should it enjoy? The FED lobbied very strongly for this role.

The third question had to do with the jungle of new products and speculative transactions that invaded the markets, not subject to any regulation or legal controls during the 'innovative' Greenspan era, and which had been key players in the crash. They were unintelligible to defenceless consumers. Derivates had been dubbed 'financial weapons of mass destruction' by Warren Buffet. Not without reason. In 2007, these transactions had reached the incredible figure of USD 445 trillion (in 2001 the figure had been USD 70 trillion).

These products are, in turn, the offspring of numerous new giants in the financial system, such as the aggressive *hedgefunds*, run by executives with salary packages based on commission bordering on the obscene, quite prepared to create any risk for other people.

A final problem facing the legislators and the FED was reform of the ratings agencies. Their conduct prior to the crisis had been lamentable. They provided a gloss of financial reliability to what were actually junk products, concealing infinite leveraging, with no solvency whatsoever, as became sadly evident later.

What came out of the FED and Treasury propositions,[21] as well as from the legislative work in Congress—quite supportive of the government—was the long Dodd-Frank Act (2,319 pages), on 'Reform of Wall Street and Consumer Protection'. The legislators spearheading the debate in Congress were Chris Dodd, a Democratic senator, president of the Banking Committee in the Upper House, and Barney Frank, also a Democrat, president of the Banking Committee in the House of Representatives, both of them from very liberal New England. Neither of them was able to reach agreement with the Republicans[22] as has been the case since then on many occasions.

Too big to fail

Following on from the topics alluded to before and beginning with 'too big to fail', the Dodd-Frank Act led to the creation of a new authority, the FDIC, for entities of a systemic nature. This authority can only make an 'orderly' intervention to wind up the entity; it cannot rehabilitate it.[22] Moreover, and this is very significant, section 214 of the Act stresses this point: 'Taxpayers shall bear no losses from the exercise of any authority under this title'. Congress specified that public funds not restored through the sale of the assets of the wound-up bank 'will be the responsibility of the financial sector'. As can be clearly seen, we are now seeing a true 'no *bail-out*' clause should repayment not be made, in the case of banks and private financial entities.

Congress opted not to re-establish the barriers between commercial and investment banking which the Glass-Steagal Act had established. This conservative stance of Congress—following the Treasury—on an episode of deregulation in the Clinton era to which responsibility for the financial crisis had largely been attributed, was compensated for by a daring move on another matter of similar significance. This was the massive use by the banks of the buying and selling of assets for the benefit, not of their clients, but of their own accounts; i.e., speculative activities breaching the traditional role of the banks, which is to be the intermediary between savers and investors. The name of this operation is *proprietary trading*.

The greatest opponent of allowing the banks to use their clients' deposits—guaranteed by the FDIC—for risky deals, which taxpayers might end up paying for, was the former president of the FED, Paul Volcker. This was the origin of the 'Volcker Rule': commercial banks which are insured by the Federal regulator, the Deposit Insurance Corporation, cannot indulge in *proprietary trading*, and unregulated financial institutions such as hedge funds, which perform many of these operations, cannot be rescued by the government.[23] This was a way of returning to the Glass-Steagal Act, which had already been overcome by the subsequent appearance *of hedge funds*.

The Treasury Department (Geithner) and the National Economic Council (Summers) were originally opposed to the 'Volcker Rule'. But President Obama tipped the scales in its favour. In such a way, that section 619 of the Dodd-Frank Act states that a banking entity may not commit over 3% of its capital to operations of the type known as *proprietary trading*, nor have shares or involvement in a hedge fund or in a private share fund. The only exceptions to this prohibition are personal operations, such as the creation of a market, or as a means of covering risk, as well as transactions in US sovereign debt.

In the same way, the government wanted all the banks to be subjected to larger capital and liquidity requirements, and for these to be particularly demanding vis-à-vis entities of systemic magnitude. This also included off-balance sheet assets.

All of these proposals, emanating from the Treasury, were incorporated by Congress into the Dodd-Frank Act, which designated 29 big banks 'Financial Institutions of Systemic Importance' (SIFI).

The FED, the highest supervisory authority

There was no doubt at all as to who should be in overall charge of overseeing the financial system. The Federal Reserve, strongly supported by the Treasury Department, was the clear winner. The FED would work with the support of the Financial Services Oversight Council (FSOC) and would oversee all the entities of systemic importance, whether they were banks or not. The FED can grant loans but cannot rescue specific entities. However, it could come out in support of a group of industries or markets, for example by purchasing financial assets.

Nevertheless, the FED was not put in charge of consumer protection; this power was granted to a new independent agency which would answer only to Congress: the Consumer Financial Protection Bureau (CFPB), overseen and financed by the FED. The notion of protecting the consumers of financial services in the same way as any other American consumer is protected, strongly advocated by Senator Elisabeth Warren, had gained political momentum to the extent that it was incorporated into the very title of the Dodd-Frank Act.

Shadow banking

The third of the most important questions about reforming the financial system referred to new products and new agents. Nobody could possibly oppose regulation, but there was another confrontation over how to do it between Republicans and Democrats, with the latter pushing for regulation and organization of these transactions with the aim of protecting the consumer and avoiding financial catastrophes.

The hedge funds as businesses were not viewed as critically by the government as the unregulated derivatives transactions which they had helped to proliferate. Nonetheless, the Dodd-Frank Act imposed the obligation to at least provide a legal register and transparent information. The Act also established specific limits on the ownership of hedge funds by the banks, as well as totally forbidding this to commercial banks, as has already been mentioned.

Congress accepted the position of the Treasury on the ratings agencies, which meant imposing a charge on the valuations the agencies put on credits, thus reducing the need for such ratings. The Act referred the matter to later studies to be carried out subsequently by the regulators.[24]

On 21 July 2010, President Obama signed the Dodd-Frank Act, after heated debates on every possible angle and an intense lobbying campaign by Wall Street.

This was the point at which the detailed, regulatory work of the regulators began spearheaded by the FED.[25] We already know the saying: 'let them make the law and I'll make the rules'. The Republicans did exactly this.[26]

10 December 2013: the Volcker Rule is born

The task of developing the Dodd-Frank Act has a lot in common with building the Egyptian pyramids. It still has not finished. Not even 50% of this extremely long Act has been able to cross the Rubicon of the numerous regulators: the USA Chamber of Commerce, the banking campaigns led by the American Bankers Association, the political parties, letter from citizens, and the interventions of the media, the governments of European countries and even the European Commission.

The five agencies charged with drawing up the Volcker Rule in detail were the following: The Federal Reserve (FED), the Securities and Exchange Commission (SEC), the Commodity Futures Trading Commission (CTFC), the Federal Deposit Insurance Corporation (FDIC) and the Comptroller of the Currency (CC). The final document produced by their 22 voting members was approved and presented on 10 December 2013. In the midst of a snowstorm, which fell on Washington the same day and forced the closure of some federal offices, the regulators voted for a 71-page text, preceded by an interpretative foreword of nearly 900 pages.[27]

Although the American regulators had already displayed their inability to prevent the bubble which had preceded the crisis, nobody imagined that the regulatory development of the Volcker Rule would take so long. It took three and a half years for agreement to be reached between the aforementioned five regulators who handle the American financial system, playing different roles and seeing things from differing angles.

A crisis like the one which began in 2007–2008 could not be allowed to happen again. Never again would the shameful spectacle be tolerated of investment banking humiliating first the depositors, by using their savings to fund suicidal speculation, and secondly, the taxpayers, by making them pay for the rescue of the biggest firms on Wall Street after the unavoidable sinking of the latter due to their own risky betting.

The way to prevent history repeating itself was regulation by means of the 'Volcker Rule' which amounts to nothing less than the direct prohibition on banks being able to claim ownership—quasi-ownership—of the deposits in their current account in order to obtain profits, not for their clients, but for the banks themselves. To this was added the prohibition on the banking sector of having relationships with or investing in hedge funds to make short term gains, and in private equity funds.

Resistance from Wall Street was, and continues to be, overwhelming. This explains why it took so long to finally draw up the rule, which, in any case, will not come into effect completely until 21 July 2015. There was serious danger of a blockade. The financial sector alleged that their own activities had nothing to do with the crisis and that US banks would find themselves at a disadvantage compared to the European ones. This *impasse* disappeared when news came out of a new J.P. Morgan scandal, known as the 'London Whale' which served to underline the need to keep to the Volcker Rule in its entirety. J.P. Morgan lost EUR 6 billion—which it did not tell the regulators about—on speculative activities of its own, using deposits to invest in derivatives.

Tough to implement

The top executives of J.P. Morgan had the gall to allege that the speculative investments which led to extremely high losses in the 'London Whale' case were *hedging* (legitimate risk cover) and not proprietary trading.

As the president of the CFTC, Gary Gensler, pointed out, the rule allowed the covering of 'specific, identified' risks to the entity, but not generic risks arising from assets and banking obligations or as part of the evolution of the economy.[28]

To this should be added the fact that the banks are allowed to deal in foreign sovereign debt, which means a change from a previous version of the rule which only allowed them to deal in US sovereign debt. The former version had brought about strong protests from governments such as the Japanese, with a powerful bond market.

The Volcker Rule will apply to all foreign affiliates of American banks, to foreign firms operating in the USA, and to Americans residents who invest in American bank funds. Thus, the prohibition on investing for your own profit will cover these eventualities.

The Wall Street protest has been raucous. The head of J.P. Morgan, Dimon said defiantly earlier this year that banks are suffering an 'assault': says he who runs a bank that has paid in the past five years a total of USD 25 billion in fines for manipulating the markets.

Banking has seen its profit margin reduced because of the demands of having more funds as back-up and abandoning their riskier activities. This is why the reaction is so violent, especially in the USA; with the support of the new Republican majority in Congress. Democrats have the leadership of Senator Warren.

Wall Street, a master in lobbying, has already achieved some progress, getting two more years to disengage from high-risk activities from the FED, which were what led to the crisis.

The boycott of Wall Street financial regulation is very visible, and at this point Obama is not as strong in this area as he is in relation to health. The battle over the financial system will be central in the new Congress of 2015–2016.

The controllers' moment

The Dodd-Frank Act created a system of control and application of the norm—the Volcker Rule—which would reside in three fundamental agencies: the Federal Reserve, in charge of the biggest holding banks, the Comptroller of the Currency, for national banks; and the Securities and Exchange Commission (SEC), which controls the business arms of the banks.

Control also extends to the *non-banking system*, which in the decade prior to the crisis had become a growing source of financial instability.

It is a question of strengthening the financial system, so that it cannot be swept away by the liquidity problem or insolvency of a single entity. Banks no longer play the same role as in former years. Overnight deposits are no longer the only, or even the principal source of funding. On the assets side, the banks have developed, very often to excess, the practice of securitizing and selling on their loans and mortgages. The banks form part of a complex chain in which non-banking intermediaries take a leading role. These are complex structures which, as Kroszner points out, are much more vulnerable to the vagaries of the market. They are liquid markets which can suddenly freeze up.[29] This and other challenges which the Obama Administration has set itself will essentially fall to the regulatory agencies, according to how stringently they approach their complex task. The aim of resolving the remaining questions still inherent in American financial reform will depend, in short, on their achieving their key objective: for banks to focus their business once more on lending, not on investing.

European Banking Union Is Still on the Horizon

If there is one subject on which the USA and the European Union's response to the crisis are poles apart, it is in banking regulation. The USA has all but finished its financial reforms. The Union is just starting on theirs; although it has been talked about for years. This is the pace in Brussels.

There has been a five-year wait for reform to be broached, despite the high-flown word of Sarkozy on the 're-establishing of capitalism'. At the Council of Europe on the 28–29 June 2012, van Rompuy was 'invited' to draw up a road map for the attainment of a genuine 'Economic and Monetary Union'. In December of that year, The Council of Europe approved the road map, which included the establishment of a Banking Union.

The creditor countries of the south are those most interested in the solution, since both businesses and individuals are still suffering higher interest rates than the creditor countries and are experiencing an unpredictable flow of credit without which it is difficult to envisage sustained economic recovery.

It is a tragedy for those companies which create two-thirds of the employment in Europe and whose situation is therefore crucial to economic growth. Small and medium-sized businesses depend on the banking sector, as it provides 80% of corporate loans.

In the USA, the opposite is true. There has been a renewed recovery in the banking sector, which makes it more inclined to lend to companies to purchase or merge with others. This dynamic has been quite clear throughout 2013. It bears hardly any resemblance to the cautious climate in European Union banks.

There are many different reasons for the lack of sufficient credit in the Eurozone. There is low capitalization of the banks because of the poor quality of many of their assets, as well as on account of their high indebtedness, which still persists—the assets represent three times the size of the economy; this factor causes peripheral Eurozone banks to base their liquidity on financing by the ECB, and in the future, on increases in capital.

New regulation of the unregulated and fragmented European financial system means starting almost from zero, if it is seriously intended, if there is a real desire to build a Banking Union. There are four actions which must be undertaken, in this order: first, handing over the supervision of all Eurozone banking entities to a supranational body; secondly, solving the complex question of the rescue and resolution of banks in difficulties, which means agreeing upon which authority will carry it out and deciding which funds will be used and who will accept the price of the rescue or the winding-up of the bank; thirdly, the fund guaranteeing deposits up to a certain level (today it stands at EUR 100,000); and fourthly, establishing the norms which will regulate the business and intermediary activities of the banks and other financial entities. There is a final requirement, which we shall see shortly, which consists of the demand for banking capital, regulated by the voluntary Basel mechanism, and which applies jointly to the USA and Europe.

We know that the USA has resolved these issues in a fairly convincing way. In Europe, we can only apply this description to the first of them: oversight.

Oversight

Regulation 1024/2013 of the Council, on 15 October 2013, with the support of the European Parliament, handed prudential oversight of those European banks of systemic importance to the European Central Bank. This came into effect on 3 November 2014, after the *stress tests* on these banks carried out by the ECB and the European Banking Authority (EBA) based in London.

The Mechanism of European Supervision (MUS) is the first pillar of Banking Union. It grants to the ECB—separately from its role in monetary stability—supervision and control of the biggest Eurozone banks, those which possess assets of more than EUR 30 billion or more than 20% of GDP. They account for 85% of banking assets in the Eurozone. This oversight capacity of the ECB extends to the three most significant entities of each participating member state, and those which have received direct financial assistance from the EFSF and the ESM.

It is understood that the ECB is better-equipped than national authorities to root out certain types of problems such as those which led to the financial disaster. However, the Commission did not succeed in extending this ECB oversight to the 6,000 Eurozone banks, which will remain in the care of national authorities.[31] The ECB will only be able to intervene in fully justified specific cases. It is likely that Germany was the main stumbling-block. Behind Germany's attitude lurks their obsession with the taboo of public opinion and of their Constitutional Court: not sharing financial risks with other countries, and thus, not mutualizing either public debt or private banking risk, especially when these are being 'resolved'. The German thesis is that national problems only have national solutions, hence their aversion to the creation of a centralized European fund to rescue foolhardy or imprudent banks.

The disappointing reform of the banking resolution mechanism

German arguments have prevailed in the regulation of the central element of European financial reform: banking resolution. In the second half of 2013, a struggle broke out between the European Commission, seeking the leading role as resolution authority[32] and Germany, which, through its 'superminister' Wolfgang Schäuble (a survivor in the current coalition government) reiterated that accepting what the Commission and other countries were suggesting, would entail reforming the Treaties and the German Constitution itself, because of loss of sovereignty. As a pretext for opposing the granting to the Commission of the power of resolution over a bank, Germany added the incompatibility of its powerful antitrust powers.

Germany wanted governments to have the last word over intervening in a financial entity; that the banking Resolution Fund should not be a single one until 2026; and that the ESM should not fund the future Resolution Fund. All of this has basically gone ahead in the agreement between the Council and the European Parliament on 20 March 2014.

The Single Resolution Mechanism, which will come into effect on 1 January 2016, will not actually be 'single'. There will be a 'resolution council' with wide ranging powers over transnational banks and those overseen by the ECB. The Council of Ministers will have the last word if there is any discrepancy between the resolution council and the European Commission.[33]

The other arm of the SRM, its financial one, is the Single Resolution Fund. The fund will be financed by contributions collected from banks on their home grounds. Over a period of eight years it will gradually change from a joint international fund to a single fund, with a top limit of EUR 55 billion. It will be able to go to the markets, but the ESM will not be allowed to lend to it. This poses serious limitations on SRM.[34]

The limit of EUR 50 billion is frankly insufficient to prevent a crisis. Many of the banks which might have to be supervised, or rescued, possess over EUR 30 billion in assets, each. Let us remember that since 2008 tens of thousands of millions of euros have been injected into EU banks.

The Banking Union model which is being outlined comes nowhere near that of the Federal Deposit Insurance Corporation, which props up American banks with a line of credit from the Treasury and establishes consistent parliamentary control, which are conspicuous by their absence from the 20 March agreement.[35]

From bail-out to bail-in. Saving taxpayers from the sins of the banks

There is a before and an after to Cyprus's rescue. It was the catalyst of a new culture in the EU, determined, like the USA, that the taxpayer should never again be saddled with the mistakes of others.

In the summer of 2013, a general consensus was reached: that in the eventuality of a bank failing, the first capital used to support it should be its own, that of its shareholders, and then that of 'junior' creditors, and holders of more than EUR 100,000.

This consensus has spread beyond the Eurozone, to include that led by Carney and the Financial Stability Board, but it incited the initial reluctance of Draghi, fearful of destabilization through loss of bond value. The IMF has also joined this consensus.[36]

The agreement took shape in both meetings of Ecofin, on 10 and 18 December 2013.

In the opinion of the Council, before having recourse to the Resolution Fund it will be necessary to reach a minimum loss level of around 8% of the bank's total obligations. Deposits belonging to individuals, small and medium-sized enterprises and microbusinesses will be accorded preference over non-preferential creditors and the deposits of large corporations. The Single European Deposit Guarantee Fund has still not come into being.

According to Ecofin, the Resolution Fund contribution should not account for more than 5% of the total debt of a bank or financial institution. If they reach this level, they will have to seek alternative sources of finance.

These decisions may appear positive. What is negative is their late arrival, because the proposed directive is the transposition into European law of what was agreed in Washington as long ago as November 2008, when the leaders of the G-20 advocated for ensuring an orderly resolution of the biggest and most complex transnational financial institutions.

Banking union without the Volcker Rule (for the time being)

There has been a similar or greater delay in the EU in another important aspect of financial reform, the possible separation of classical banking activities from capital market activities, which would mean breaking down the universal banking model prevailing in Europe, with big banks at its head.

In the UK, the banks must separate the said activities into different subsidiary businesses within the group. In the EU, as such, there are no concrete measures which can be compared to or correspond to the Volcker Rule, save the report issued by Erkki Liikanen, Governor of the Central Bank of Finland, favouring the separation of activities model.[37] This report inspired the proposal which the Commission presented on 29 February 2014, prohibiting banks from indulging in *proprietary trading* (the Volcker Rule), and making it possible for the supervisor to transfer high risk negotiating activities to an independent unit within the affected banking group.[38]

Legislation in this respect is purely national, and this has been made use of by France and Germany to approve a regulation which maintains the unity of the banks—the latter being much more important in the financial sector in the EU than the USA—and which protects their investment capacity to the hilt.

It should also be pointed out that the EU lacks legislation at community level on the non-banking financial market, the hedge funds and other funds which deal in sophisticated *over-the-counter* financial products.

This vacuum is not good. An increase in banking regulation will produce the tendency to transfer investment and risk to the *shadow banking system* which is much less regulated and to which the ECB enjoys no access.[39] The regulation of the shadow banking system has until now been less fortunate than the directive agreed on 14 February 2012 between the Council and the Parliament, on transactions in goods as important as cereals or energy.[40]

In spite of everything, attempts on the part of the Commission to stimulate a now practically inexistent European capital market, or non-bank market, in order to boost the financing of European companies. In this way, products such as asset-backed securities, covered bones, corporate bonds and private placements will be strengthened.

Basel III and Capital Requirements

The excesses which led to the financial crisis showed the other side of the coin in their deficits. The biggest, the lack of sufficient capital in the banks with which to meet the indebtedness they had got into in order to speculate, instead of attending to their natural business, which is lending.

The requirement of capital is a principle of guarantee which, until the crisis, had been nationally overseen, without prejudice to the existence since 1974 of a supranational body, the Basel Supervisory Committee. The Committee did not possess legally binding powers, but it could make recommendations about proper conduct in the banks with a certain weight. It has been a kind of supervisor of supervisors.

Here follows a quick description of the evolution of this subject, with a modest disavowal as to its technical dimensions and regulatory complexity.

The first formal Basel agreement, known as Basel I, was on banking capital. Risk is what determines how much capital a bank must hold in reserve. The guidelines set out by the Committee distinguish between Tier 1 (shares, preference shares and other high quality capital) and Tier 2 (everything else). Basel I stipulated that banks which operate in various countries must have capital equivalent to 8% of its risky assets.

By 1992, the majority of G-10 countries, the most advanced economies had adopted the Basel I directives.

The same was true of many countries with emerging markets in search of financial credibility. Nonetheless, capital ratios varied from country to country because it was not easy to measure the risk.

The crises of the 1990s swept away Basel I and led to Basel II, with much more precise capital directives. Basel II continued with the criteria of weighing credit risks. In accordance with these risks, the bank must hold a specific level of its own funds in reserve, to avoid insolvency. Basel II was not observed by the Anglo-Saxon block. The USA, the UK and Australia announced that they would only apply it to large international banks.

In 2008, it was realized that Basel II could no longer protect banks during a severe financial crisis, that its view of supposed stability in the markets was not correct and that banks needed more quality capital, more resistant in times of crisis, because in the latter case capital and its value sank, in an expression of what economists term 'procyclicity'. Basel II granted too much discretion to financial institutions.[41]

The Great Crisis did away with Basel II. It was now the era of Basel III, which, taking to heart what had happened, gave a greater role to liquidity risk, which had been forgotten for such a long time previously owing to the superabundance of money in the golden years prior to the crisis. The other key element of Basel III is the strengthening of the demand for quality capital.

The Basel Banking Supervisory Committee's new requirements for capital compelled the banks to hold capital equivalent to 7% of its assets subject to risk, which do not represent all the assets it possesses. The percentage on total assets is a minimum of 3%, which is truly meagre when confronting hypothetical financial difficulties, since the capital (3%) remains unchanged whatever the quality of the assets may be.

The new requirements were agreed in December 2012 'Global regulatory framework to strengthen banks and banking systems' and were applied in the EU by means of a regulation and a directive in 2013, thus creating harmonized guidelines regarding insolvency.[42]

From 2010, the Basel III agreements have been made more palatable by the Committee presided over by Stefan Ingres, giving way to pressure from the financial industry, as Europeans bonds lost value and liquidity because of the crisis.[43]

To convince the Committee, the banking industry alleged that harshness in capital demands would endanger growth, because it would force the banks to take on more risk.

The other weapon used in the industry's argument, and repeated tirelessly, was that if more capital is demanded, it is necessary to reduce credit to businesses and households. This is false, as has been demonstrated by Admati and Hellwig in their magnificent book.[44] If a bank has to have more capital, it can look for more and in this way have funds for lending and investing. What happens is that banks prefer to get into debt rather than increase their capital. Since they know that the state and the taxpayers will come to their aid, it is cheaper for them to issue debt than increase capital, which has to be rewarded with high dividends. For this reason, banks are always more indebted than businesses in other sectors of the economy. The ECB's policy of granting unlimited credit to the banking sector at 1% is an extreme case of benevolence and favouritism.

Short term debt, without sufficient capitalization, is a very high risk factor. In 2007–2008, the banks had very little capital (2%) compared with their level of assets, and they were unable to respond to the rapid and far reaching devaluation of these assets, something which called their solvency into question. Besides, the banks had—and still have today—a high level of interconnection with other banks and other non-banking financial entities, all of which means that one default soon spreads like wildfire ('too interconnected to fail').

These reasons are what led the Federal Reserve to approve new capital requirement rules which came into effect on 1 January 2014. American banks need to hold reserves at a ratio of 7% of high quality assets (Tier 1) for those assets considered risky. If they are international banks, 2.5% more must be added to this percentage, and a ratio of 3% more capital as regards debt, i.e., assets.[45]

The USA has moved faster and further than Basel. On 24 October 2013, the FED estimated that banks subject to the new regulation would have around two and a half trillion dollars in quality liquid assets. The starting date for these rules, not at all to the liking of Wall Street, was brought forward to 2017.[46]

Protests from European banks operating in the USA were soon heard, pointing out that these demands did not exist in their home countries. The FED did not change its stance, which was based on the need to demand a special effort from entities whose size made them invulnerable to failure, because the state would help them, giving them a considerable advantage and putting taxpayers at risk.

Regardless of what has just been stated, so-called *moneymarket* funds and funds of financial societies which operate as '*shadow banks*' are not regulated in the USA, which leaves a gaping hole in a financial market in which they account for two-thirds of the business, as opposed to a third in the regulated banking sector. It was only in October 2014 that the Basel Committee began to establish regulation more amenable to 'shadow banking' in so far as the guarantees they must provide to obtain short term credit from the conventional banks are concerned.

In Europe, capital requirements for banks and insurance companies are much more lax than in the USA. The ratio of capital to assets is, according to Basel III (and the EU), 3%. Even more. Basel has agreed to relax its valuation of some risks to limit capital demands. The implacable banking *lobbies* won over the Basel Committee regulators. This is especially inconvenient for the EU, because European banks are bigger and systemically more significant than the American ones, which make them too big to be rescued by a single government or central bank, as Gert Wehinge (OECD) points out.

The Basel Committee rounded off its 'surrender' by increasing the time limit to 2019 for the banks to start adapting to the Basel III agreements, i.e., four years longer than 2015, which was the initial timespan.

The Power of the Financial Markets

The crisis revealed an open secret. Banking—and the totality of the financial markets—possess exceptional and extraordinary power. So great that it has been dubbed 'systemic'. It is structural and transnational power. It can only be compared to political power itself, although without the democratic legitimacy of the latter. Citizens have discovered that their political representatives cannot handle the demands and dictates of the 'markets'. This fact, which is dreadful for democracy, forms part of the legacy of the Great Crisis.

The crisis which began in 2007 became truly visible when it attacked the very heart of the state, its fiscal and budgetary sovereignty. Then, the enormous debt was called 'sovereign'. But the crisis was, has been and continues to be a banking crisis in Europe, where the vast majority of monetary transactions are managed or facilitated by regulated banks. The malaise is in the banking sector, and even more so, in the whole of the financial system (stock exchanges, investors, aggressive funds, products, etc.); it does not reside in sovereign debt.

It is not difficult to understand the financial nature of the crisis. The world economy is 'financialized'. It is unthinkable without reference to money. It is the face of modern or post-modern capitalism; of the capitalism of globalization. Each economic operation has a financial image. Given that the economic tool par excellence is money (cash or virtual), the economy is ineluctably run by the 'moneymen', the banks and financial entities.

The phenomenon of 'financialization' appears rather enigmatic. The real or 'physical' economy took a long time to monetize, but once this transmutation had taken place, it became irreversible. Money is just another commodity, in the words of Milton Friedman. It is the biggest springboard to power in current society. Whoever can 'create it' becomes almost omnipotent. This is the central transformation of the capitalist economy, which explains the change that started with the end of the gold standard and the beginning of deregulatory neoliberalism.

Until the era of Reagan and Thatcher—when the current crisis was engendered (see Chapter 2)—the state was capable of controlling the creation of money. Since then, an almost unbeatable competitor has emerged: the financial system. This was the end of Keynesianism. It is the inability of political power to carry its popular mandate to its final consequences. Reagan and Thatcher meant the 'surrender' of the political right to the economy, something which was also accepted by the Blairite left, and which has a clear Anglo-Saxon flavour.

What has happened? The banks are able to create money. Not only the central banks. Also private banks, with assets[47] which are multiplied by debt upon debt, in a process which has already been explained and which in total represent several times the amount of GDP of major countries. They are too big to fail. The state and the taxpayers—the real economy—always have to save them.

However, they bear no relationship to the basic economy. They escape. They create a world with its own laws, its own authorities and its own culture. It is the most profitable sector of the entire contemporary economy.

The financial services industry has become consolidated by a crisis which it invented. In 2013, the sector's performance returned the greatest profits: an increase of 13%. Currently, it accounts for 30% of all corporate profits in the USA, its most user-friendly territory. This is what Krugman terms 'profit without productivity', which is when profits increasingly reflect 'market power' more than productivity. This is 'monopoly income', which does not reflect the actual return on an investment but rather, more strongly and disproportionately, the fact of market domination. The financial industry has the structural power of a market.

The financial 'system' represents the arteries of the economy, but through them it subjects the productive body to constant pressure. But this is not a technique; it is a power, belonging to owners with names and surnames. Very few, because financial wealth is incredibly highly concentrated. They have managed to seize control of the mechanisms which penetrate the real economy. They condition it. They make it so dependent that this economy, wounded by financial powers, has to run to help them if they take ill, victims of their own excesses. Credit is the leader of the economy. The latter is the hostage of the former.

This is the contradiction. The financial system is a gearbox on which everyday social and economic functioning depends. In other words, it controls an apparatus of overwhelming power. However, it is not public power. It is the greatest of private powers; resistant to public power and liberalized by the latter, by means of the deregulation of capital all over the planet. The result is that in a zero endgame, the expansion of financial power stifles—'dwarfs', we would say in footballing terminology—the arena of political power.

Once there is a clash between social democracy and the economic hegemony of the financial system, we have the makings of a real crisis, i.e., the difficulty of continuing to reproduce the social model of Western culture. This is what we are experiencing now.

As a unitary state, the USA has been able to direct its policies in such a way that financial regulation at present seems to be controlling the critical loss of direction which has just been described. The European Union has not been able to do so, because the old order (state control) just will not die off, so that the new order (true political union) still cannot be born. The crisis has caught Europe halfway there, and under these conditions, it has not been able to triumph over the financial hieroglyphics.

Banks take over from banks

The great banking sector shows off its power especially in the persistence and irreversibility of what has been the slogan of the crisis: too big to fail. The regulatory attempts to prevent the state from rescuing a systemic bank have proved useless. The markets can hardly believe their luck: and this constitutes a privileged position compared with the smaller banks.

It is true than the flow of capital in the world (USD 4.6 trillion in 2012) is less than in 2007 (USD 11.3 trillion) and that the real economy is languishing, but the big banks and Wall Street are bigger now, have more assets and greater profits (the six major US banks made USD 76 billion in 2013) in a centralizing process catapulted by the crisis itself. In the second half of 2014, the banking industry in the USA registered the second highest profits in at least the last 23 years (USD 40 billion).

Despite the attenuating of the debt effected by the banking sector in the last few years, the four biggest US banks have 3,675 subsidiaries, 8.6% more than five years ago.[48] According to Mark J. Carney, if this tendency continues, the assets controlled by the British banking sector will grow by 2050 to represent nine times annual GDP.[49]

The sheer size of the banking sector determines its deep complexity. Banks are too complicated and are too interconnected for the state to control, or regulate, or get tax from their gutful of assets, whether traditional or derivative, whether liquid or not, whether visible or hidden.

It is this complexity that determines the increase in systemic risk.[50] One example of this is the policy which the major USA banks have been pursuing over the past few years and which partly explains the increase in profits. It is the sharp reduction in the reserves held against potential losses. The regulators have already warned them that this is a risky position to adopt.[51]

While the US banking sector is more or less the same size as its economy—and the banking sector in Japan, Canada and Australia double theirs—the Eurozone is three times the size of annual GDP (EUR 32 trillion).

Eighty per cent of credit in the EU is channelled through the banking sector. This is why one of the main problems is the absence of credit, or rather the scarcity of credit, for the reasons previously mentioned.[52]

The serious 'bank dependence' of the European economy highlights this even more than in the USA. The market power of the Union's banks explains the 'systemic uncertainty' swirling around the state of their balance sheets and the percentage of toxic assets they may contain.

The ability of the Eurozone to recover economically is dependent on this, to a significant extent.

The other banks … in the shadows

The other face of the banking business has already been alluded to, the one which profits from public generosity towards financial activities which are totally lacking in any kind of regulatory straitjacket, the shadow banking sector. The latter has experienced dizzying growth, especially, as is obvious, in the USA. And it will grow even more when the new regulations for traditional banking come into effect.

The hedge funds—an inappropriate name—have spearheaded this race. Their assets increased from USD 40 billion in 1990 to almost USD 2 trillion in the run-up to the crisis. Despite this, they now hold assets of around USD 2.3 trillion, a fifth of US GDP. Hedge funds have moved into attracting pension funds and public entities. Greater stringency in banking regulation encourages this flight of investment monies towards centres of power not subject to restriction, at least at present.

Hedge funds are speculative funds designed to make greater profits—at greater risk—than the regulated banking market, and they take advantage of this at times of straitened availability of urgency. The hedge funds' higher interest rate allows them to reward investors who have entrusted their money to the fund. And it has also been noted that hedge funds are assiduous tax haven clients, as should be expected given their '*shadow*' nature.

Private equity companies belong to the same family as hedge funds, with a record number of businesses in 2013 buying and selling companies, and enjoying the confidence of pension funds and plutocrats. The same is true of the enormous (EUR 1 trillion) *money market mutual funds*, private short term capital funds. They are all back in fashion.[53]

Non-financial companies, on the prowl for funds, could also be included in this broad definition of those operating beyond the bounds of normal banking sources. Banking credits have fallen and corporate bonds have risen, especially in countries experiencing the most severe credit drought. Investors have been keen to buy such profitable bonds.[54]

Shadow banking has recovered from the crisis. The value of financial assets in power of money-market fund, hedge funds, trust companies and financial firms, different from banks, reached 25.2 trillion dollars in 2013, surpassing the level they were at prior to the crisis. Yet another piece of evidence demonstrating the vitality of the financial system and its dominance over the real economy.

Shadow banking represents a third of the US financial system. It accounts for more than the total of all the banks together. It constitutes a huge risk because, being much less regulated than the banks, it can enter into dodgy, high-risk deals, based once again on a pyramid scheme.

Financial innovation and systemic risk

The *boom* in banking and in the entire system of financial power in the years prior to the crisis—and which did not stop either before or after it—would not have been possible without the invention, starting in the 1990s, of a wide variety of products which have proved to be a dagger plunged into the West's economic body. They almost all stem from 'derivatives', so called because they had their origin in the need to cover credit operation risk, which is done by paying a premium, just as for any type of insurance. The first to appear, of the type which is dealt with in the first part of this book, were *credit default swaps* (CDS). The issuer of CDS (outside of the banking sector, in other words *shadow banking*) agreed to pay back to the lender all the credit issued if the person who had taken out the credit could not repay it.

CDS were enormously successful. Credit operations hit the roof in the casino of capitalism. In 2007, they accounted for (i.e., they insured) USD 60 trillion,[55] and they are still in operation.

Another financial product which was all the rage in the Western world in the first decade of the 21st century was securitization or packaging—followed by distribution—of mortgages, many of which were of extremely low quality, which did not prevent the arrogant, irresponsible ratings agencies from assessing them as risk-free operation. In 2007 they accounted for more than USD 2 trillion. Six years later, new types of assets packaged for sale to investors keen on risk started to reappear in banking circles.

Among these innovations, the tireless and uninterrupted 'repo' market which buys up assets should be mentioned: banks and institutional investors offer their assets as a surety—with a repurchase agreement—in exchange for millions of dollars in short term loans, in other words, enormous and immediate liquidity.

Many of these 'innovations' are based on technological progress, which makes it possible for any number of swift transactions to take place. This is what happens with high frequency *trading*, which accounts for half of these transactions in Europe and even more in the USA. Technology allows these new professionals—the *traders*- to launch thousands of buy or sell orders from banks, hedge funds or other financial institutions in a single second.[56] The opaque, manipulative and speculative nature of this *trading* is clear. There is no other explanation.[57] Banks which work with derivatives, or who make use of *trading*, are aware that these operations do not appear on their balance sheets. In this way, the bank appears less leveraged than it actually is.[58]

All of this is apparent in the systemic power of the financial markets, banks, non-banks and products manipulated by all and sundry. They are still bobbing around, like a cork on water.

Control Over Financial Power

Can the financial powers be controlled by the political powers?

This question cannot simply be answered with a yes or a no. It depends on which political power. Financial power cannot any longer be efficiently controlled only by a nation-state. It would be possible for the European Union to do so, but in a nuanced way. However, a strong G-20 in agreement with the objectives, with the support of the USA, could do so, in a totally un-nuanced way. This means that control is possible. What is needed is the will to exercise it.

There are basically two types of problem: on the one hand, the appropriation by the financial system of a substantial and disproportionate amount of the wealth produced, due to the fact that they enjoy the privilege of using other people's money to turn a profit. On the other hand, there is the impoverishment of our entire society, if the risks taken by banks and investors go awry, as has happened in recent years.

The way to tackle the first problem is essentially by taking political decisions at European level—which will establish economic and fiscal control over all financial activities, both legal and illicit.

Dealing with the second problem means supranational regulation of the financial system. The one we have had up until now is clearly unfit for purpose as regards the risk of holding assets several times the size of global GDP. Power goes hand-in-hand with risk. The vast political ability to create risk represents the measure of financial power. If political power cannot neutralize this risk, democracy wavers.

Naulot hit the nail on the head when he stated that the systemic risk which is under discussion today is different in nature to what existed years ago. It is like comparing conventional war with nuclear war. World finances have turned into an enormous 'nuclear power station' constructed without any attention to safety regulations. Because the interconnection and the sheer size of the operations, along with the lack of transparency, is unsustainable without political control—which does not yet exist.

All of this can only be put right with a clear road map leading to control of the market, which is almost a contradiction in terms.

The minimum reforms required

A regulatory road map for the financial markets must have one clear and unequivocal objective: to exorcise the systemic risk inherent in growing centralized and globalized financial power; in other words, the power concentrated in the largest and most international institutions.

The European Union will have to come up with an authority (the ECB, the Commission or the Council of Europe—or a body of that ilk) with the power to exercise control over the movement of capital,[59] and able, should it become necessary to do so, to staunch the haemorrhage of a financial crisis, the possibility of which is not preposterous in view of the overwhelming pattern of risk still apparent in the West's financial system.

In order to avert this hypothetical catastrophe, it is time to approve anti-risk regulation of the entire financial power structure, bearing these principles in mind:[60]

1. Reform of insurance, which has still not taken place.
2. Banking reform, particularly the separation between the deposit banking and investment sectors; the abolition of executive bonuses; the publication of profits and taxes in each member state, exactly as demanded by the European Parliament; the setting of reserve quotas for high risk capital. These are still small and unclear. Basel III did not take away the ability of financial entities to set the risk value on their assets. Ways of getting into debt are endless. The banking sector has to be reduced in size, i.e., 'too big to fail', and it must be less complex to control. However, what is actually happening is the opposite, and for this reason it is essential to impose a tax which will dissuade banks from growing any larger.
3. Reform of the derivatives market to get rid of its opacity and the risk intrinsic to a product which was designed precisely to speculate on this risk.
4. Regulation and supervision of the silent shadow banking sector and hedge funds, who make such great use of these financial innovations and who have grown to account for a fourth of global finance.

5. The prohibition on short selling sales and on all financial procedures and products of an extremely complex nature, which are intrinsically open to abuse and to systemic risk.
6. Drastic reduction in financial speculation on the major raw materials markets.
7. Legal regulation to punish financial agents who indulge in forbidden risky behaviour that has a serious effect on financial stability. This final point is perhaps the most effective preventative measure against financial and tax abuses. White collar criminals are more afraid of prison than anything else. Fines are 'discounted' and absorbed by the markets.

These reforms must have a common purpose: the transparent publishing of accounts, a prerequisite of any serious control, and a reduction in size of the financial system.

In the last analysis, what is intended is that the financial system should stop covering up systemic power and risk, which are totally sterile and useless, and start serving the man or woman in the street.[61]

The money in circulation—both real and virtual—is several times the amount of the wealth actually created, which it supposedly represents as a means of avoiding a return to the mediaeval barter system. Global financial assets four times the size of GDP were the start of the crisis. The financial markets therefore devote most of their activities to pure speculation. There is no added social value for society. The meaning of shadow banking, *trading* in the dark, inflated derivatives, tax haven transactions and deals done in nanoseconds is nothing more than casino capitalism. And we already know that in casinos the house always wins, not the players. This type of financial capitalism puts the entire economy constantly at risk and has wreaked enormous damage on our social model and on citizens' rights, as well as widening the equality gap between individuals, social classes and countries.

'True and complete' reform of the financial system, as promised by the Council of Europe in 2008, must do away with this 'casino'. It must be radical. It must ensure that everything that is obviously superfluous in the financial system vanishes: its exaggeratedly useless size; its lack of transparency; its speculative self-absorption; its disconnection from social needs; its abuse of its dominant position.

Regulation to endow the financial system with solidity only has advantages. Absence, not excess, of regulation and oversight was what made the financial crisis possible.[62] The arguments put forward in an unceasing stream by banking industry pressure groups, such as the danger of a fall in the availability of credit and in financial activity, have no basis whatsoever in reality. They are what Admati and Hellwig call 'the story of the big bad wolf'.[63]

Unfortunately, as we have seen before, neither the Dodd-Frank Act in the USA[64] and its regulatory advances, nor current European Union directives head in the direction of making a clean break with everything that led to the Great Crisis. There is an interesting European initiative which emerged in 2010 and which would mean taking a truly encouraging step towards a thaw. This is the taxing of financial transactions. However, in 2013 it was shot down from all angles and it is currently in the balance and undecided.

The Financial Transaction Tax, an Instrument to Curb Financial Power

An initial response to the plunge in income from taxation in Europe was the establishment, in national arenas, of a tax on banking profits. In 2010 there were already at least 10 countries who either applied it or intended to introduce it: the United Kingdom, Germany, France, Belgium, Denmark, Cyprus, Austria, Portugal, Hungary and Sweden.[65]

Nevertheless, the most concrete proposal came from the European Union as such: the creation of a tax on speculative financial transactions.

The truth is that since the explosion of the sovereign debt crisis in 2010, the idea of a tax on financial transaction (henceforth FTT) had started to be bandied about at the meetings of European institutions and was then taken up by the Commission which started to work on the idea.[67] However, the proposal took off on 16 August 2011 when a Franco-German meeting put it on the agenda of the European Union. An initiative of the European Socialist Party and some alternative groupings (Attac) was skilfully commandeered by the French (Sarkozy) and German (Merkel) governments, who realized the political clout of the proposal and were in need of financing at the lowpoint of the crisis.

At that stage, their positions were still quite timid. The only FTT that could be envisaged was one that could be applied simultaneously throughout the Union, to prevent any discrimination in competition. It was understood that the United Kingdom would not accept it and that many countries would find it difficult to proceed without the *nihil obstat* of the City of London. It was also clearly unlikely to be welcomed by the markets. On the day after Merkel and Sarkozy's meeting, the German stock exchange fell by 5.8% and London by 2.8%. The Association of European Financial Markets said that the cost of the tax would hit growth.

The Commission's reaction was swift, realizing that the political route was free of obstacles. It unanimously formalized its proposal during the following month (on 28 September) with a view to bringing it into effect on 1 January 2014.[66] This date would not be honoured.

The tax receipt figure estimated at EUR 57 billion by the Commission at that point would not be reached either. The text presented, in the light of which this tax figure was arrived at, foresaw a minimum tax rate of 0.1% for all buying and selling transactions relating to shares and bonds if at least one participating entity was based in the EU for tax purposes; and a rate of 0.01% in the case of derivatives transactions, the financial instrument blamed for causing the crisis.[67]

The proposal, as was expected, did not receive the unanimous support of all the governments, which is why 11 of them have had to apply it through a process of enhanced cooperation.[68] The sponsor countries (Germany, France, Italy, Spain, Belgium. Portugal, Austria, Greece, Slovenia, Slovakia and Estonia) produce two-thirds of the wealth of the EU.

The FTT taxable base in the final proposal which the Commission presented on 14 February 2013 is very broad. The explanation of the thinking behind the text clarifies thus (3.3.2): 'it aims at covering transactions relating to all types of financial instruments as they are often close substitutes for each other. Thus, the scope covers instruments which are negotiable on the capital market, money-market instruments (with the exception of instruments of payment), units or shares in collective investment undertakings [...] and derivatives contracts', as well as other structured products (securitization).

The proposed FTT applies to business transacted in official markets and also where applicable to *over the counter* transactions. One of its aims is to prevent the trading of financial instruments between the independent entities of the same group. It is a tax on the virtual economy, not on the real one.

It is a tax on the economic crisis unleashed by the reckless, sometimes criminal, action of the financial markets. The FTT does not affect transactions carried out by businesses or citiziens, nor does it affect loans, payments, insurance, bank deposits, etc. The tax is intended as a way of addressing purely speculative movements in the financial economy, but it clearly has a tax-gathering aim which Tobin's 1972 proposal did not include. It is also a way of combating tax evasion and tax havens.

Moreover, it is a fair tax. The financial sector must pay, not in reparation for its sins, but because it must pay back—only partly—what it received in rescue funds, about 20% of GDP of the European economies. This damage to GDP must be counterbalanced by a contribution from the financial sector, since this sector has enjoyed the greatest income in the last few decades, as well as being in a position of privilege from a taxation point of view since it does not pay VAT.

A FTT of substance, not merely a symbolic one, would set a limit on the phenomenal number of transactions clearly inimical to social and economic progress, transactions which may then turn out to be toxic insofar as regards their ability to create systemic risk. A FTT would put a brake on the growth *ad infinitum* of short term *trading* and would enforce more responsible behaviour.

The latent political objective of the FTT is to place responsibility for the crisis on the financial sector and to focus European economic debate on this area. The crisis was not brought about as the result of poor administration in the countries of the south. The key responsibility falls on financial power, which has 'power' and consequently responsibility for it deeds, whether correct or not.[69]

The FTT, moreover, grants a new political dimension to European institutions in the form of tax-raising and spending power, not just a supervisory and disciplinary role.

The most significant contribution which the FTT makes to all those who have been hit by the crisis, is, in my judgement, the creation of the best instrument of control over financial power that has ever been invented. And I believe that this is what makes it so painful to the 'sacred cows' of the markets. This is definitely what after calm beginnings unleashed a battle whose final outcome cannot yet ensure a happy ending for those who believe in the will of the Union to confront what it at one time referred to as 'true and complete reform' of the financial system.

Heads

The FTT was one of the most inspiring and mobilizing ideas of recent decades. It managed to garner the enthusiastic support of the most unlikely persons and institutions. From multimillionaire investors to NGOs promoting equality all over the planet. From progressive parties to conservative parties. From national parliaments to supranational institutions.

People like Bill Gates, Warren Buffet and George Soros have applauded the FTT as a means of combating world poverty. Bill Gates defended it passionately at the G-20 summit in 2001.[70]

The European Parliament adopted a positive legislative resolution on 3 July 2012 on the proposed directive relating to the FTT, a resolution which it endorsed on 12 December.

The Parliamentary Assembly of the Council of Europe passed a resolution on 5 October, 2012 in which it hailed the FTT as a 'return to social justice' in response to the grave errors of the financial markets, which had proved incapable of ensuring sufficient financing of the real economy.[71] The Assembly highlighted the clear majority support of European citizens for the idea of a European tax on financial transactions.

At the same time, hundreds of economists and 50 major financiers wrote to David Cameron calling for a FTT or 'Robin Hood tax'.

Everything appeared to be going well for the FTT. But the power of finance had been underestimated. A power so difficult to control that it simply was not prepared to meekly accept any such gimmick.

Tails

As soon as news of the FTT spread, market *lobbying* sprang into action. They also had their economists, such as the famous—unwillingly so—Kenneth Rogoff who launched into a criticism of the FTT supposedly to help tax-gathering, which would be negatively affected if the aforementioned tax were to be implemented.[72] This was a different version of the Laffer curve.

The conservative and liberal Anglo-Saxon press (*The Economist, Wall Street Journal*) all had their say, employing the argument that the extension of the FTT beyond the specific borders of the sponsor countries was a kind of imperialism.[73]

The most powerful non-financial French business federations protested loudly about the unacceptable costs of the FTT. The London Chamber of Commerce and Industry did likewise.[74] German industrial companies joined in.

This type of fierce resistance on the part of private banking had been foreseen but not such an acrimonious reaction from the central banks. The then Governor of the Bank of England, Sir Mervyn King, summed it up like this: 'I could not find anyone within the central banking community who thinks it's a good idea'. As was to be expected, the Bundesbank came out in criticism of any unorthodox proposal that might damage its untouchable markets. Nor did the Bank of Spain express any support. The Bank of France was explicit in its criticism. Its Governor, Christian Noyer, harshly attacked the 'Robin Hood tax' again and again, since he considered it an 'enormous risk' to financial stability, without bothering to assess the risk implicit in an uncontrolled, deregulated financial system. Noyer coolly alleged that the FTT would destroy entire areas of the financial industry and lead to a massive brain drain, which would damage the entire economy. According to Noyer, this would happened because of the increasing cost of capital to governments and corporations, and a fall in liquidity.[75]

Christian Noyer was bluntly expressing, what was now the implicit doctrine of the European Central Bank itself, which offered to revise the text of the Commission's proposed directive. Particularly, the section referring to the 'repo' market for the repurchase of shares (a more opaque market than any other) on which Treasury bills are temporarily exchanged for cash and which is a vital source of day-to-day liquidity. Both Noyer and Weidmann, the President of the Bundesbank, have demonstrated their preoccupation with this market.[76]

The Commission even came under 'friendly fire' in early September 2013. The actual judicial services at Berlaymont launched a missile against the proposed directive, alleging that it was contrary to European legislation and international treaties, on account of exceeding the jurisdiction of the Union and seeking to tax contracts drawn up in London, America and Asia.

And all of this opposition to a really modest tax on some transactions which already entail other costs (commission, management, etc.) about which no one has anything to say. Not to mention *stamp duty* in the United Kingdom, which is an indirect tax on stock exchange deals. What is clear is that the lack of a FTT on financial services explains the abuse of transactions, which creates chronic instability.

Despite these arguments, the political chain supporting the FTT began to be weakened by the government of the country which had spearheaded the campaign for a FTT, France, and by the party which had done most for it, the French Socialist Party. Pierre Moscovici began to unsettle things, in other words, to water down the wine, by distorting the objectives and fiscal instrument which the Commission, had quite correctly introduced into the original formal FTT proposal.

After the German elections in September, the FTT recovered ground. The coalition government pact, which included the Social Democrats, reaffirmed the pledge to 'swiftly implement' a financial transactions tax with a broad remit to include 'shares, bonds, investment certificates, monetary transactions and derivatives contracts'. Insofar as currency transactions are concerned, the coalition's manifesto introduces one condition: the tax must be structured so that it avoids 'negative effects on instruments for pensions, small investors and the real economy'.

At the beginning of 2015 Hollande, after the failure of Ecofin in December 2014, has tried to recover the Financial Transaction Tax with a basis as wide as possible in order to put it into practice in 2017. A position more in favour of stimulus than that held by France up until this time, which was to limit the FTT to shares and a small proportion of derivatives (CDS), faced with pressure on the part of the French banks and, as always, the threat of off-shoring. But the basis of the tax is a key question. Derivatives represent 85% of strictly financial transactions, and if they are not included, the tax becomes pointless. Today, Moscovici is on the other side: he's the European Commissioner for Economic Affairs.

At the time of finishing this book in February 2015, the situation regarding the Financial Transactions Tax can be defined by the French word 'impasse'.

Conclusion

The Ice Age Will Not Last Forever

As far as I've been able to read on Wikipedia, the last glacial period, or Ice Age—known as the Würm glaciations—began about 110,000 years ago, was at its height 20,000 years ago, and had its collapse 10,000 years ago. Since then, we have enjoyed what scientists call the 'interglacial period'.

During the Ice Age, large areas of the Earth from the icecaps to near the tropics were covered by ice, especially in the northern hemisphere. The climate cooled worldwide and the volume of seas, lakes and rivers went down as most froze. Greenland and Antarctica have retained their glaciers since then (with a serious danger of shrinkage in the Arctic because of the phenomenon of global warming).

The Ice Age is the metaphor of the Great Crisis that has plagued the West. This has not been transient in nature. It has being going on now for seven years, particularly affecting the northern hemisphere—as in the Ice Age—but its effects extend to the entire global economic system.

The Great Crisis has first and foremost frozen money, the food of the economy in our era, just like the water nourishing our planet; it has frozen the arteries of the system, banks and financial institutions, just as the Ice Age paralyzed rivers; and above all, it has frozen the heart of the economy, the rhythm of its production and employment, and has plunged us into a period of winter hibernation, bringing growth and employment screeching to a halt.

The Great Crisis has forced South-North migration, as the Ice Age forced our human ancestors to go from Asia to America. The Great Crisis, in short, has damaged the deep structure of the welfare state, in the way that glaciations hindered the flourishing of life. The Great Crisis, which has been studied in some detail in these pages, is not a mere parenthesis in a supposedly continuing development of economy and society in Europe and America (neither was the Ice Age). In fact, it has completely transformed them, and has put in their place a different model, one which predominated in the middle of the last century.

In the early years of this century a series of transfers of power have occurred that the crisis has consolidated, and this transfer has always gone in the same direction: with a focus on the most powerful, i.e., on the possessors of wealth with the highest capacity for hegemony—that is to say, the financial and transnational—and on the governments with most leeway, the creditors. Transfers of an economic, political and social nature which have a lasting, structural (and not cyclical) character.

Transfer of wealth: the hegemony of financial markets and multinational companies. The loss of taxation ability of the State

The crisis is financial in nature. We have said so on many occasions. The era of neoliberalism has served to pave the way for the undisputed domination of the money lords—lords of the money of others, of course, the magical domain of the money masters giving them the ability to create money in the form of credit, creating a seductive debt for those on the other side of the table.

Financial markets have produced a transmutation of power, bringing democratic institutions to their knees, the latter powerless to manage such complex entities, or to set and apply rules for those who create systemic risk. Finance has increased its power because it has transferred wealth to its closed shop, and has made the economic world revolve around it.

Financial institutions grew exponentially before the crisis thanks to the deregulation imposed in their favour by political powers; then, as a natural consequence, this led to the Great Crisis; they have forced taxpayers to save them from collapse and disappearance; they have been strengthened by all this and have even increased their profits, although the economic crisis is not yet over. Financial institutions, in the light and in the shadows, are now fewer in number, but they are larger; they have made the systemic risk higher and lowered their capital requirement. They drip-feed credit to needy businesses and consumers, bearing no relation to the low interest rate set, unsuccessfully, by the ECB in the Eurozone.

The other sector that has been strengthened is the transnational one, just like the financial one, protagonist of globalization. Multinational companies have also achieved a huge transfer of wealth to their advantage, especially in two ways. The first, through favourable credit conditions that financial markets provide to their bond issues or their increases in capital; conditions which SMEs can only dream of aspiring to, despite the fact that SMEs are the businesses which create the most employment.

The other, scandalous and illicit, way of gaining profit for multinationals is tax evasion and tax avoidance, as we have seen in Chapter 6. Evasion, thanks to tax havens, has been incomprehensibly allowed to exist—as has the avoidance of corporate tax rates by way of an aggressive fiscal optimization strategy, causing a huge hole in the public purse, in both Europe and the USA. Only in recent years have we begun to react, but too late and without the essential coordination necessary to tackle this problem.

Tax evasion and tax avoidance by multinationals have strong support in states such as Ireland, Luxembourg and Austria which assist in this process in order to attract capital—in one way, quite sterile and opportunistically—with the appeal of very low corporate tax rates.

These transfers of economic power are not anecdotal. They form an essential part of the Western 'Economic Constitution' model in this new century, which coexists with its 'political constitution'.

Changing social models: the weakening of the Welfare State

The austerity policy, which (so clearly) prematurely took the place of a stimulus policy in the economy of the European Union—unlike in the USA—has a scapegoat: the much-loved but also much-maligned Welfare State.

Actually, the first victim was the state itself, *tout court*. The Great Crisis is the sign of a state already weak in the face of the emboldened markets and, simultaneously, of a state that further weakens itself by denying tax authorities the opportunity to address the most cruel and antisocial effects of this crisis.

The Welfare State is not just a belated addition to the contemporary state. It is the whole form and policy that the state adopted in the second half of the twentieth century in Western Europe and, undoubtedly to a lesser extent, the USA. The Welfare State was surrounded by a whole constitutional structure, guaranteeing social rights and political rights, which have been supplemented by environmental rights in recent years.

This architecture has been eroded by the termites of the policy of adjustment imposed on the so-called 'peripheral countries', the Southern European ones. These termites are responsible for what I have called in Chapter 5 the 'Four Horsemen of the Apocalypse' of 'unemployment, underemployment, poverty and inequality'.

The democratic majority is reluctant to swallow this bitter medicine, and clings to the social contract in Europe born of the Second World War, that has the Union as one of its guaranteeing elements. Therefore, the fragmentation of Welfare means the fragmentation of the European Union itself. Their fates are linked. This is what makes the change in social model so serious, and its rescue and restoration so urgent.

The Ice Age and its alternative

In Europe, then, we are living through a situation that involves more than a crisis. It is a deregulated production model based on anaemic growth and on arbitrary credit. It is a political model with decreasing powers of the state, devoid of taxation power thanks to tax avoidance and evasion, and therefore the power to be able to direct investment and spending. It is a social model in real crisis, in which the rights to major public services, pensions, harmonious labour relations, have lost their former judicial and constitutional backing, to return to a model of low wages, job insecurity and loss of bargaining power by trade unions.

All these changes in essential elements of the state of advanced capitalism tell us—and this is the central thesis of this book—that we have entered a new economic and political era, different from the one dominant in the twentieth century in Europe and the USA: eroded social protection, tax authorities humiliated by the power of transnational capital, financial in nature, in a context of devaluation and inequality in wages and wealth, with growth close to zero, and stagnating production and prices.

For this reason, leaving the crisis and moving towards a state that guarantees all social rights, i.e., rescuing the Welfare State and adapting it to the knowledge society and the global economy, means a profound transformation of the panorama before us.

It is necessary to practice a Europe-wide economic policy of investment and demand stimulus, publicly funded, in part via mutualized debt, and partly through direct taxes on the very wealthy and corporations, as well as the financial transactions tax. This should be backed by the ECB with an expansive monetary policy, not only aimed at financing banks as the indispensible middlemen between the ECB and the real economy. The ECB has to evolve towards a monetary policy, conventional or unconventional, which mirrors that followed by the Federal Reserve.

The effort of the G-20 and the EU has already addressed, and with absolute determination, the huge tax evasion based in tax havens. This implies directly prohibiting any transaction with opaque jurisdictions and harmonizing real rates of corporation tax below 20%. Alongside this, the EU has to agree to legislation to prevent tax avoidance by multinationals.

The third element of a reform that attacks the foundations of the crisis consists in regulating the financial system, with different objectives: reducing its economic weight; avoiding systemic risk with capital requirements of near 10%; and also implementing a European Banking Union with a centralized authority, resolution funds and deposit guarantees sufficient to serve as a firewall in the case where the fall of a financial institution cannot be shouldered by shareholders, creditors and depositors with an excess of EUR 100,000. Never again should the bill be footed by the taxpayer.

This programme of radical democratic reforms can be tackled by a political power that even the USA only has when the most progressive forces dominate Capitol Hill—which is not the case now—and that a European federal policy alone could provide, although we are still far from this in realistic terms. This is the real challenge for the Old Continent. If we do not respond to it, it will take a long time before we manage to leave the Ice Age behind.

Bahía de Cádiz, February 2015

Notes

PART I The Great Crisis

Chapter 1 The Thirty-year Crisis

1. Robert Skidelsky, *Keynes: The Return of the Master*, 2009, p. 28.
2. Aldo Giannuli, *Uscire della crisi è possibile*, 2012, p. 45.
3. Luciano Gallino, *Finanzcapitalismo. La civiltà del denaro in crisi*, 2011, chap. V, pp. 107 et seq.
4. Paul Ormerod, *The Death of Economics*, 1994, p. 199.
5. Jeffrey D. Sachs, *The Price of Civilization*, 2011, p. 61.
6. Cf. Diego López Garrido, *Economic Rights and Fundamental Freedoms in the European Community System*, 1986, pp. 15 et seq; and *The Treaty of Maastricht*, 1992, pp. 42 et seq. This treaty banned capital controls.
7. Stephen S. Cohen and J. Bradford Delong, *The End of Influence. What Happens When Other Countries Have the Money*, 2010, p. 110.
8. Michel Albert, *Capitalism vs. Capitalism*, 1993, p. 1.
9. Vid Giannuli, op. cit., p. 57.
10. José V. Sevilla, *El declive de la Socialdemocracia* [the decline of social democracy], 2011, ch. III.
11. M. Albert, op. cit., p. 248.
12. Binyamin Appelbaum, *International Herald Tribune* (hereinafter IHT), 24–25 December 2012.
13. Joseph E. Stiglitz, *Le Rapport Siglitz. Pour une vraie du système monétaire et réforme financier international*, 2010, p. 69.
14. OECD, *Economies in Transition*, 1989, ch. 1.
15. Figures quoted in Giannuli, op. cit., p. 67.
16. Louis Hyman, *Borrow: the American Way of Debt*, 2012.
17. Raghuram G. Rajan, *Fault Lines: How Hidden Fractures Still Threaten the World Economy*, 2011, p. 51.
18. Ibid, p. 146.
19. José V. Sevilla, op. cit., pp. 399 et seq.
20. Gallino, op. cit. p. 59.
21. Cohen and Delong, op. cit., p. 111.
22. Nouriel Roubini and Stephen Mihm, *Crisis Economics: a Crash Course in the Future of Finance*, 2011, p. 19.
23. L. Hyman, op. cit., p. 246.
24. Quoted by Carmen M. Reinhart and Kenneth S. Rogoff, *This Time is Different: Eight Centuries of Financial Folly*, 2011, pp. 232 et seq.
25. Richard Duncan, *The New Depression. The Breakdown of the Paper Money Economy*, 2012, pp. 49 and 61.

Chapter 2 Shock

1. Jacques Attali, *La crise et après?*, 2009, p. 69.
2. François Morin, 'The global financial crisis and new system orientations' in S. Amin, E. Altvater, F. Morin, P. Gowan, *Crisis Financiera, económica, sistémica*, 2010, p. 57.
3. Jacques Adda, *La mondialisation de l'économie: de la genèse à la crise*, 2012, p. 271.
4. International Labour Office, 8th European Regional Meeting, Lisbon, 2009, pp. 2–3.
5. Roubini and Mihm share this view. See op. cit, pp. 136 et seq.
6. Ibid, p. 148.
7. Joseph Stiglitz, Freefall: America, Free Markets and the Sinking of the Global Economy, 2011, p. 253.
8. Roubini and Mihm op. cit., pp. 153 et seq.
9. Ibid, p. 155.
10. Richard Duncan, op. cit., pp. 68 et seq.
11. *Financial Times* (hereinafter FT), 20 March 2009.
12. Raghuram G. Rajan, op. cit., p. 132.
13. J. Adda, op. cit., pp. 281 et seq.
14. Ibid, p. 283.
15. Only the series of investments in schools and hospitals contemplating spending EUR 18 billion in two years. Tax cuts for businesses and citizens approved by CDU/CSU and SPD reached EUR 9 billion for the period of time between 1 July 2009 and late 2010. It was the largest aid package approved since WWII.
16. El País, 3 June 2009.
17. Cinco Días, 26 October 2009.
18. Specifically, the decisions taken at this point were:
    - To establish a new Financial Stability Board (FSB) with greater powers, including all G-20 countries, Spain and the European Commission.
    - The FSB will collaborate with the IMF to provide early warning of macroeconomic and financial risks, and steps to overcome them.
    - Remodelling of national regulatory systems so that the authorities can detect and take into account the risks.
    - Extension of regulation and oversight to all institutions, instruments and systemically important financial markets. This will include, for the first time, the systemically important hedge funds.
    - Applying strict principles on pay and salary compensation.
    - Taking action, once recovery of a crisis is assured, to improve the quality, quantity and international consistency of capital in the banking system. In the future, regulation must prevent excessive leverage and require the accumulation of capital buffers in good times.
    - Taking action against non-cooperative jurisdictions, including tax havens. To this end, we can deploy sanctions to protect public finances and financial systems and to end banking secrecy.
    - Expanding monitoring and requiring registration of ratings agencies to ensure they meet the international code of good practice, particularly to prevent unacceptable conflicts of interest.
19. See Brian Keely and Patrick Love, *De la crise à la reprise. Causes, déroulement et conséquences de la Grande Récession*, 2010, p. 12.
20. Ibid, p. 53.
21. R. Duncan, op. cit., p. 75.
22. Ibid, p. 74.
23. Quoted by Paul Krugman in 'End this Depression Now!', 2010, p. 143.

PART II The Reaction

Chapter 3 The Failure of Austerity

1. The State of the European Union. The Failure of Austerity. Fundación Alternativas and Friedrich-Ebert-Stiftung, 2013. Accessible via Internet on the website of the Fundación Alternativas.
2. See M. Albert, op. cit., p. 118.
3. Mark Blyth, *Austerity: The History of a Dangerous Idea*, 2013, pp. 141 and s.
4. Ibid, p. 2.
5. Guillaume Duval, 'La genèse d'une crise' in *Comprendre la Crise*, Alternatives Economiques Poche, no. 58, December 2012, p. 64.
6. See Mark Blyth, 'The Austerity Delusion' in *Foreign Affairs*, May–June 2013, p. 42.
7. Neil Irwin, *The Alchemists*, 2013, p. 208.
8. *The Guardian*, 20 February 2010, p. 17.
9. Communication from the European Commission, June 2010.
10. See statement of the Eurogroup, 11 April 2010.
11. See Statement of the Eurogroup, Greece, 16 November 2010.
12. M. Blyth, op. cit., pp. 235 et seq.
13. Andrew Farlow, *Crash and Beyond*, 2013, p. 253.
14. Data provided by Peter Mathews, 'A politician's perspective on debt and default' in *What if Ireland Defaults*? 2012.
15. Regulation no. 407/2010 was adopted by the Council on 11 May 2010. It is intended to 'provide financial assistance from the Union to a Member State that is in difficulties or is seriously threatened by a severe economic and financial disturbance caused by exceptional occurrences not under its control' (Article 1).
16. A. Farlow, op. cit., p. 260.
17. Blyth, op. cit., pp. 237 et seq. The author makes a suggestive comparison with Iceland, where the government decided not to rescue the banks.
18. Quoted in M. Blyth, op. cit., p. 66.
19. Ibid, p. 67.
20. A. Farlow, op. cit., p. 282.
21. *The Economist*, 16 July 2011, pp. 9 and 67.
22. The legal texts were approved by the 27 in the European Council on 23 and 24 June 2011, and the finance ministers signed it on 12 July.
23. For an extensive study of the constitutional reform of Article 135 EC, see Diego López Garrido (dir.) And Maria Luz Martínez Alarcón (coord.), Reforma Constitucional y estabilidad presupuestaria [Constitutional reform and budgetary stability]. Article 135 of the Spanish Constitution, 2013.
24. For a political critique of the treaty, see L'Europe maltraitée, 2012.
25. Aquí Europa, 21 September 2011.
26. Quoted in L'Europe maltraitée, op. cit., p. 3.
27. M. Blyth, op. cit., p. 4.
28. Diego López Garrido, 'Introduction' to the Report on the State of the European Union, 'Twelve months of economic despair', op. cit., p. 18.
29. Osservatorio di Politica Internazionale, 'L'Europe a political compact verse: Opzioni per uscire dalla crisi' no. 58, June 2012, p. 10.
30. Data provided by the Department of Economic and Budgetary Analysis of the Spanish Congress of Deputies.
31. Youth unemployment was, in the third quarter of 2012, double that of adults with low chances of obtaining employment, and especially stable employment. See figures in the

Communication from the Commission, COM (2012) 727, dated 5 December 2012. For a detailed study of job quality in its evolution during the crisis, see 'Tendances de la qualité de l'emploi pendant la crise: Une approche comparative européenne' Centre d'Etudes de l'emploi, March 2013.

32. In euros, constant of 2005. 'Comprendre la crise' in Alternatives Economiques, op. cit., p. 78.
33. Autumn Statement 2012. HM Treasury, December 2012, CM 8480.
34. A. Farlow, op. cit., pp. 248 et seq.
35. J. Stiglitz, 'Les Illusions perdues des maîtres du monde', *Les Echos*, 14 February 2013, p. 10. IMF, WO/13/1, <www.imf.org>.
36. Germany in 2012 reached a record 41.5 million people employed, 416,000 more than the previous year, according to the Federal Statistical Office (Destatis). In 2010 and 2011, German GDP grew by 4.2% and 3%, respectively, following the sharp decline of 5% in 2009. Like the entire Eurozone, Germany contracted at the end of 2012 in terms of GDP (0.6%) and also in terms of private investment, but its strong export orientation (4.1% in 2012), and growth in the US and Asia, made its recovery immediate. In fact, Germany had in 2012 a surplus (0.1%) for the first time since 2007.
37. According to a report from Intermon Oxfam, 'Crisis, inequality and poverty', from now until 2022, 40% of Spaniards will be in a situation of social exclusion. Quoted in El País, 14 December 2012.
38. Remarks on a visit to Marché de Rungis (Val-de-Marne) on 27 December 2012. *Le Monde*, 29 December 2012, p. 1. France has destroyed 750,000 industrial jobs in a decade, according to Louis Gallois' report on the competitiveness of the French economy, at the request of the President. The report is clearly contrary to regulations and favourable towards tax cuts for businesses, as well as a reduction in the social safety net. F. Hollande reacted by proposing a competitiveness pact between government and business in the second economy of the Union.
39. CESifo World Economic Survey, Munich, April 2013, p. 4.
40. The UK grew during this period by 3.4%, compared with 3.4% France, Germany (3.7%) and the USA (4.9%). The UK economy is now smaller (3%) than it was in 2008.
41. *The Guardian*, 25 January 2013, pp. 1–2. See 'Business analysis' on p. 29. The government proposed achieving a balanced budget within five years, in 2018, applying a strict austerity policy.
42. Not all were critical voices in the press. The editor of the *Financial Times*, Chris Giles, adopted a position in support of Osborne. *Financial Times*, 14 March 2013, p. 9.
43. Regional Economic Prospect in EBRD Countries of Operations, January 2013. EBRD Office of the Chief Economist. Available at www.ebrd.com.
44. However, in 2006–2012, federal government officials fell by 74,000, while the private sector increased (203,000 jobs each month of the first quarter of 2012).
45. The *Financial Times* wrote a laudatory editorial on 7 February 2013, p. 8.
46. Floyd Norris, 'Downturn Takes hold far and wide', *International Herald Tribune*, 23–24 February 2013, p. 15.
47. The *sequester* is part of the Budget Control Act Barack Obama signed in August 2011. Economists feared a recession faced with the billions of dollars in fiscal contraction.
48. The Commission presented to the General Affairs Council of 11 December 2012 the annual growth prospects study of 2013. It proposed reforms focusing on five priority areas. The first was 'further fiscal consolidation, growth-friendly'. This was the term used by the European Council on 14 and 15 March 2013.
49. Another interesting statement is that relating to the fight against tax fraud (paragraph 6 of the conclusions). See the 'position of the Council for European Affairs on the

European Council of 14-15 March 2013' of the Fundación Alternativas (see website), paragraph 6, on taxation and tax havens.

50. For example, in the G-8 May 2012.
51. 88.2% of GDP in Spain, which reflects an increase of 15.2 points in one year. In the EU 17, the increase was 4 points; in the EU 27, 2.6 percentage points of GDP.
52. Quoted by David Wessel, 'Trying to Calculate the Cost of Uncertainty', *Wall Street Journal*, 5 December 2012, p. 7.
53. President Obama enacted on 10 April 2013 the corresponding decree, introducing in Congress the draft budget for the fiscal year 2014.
54. This was the opinion of renowned British columnists, like Martin Wolff, 'America's tax policy is not in crisis', *Financial Times*, 23 January 2013, p. 9.
55. This is the legislative proposal put forward by Republicans in May 2013 in the House, without the intention of letting it prosper.
56. An example of the latter sector includes Allianz and the German Commerzbank insurance company. Michel Heise, chief economist of the first, defended austerity: 'The bitter medicine that these countries have to take has begun to take effect'. Jörg Krämer, chief economist Commerzbank, stated in March 2013: 'The last thing Germany needs is fiscal stimulus'. To Krämer, low interest rates set by the ECB are sufficient stimulus, and it would be 'stupid' to add more. *Financial Times*, 30 November 2012, p. 3 and 14 March 2013, p. 4, respectively.
57. *Financial Times*, 30 November 2012, p. 3.
58. 'Europe's Austerity Fable', *Wall Street Journal*, 24 April 2013. The WSJ thesis was shared by some columnists in the *International Herald Tribune* (29 April 2013). Hugo Dixon noted that the Euro crisis had not been produced by austerity but stemmed from an uncompetitive economy where the 'Welfare State was too generous, work had excessive privileges and social services were inflated'.
59. Kenneth Rogoff and Carmen Reinhart, *This Time is Different*. Another conservative reference, the authors Alberto Alsina and Silvia Ardagna, minting of the term 'expansionary austerity'.
60. R. Pollin and M. Ash, 'Why Reinhart and Rogoff are wrong about austerity', *Financial Times*, 18 April 2013, p. 9.
61. 'Debt and Growth', *Wall Street Journal*, 1 May 2013, p. 14.
62. Jean-Marc Vittori, 'Lorsque la France réduisait sa dette publique'. *Les Echos*, 29 October 2012, p. 14.
63. In this regard, some critical economists in Galway (Ireland) developed a text that was released in November 2012. This argued that an increase in austerity measures would lead to massive default. See 'A Politician's Perspective on Debt and Default' in What if Ireland Defaults?, p. 237. In the same direction, the Institute of Macroeconomics and Short-Term Research (IMK) in its 2013 outlook report requested by Angela Merkel a 'radical shift in its strategy'.
64. *Financial Times*, 7 January 2013, p. 7. See also the article 'Austerity is the actual obstacle to economic reform' in FT, 25 February 2013, p. 9.
65. 'Europe's bitter tonic', *International Herald Tribune*, 16 April 2013, p. 6. 'European stagnation', IHT, 6 May 2013, p. 8.
66. Some columns of P. Krugman in the IHT, published in the period of February, March and April 2013, are especially recommended: 'Looking for Mr. Goodpain' (2–3 February 2013, p. 7); 'Zombie economics' (16–17 February 2013, p. 9); 'The market speaks' (9–10 March 2013, p. 7); 'The urgent need to purge' (6–7 April 2013, p. 7). They are noteworthy articles published by Krugman in the crucial period of February, March and April 2013, when the doctrine of austerity began to be in crisis. However, it stands

out above all the aforementioned long article in The New York Review of Books entitled 'How the case for austerity has crumbled' (June 6, 2013, vol. LX, Vol. 10, pp. 67–73).

67. FT, 15 February 2013, p. 8.
68. M. Wolff, 'Britain's austerity is indefensible'. P. Stevens, 'The New Deal for Europe: More reform, less austerity', FT, 26 April 2013, p. 7.
69. Highlights include two editorials in *The Guardian*: 'Austerity: an idea on trial' 22 April 2013, p. 28; and 'Spending review. Vital, bloody and pointless', 1 May 2013, p. 28. See also articles in the same newspaper Seumas Milne 'Europe's Flesheaters now threaten to devour us all' (27 March 2013, p. 38) and 'Ed Miliband will fail if he locks himself into Tory austerity' (1 May 2013, p. 26).
70. OECD, Economic Review Reforms 2013. Going for Growth, 2013. At a meeting in Paris, at the headquarters of the OECD, 27 February 2013, with the Committee on Economic and Security and the Political Committee of the Assembly parliamentary NATO, in which I participated as vice president of the first commission, Sebastian Barnes, chief economic adviser to the OECD economist, explained the position of this in a lecture entitled 'the economic outlook and the Euro crisis'. It made clear that the first policy that should be applied according to the OECD was fiscal consolidation.
71. Olivier Blanchard and Daniel Leigh, 'Errors in Forecasts of Growth and Fiscal Multipliers', January 2013.
72. See article about Joaquín Estefanía 'Errors that lead to suffering' in El País, 7 January 2013, p. 23.
73. IMF World Economic Outlook. Transitions and Tensions, 2013. David Lipton, deputy managing director of the IMF, European Central Bank requested the use of unconventional measures such as buying bonds to increase lending and stimulate the economy.
74. A. Lowrey, 'IMF talks of growth but pushes for austerity', IHT, 16 April 2013, p. 15. 'EU leaders and IMF closer on crisis cures', IHT, 22 April 2013, p. 15.
75. José Manuel Barroso launched the phrase 'Countries with a high risk premium do not have the luxury of choice'. The European Commission has moved in this direction, at all levels. So, Marco Buti and Nicolas Carnot, economists Commission published a lengthy article defending the adjustments and structural reforms. Ecofin Brief, issue 2, March 2013. Available at europa.eu/economy-finance/publications.
76. In March 2013, representatives of the Troika, after verifying the implementation of the adjustment programme in Portugal, the Portuguese government agreed with the revision of the deficit targets. 5.5% of GDP was established in 2013 (instead of 4.5%); 2014 4% (instead of 2.5%); and by 2015 the target was set at 2.5% of GDP (ECB, 15 March 2013. Available at www.ecb.int).
77. According to Eurostat, the deficit in the EU 17 was, in 2012, 3.7% of GDP, from 4.4% in 2011. In the EU-27, the deficit was 4%, from 4.4% in 2011. The Eurozone debt amounted to 90.6% (87.3% in 2011); and the EU 27 amounted to 85.3% (82.5% in 2011). In Spain, in 2012, the deficit was 10.6% of GDP, including the cost of banks rescued. France had a deficit of 4.8%. In the US, the 2012 deficit exceeded 8% of GDP. In Japan, the deficit was more than 10%.
78. The Australian Government, which had suffered a sharp drop in revenue, presented a budget in the first half of May—four months from the elections—abandoning the path of cuts and focusing on growth and investment in health, education, infrastructure and employment. It thus joined the upward trend favoured by Abe in Japan.
79. Spain and Italy fell by 0.5% and France 0.2%, officially entering a recession. Germany grew by 0.1% thanks to consumption, just the opposite of France. (See *Le Monde*, supplement Eco-Enterprise, 16 May 2013.) Finland yielded 0.1%, as Holland. The EU fell by 0.1%.

80. That figure is USD 200 billion less than the projected deficit by the agency three months earlier. The Congressional Budget Office estimates that in 2015 the US deficit will drop to 2.1%; and then gradually grow the rest of the decade, as a result of the economic recovery. See 'US Budget gap less stimulating than expected' IHT, 16 May 2013, p. 14.
81. International Herald Tribune, 18-19 May 2013, p.11
82. The private sector activity in the Eurozone fell again in May.
83. Diego López Garrido, Nicolás Sartorius and Carlos Carnero, 'We cannot wait for the German elections', El País, 21 May 2003.
84. Spain, France, Poland and Slovenia extend their terms by two years. Portugal, Belgium and the Netherlands, a year. In the latter, the Commission recommended eliminating tax deductions for mortgage interest, one of the most sensitive policies in the Netherlands.
85. The Commission criticized that France had raised the minimum wage in the previous year.
86. Finland had a national debt of 53% of GDP and a deficit of 1.9% in 2012 (Eurostat).
87. FT, 27 June 2013, p. 4.
88. The Deputies Congress encourages the government to break the vicious cycle between banking and sovereign debt through direct recapitalization of Eurozone banks by the European Stability Mechanism in order to end the fragmentation in financial markets resulting in very different conditions of financing for companies in different countries of the Eurozone.
89. See the position of the Alternatives Foundation on the European Council of 27 and 28 June 2013 on the website of the Foundation.
90. In the Euro area employment rate rose slightly for the first time since 2011 (by 0.1% to reach 63.5% total).
91. Bank lending to non-financial companies in the peripheral economies had declined by EUR 137 billion between late 2011 and the third quarter of 2012, 1.1% of EU GDP. See N. Ferguson and Pier Paolo Barbieri, 'The EU's feeble war on unemployment' IHT, 4 April 2013, p. 8.
92. Anatole Kaletsky, 'Austerity is falling out of favour', IHT, 26 July 2013, pp. 14 and 16.
93. The Eurozone debt rose EUR 150 billion in the first quarter of 2013 to reach a total of EUR 8.75 billion, i.e., 92.2% of Eurozone GDP (in the previous quarter debt was 96.6%). Ireland, Greece, Portugal, Italy and Belgium were above 100% of GDP. Spain, whose national debt was 40% of GDP in 2008, reached nearly 90% in 2013. See B. Blackstone, 'Berlin Dealt Setback Over Austerity' WSJ, 23 July 2013, pp. 1 and 4.
94. In July 2013, business in Germany rose more than expected and faster than in the past five months. It was a sign of recovery in the Eurozone; but only in terms of growth, not in employment or debt.
95. The Institute for Global Economy in Kiel estimated that in 2011 Germany was spared in debt interest EUR 11.1 billion. These data were cited in the article by Nicholas Kulish, 'Pressure builds on Merkel amid anti-austerity clamor', 4–5 May 2013, pp. 1 and 3.
96. Sebastian Dullien, 'A German model for Europe?' At the European Council on Foreign Relations, July 2013, pp. 4 and 6. See Adam Posen (president of the Peterson Institute), 'Germany is being crushed by STI export obsession', FT, April 4, 2013, p. 7.
97. See Marcel Fratzscher, 'The costs for Germany if the Eurozone collapses' in *Europe's World*, 1 October 2013. The author refers to the three illusions that the Germans have: Europe hinders its economic success, other European governments just want German money (hence appeals before the Constitutional Court of programmes ECB asset purchase), and that the crisis is the fault of the Euro. Therefore, many Germans did not want Germany to lead Europe.
98. See J. Ewing, 'No bounce for Europe in rebound by Germany', IHT, 4 April 2013, pp. 1 and 17.

99. In a study for the European Commission prepared by Jan in't Veld, it is noted that the contractionary fiscal policy conducted between 2011 and 2013 has produced an accumulated loss of 18% annually in Greece, 9.7% in Spain, 9.1% in France, 8.4% in Ireland, and even 8.1% in Germany. Data taken from the excellent article by Martin Wolff, 'Germany is a weight on the world', FT, 6 October 2013, p. 9. The conservative replication of the Keynesian article Wolff was given the following day by Simon Nixon, analyst for Europe Wall Street Journal, in an article entitled 'US Treasury Has it Wrong on Germany', WSJ, 11 October 2013, p. 4.
100. Alert Mechanism Report, 2014, COM (2013) 790 final.
101. See articles by: Susanne Wasun-Rainer, German Embassy in France, published in *Le Monde* (21 November 2013); Karl-Theodor zu Guttenberg, German minister several times in INYT (27 October 2013, p. 9); Clemens Wergin in INYT (22 November 2013, p. 9) and Heribert Dieter in WSJ (1 November and 29 December 2013, p. 13). The arguments are matched in terms of the positive contribution that the solvency of Germany contributes to the EU and other regions in terms of job-creating investment.
102. Annual Economic Report 2013/14. German Council of Economic Experts. The title of the report is Against a Backward-looking Economic Policy.
103. European Economic Forecast, European Economy 7/2013, European Commission, autumn 2013.
104. OECD Economic Outlook, vol. 2013/2, OECD Publishing (Preliminary Version).
105. The figure has even more value because the US came to get a good result from growth in the second quarter 1.7%, driven by the pull of consumption, and the boom of shale gas. In the first quarter of 2013 the growth was 1.1%.
106. The strength of US consumption is remarkable. In the fourth quarter of 2013, spending on restaurants and hotels grew 10%, the biggest jump in the last 20 years. See N. Shah and S. Portlock, 'U.S. Economy Growth Starts Hit Stride 'WSJ, 31 January–2 February 2014, p. 7.
107. These are figures cited by Martin Wolff in 'Germany's strange parallel universe', FT, 25 September 2013.
108. On 22 January Eurostat established the Eurozone debt in the third quarter of 2013, at 92.7% of GDP (from 93.4% last quarter). It is the first time that it had dropped since 2007. The EU debt amounted to 86.8% of GDP (from 86.7% last quarter).
109. European Economic Forecast, European Commission, winter 2014, p. ix.
110. Christine Lagarde warned (15 March 2014) in Washington risk of deflation that would be disastrous for recovery.
111. Report quoted in an article by Paul Hannon, 'After Crisis, US Better Off than Europe', published in WSJ, 6 October 2013, p. 11.

Chapter 4 The European Central Bank and the Federal Reserve Take on the Crisis

1. Between October 2008 and May 2009, the interest rates set by the ECB declined 325 basis points to stand at 1%. After an increase which nobody understood, to 1.5% between spring and summer of 2011, the interest rate dropped back to 1%. See Papadia and Carlo Francesco Santini, Towards the European Banking Union, 2012, p. 125.
2. The ECB relaxed the requirements for assets that were given as security (collateral) of loans to financial institutions, and also in May 2009, launched the 'Covered Bond Purchase Programme (CBPP) 'acquisition bank bonds, up to EUR 60 billion (figure

reached in May 2010). See article by Antonio Millaruelo and Ana Río, 'Unconventional measures of monetary policy by the ECB throughout the crisis in the Economic Bulletin of the Bank of Spain', January 2013, p. 91.

3. E. J. Adda, op. cit., p. 273.
4. The deficit in the Eurozone rose from less than 1% in 2007 to 6% in 2010 (Ireland reached 32%). In the G-7, the national debt increased thirty points of GDP over the same period. In 2009 it exceeded 100% of GDP.
5. John Plender, 'Monetary Policy: Back under control', *Financial Times*, 11 December 2012, p. 7.
6. In discussing the advantages and disadvantages of an independent status for a central bank, see F. Papadia and C. Santini, op. cit., pp. 28 et seq.
7. Recently the minutes of the IMF of decisions on 10 May 2010 have been made public. According to them, a part of the agreement that night between Germany, France and Holland with the IMF, to commit EUR 30 billion in aid of to Greece, was that the banks in these countries wouldn't get rid of Greek debt. The three countries breached the agreement. Its banks sold Greek debt hastily so that the EUR 122 billion that had this debt were reduced by half a year later and EUR 34 billion at the end of 2013. See article by Luis Doncel, 'Berlin and Paris fail to comply with Greece' in El País, 1 February 2014, p. 17.
8. In practice only 16 billion was covered, because of the revival of the private market for covered bonds.
9. The ECB announced it would continue to accept collateral to provide liquidity to Portuguese banks for Portuguese debt, even though they didn't meet the minimum qualifying requirements. This produced a relaxation of tension in the markets.
10. For example, in the meeting I had with the Irish authorities in September 2011, I transmitted to them the favourable position of Eurobonds. The Irish government supported it.
11. Trichet at the subsequent meeting of Luxembourg finance ministers snapped at the French delegation: 'You're going to destroy the Euro', according to Neil Irwin in *The Alchemists*. Three Central Bankers and a World on Fire, 2013, p. 291.
12. The ECB reactivated in July 2011 purchases of debt on the secondary markets, likewise the provision of liquidity, reintroducing in August 2011 auctions at SS six months and a year. Millaruelo A. and A. del Río, op. cit., p. 95.
13. N. Irwin, op. cit., p. 304. The Harmonised Index of Consumer Prices in the Eurozone shows that in the crisis years (except 2008) annual inflation remained around 2%. See Domènec Ruiz Devesa, 'The European Central Bank in 2012' in *The State of the European Union*, op. cit., pp. 95 et seq.
14. Since the programme's launch in May 2010, the ECB had acquired bonds worth EUR 183 billion.
15. El País, 3 November 2011.
16. There were two liquidity auctions held in December 2011 and in February 2012, which encompassed those previously scheduled for October and December 2012. A second auction was attended by 800 entities, of which 460 were German. The auctioned amount was distributed among Italian banks (approximately EUR 260 billion), Spanish (EUR 250 billion), French (EUR 150 billion), Irish (EUR 135 billion), German (EUR 100 billion), Greeks (EUR 80 billion), Portuguese (EUR 50 billion) and others (EUR 175 billion). The large amount auctioned made Josef Joffe say that Europe was like the 'Lance Armstrong economy' (WSJ, 23 January 2013, p. 21).
17. Josep M. Bricall, *Five Essays on the Crisis*, 2013, pp. 175 et seq.
18. According to the July 2011 stress tests on European banks, the value of Greek government bonds held by commercial Greek banks was 25% of GDP in Greece; in the case of

Spanish banks it was 20% of Spanish GDP; in Portugal, 10%. However, in the German and French banks, the value of its GDP on sovereign bonds which were on their balance sheets of countries with funding problems (Greece, Portugal, Spain, Italy, Ireland) was 5%. See J. M. Bricall, op. cit., p. 181.

19. D. Millet and E. Toussaint, *AAA, Audit, Annulation, Autre Politique*, op. cit., p. 86.
20. Agreement of 29 June 2012.
21. Expansion, 24 November 2011.
22. The OECD assessed at EUR 130 billion the public funding needs of Greece, Ireland and Portugal for 2012. Italy, at EUR 400 billion. OECD, PE, 2011.
23. J. Adda, op. cit., p. 312.
24. See www.imf.org.
25. During the first half of 2012, a portion of capital movements responded to international banking operations to cover the potential risk of denomination. Cechetti in Millaruelo A. and A. del Río, op. cit., p. 96.
26. In the OTM, the ECB has no preferred creditor status, so as not to crowd out private investors. Purchases are completely sterilized by the sale of securities, so the liquidity injected is drained. (see Monthly Bulletin, ECB, September 2012). The opposition of the Bundesbank was, of course, absolute.
27. BCE, Opening Statement at Deutscher Bundestag, 24 October 2012.
28. The figure of EUR 33.9 billion (15.5%) corresponded to Greek debt; EUR 22.8 billion (10.5%), Portuguese debt, and EUR 14.2 billion (6.5%), and Irish debt. These are figures released by the ECB in the interests of maximum transparency in monetary transactions.
29. Unconventional monetary policy measures of the Eurosystem increased the balance by 150% from July 2007 to late 2012. Rather less than the growth in the respective balances of the Federal Reserve and the Bank of England.
30. M. Draghi Conference at Bocconi University (Milan, 15 November 2012) on 'the ECB's monetary policy and its transmission in the Euro area'.
31. In the second half of 2012 (September to December), countries with financial assistance programmes, as well as Italy and Spain, were receiving net capital flows of over EUR 90 billion.
32. In the past three months, the Euro was revalued by 20% against the yen; 8% against the pound sterling; and 7% against the dollar.
33. Giorgio Barba Navaretti "The Currency Weight", *Il Sole 24 Ore*, 8 February 2013, p. 8. In most, the price is more important than value added. F. Rampini, 'L'euro debole salva Italia', *La Repubblica*, 10 February 2013, p. 22.
34. In July 2012, the Euro was trading at USD 1.21. The highest exchange rate the Euro reached was at USD 1.60, in April 2008, when the financial crisis in the United States was at its peak.
35. This was not a problem for the Bundesbank. Its president, Jens Weidmann, hastened to warn European leaders before the meeting of G-20 finance ministers on 15 February that any policy designed to weaken the currency would lead to inflation.
36. In February, the Euro moves from its high of USD 1.37 to USD 1.30.
37. Statement by Mario Draghi in Frankfurt am Main, 7 March 2013.
38. Since the launch of the WTO, the interests of ten-year bonds of states and corporations has declined significantly. Neither had the ECB opened up to countries with bailout programmes already underway, such as Ireland, it is not well understood why.
40. In the USA it is easier to accept such a formula because its capital market, without the interposition of banks, plays a more important role in Europe.
41. In Spain, according to the ECB, the interest rate payable on small loans to SMEs is 2.3 points higher than the bulkier loans, which are used by large companies. Data exposed

by Mario Draghi to the Committee on Economic and Monetary Affairs of the European Parliament in Brussels, July 2013.

42. From the ECB's decision to open the hand, securitized bank loans do not have to be triple A, the demand being reduced to A.
43. In Spain, 87% of financial assets are held by banks and credit institutions; in Italy, 85%; in Greece, 96%. In the USA, by contrast, only 30% of assets are possessed by banks.
44. Hence, the IMF, in its annual assessment of the Eurozone, set as a priority area for action to clean up the balance sheets of banks. IMF Survey, 8 July 2013.
45. Matthew Dalton, 'Europe's other brake: Private-sector debt' WSJ, 16 August 2013, p. 4. The official policy in the European Union is that the deleveraging of banks should be preferably reinforcing the capital, rather than reducing the equity balance. One of the possible formulas can be converting creditors into shareholders.
46. For an extension on the financial thinking of Walter Bagehot, see N. Irwin, op. cit., pp. 28 et seq.
47. For the first time, the US Treasury after Bernanke's words sold five-year bonds at a real interest rate below zero (–0.55%). The announcement drew criticism from the American political right and the German government (Schauble) due to the danger of inflation, which did not occur, because the banks did not increase their loans to individuals. In fact, the Euro rose 1%.
48. Predominantly, between three and 10 years.
49. The FED announced it would reinvest the principal of debt assets that were maturing, to maintain its balance stable at USD 2.8 trillion, i.e., three and a half of that which had occurred when Lehman Brothers fell.
50. The objective was to lower long-term interest rates. The difference with QE2 is that in Operation Twist short-term bonds were sold, something that QE2 didn't do. Thus, the new operation was neutral from the point of view of the balance of the FED.
51. Since the programmes started buying assets from late 2008 until late 2012, the FED has accumulated USD 9 billion of shares in mortgages and more than a trillion of Treasuries long term.
52. The minutes of the FED meeting January and March 2013 showed the growing concerns of a section of it because maintenance of QE3 produced undesirable financial turmoil such as investors, with interest rates so low, being tempted to take too many risks for higher returns, with negative effects on banks exposed to such risks, as occurred in 2008. However, for most around Bernanke, it was much greater the damage done to the economy by high unemployment than the existence of such risks.
53. It was the same thought that the IMF maintained in its report on US June 2013. The FED, says the report, should be progressively abandoning the asset purchase programme to increase the resilience of the financial system.
54. These 10 countries, with Iran, sanctioned form what Goldman Sachs calls the 'Next 11' economies.
55. In May, unemployment rose a tenth, from 7.5 to 7.6%, but it was interpreted as a positive thing, because it indicated that people began to rely on finding a job and returning to join the list of jobseekers. When the FED launched QE3, unemployment was at 8.1%. This means that over 200,000 jobs were created in the month during QE3, compared to over 140,000 jobs the month before the launch.
56. Editorial, Wall Street Journal, 'Bernanke Rides the Bull', 20 June 2013, p. 16. See also Daniel Malpass, 'FED Policy Is a Drag on Recovery', WSJ, 3 June 2013, p. 16.
57. P. Krugman, 'FED's interest in recovery Seems to be tapering' in *The Irish Times*, 25 June 2013, Business Your Money, p. 1.

58. US bonds rose to 2.47% (1.6%) a month earlier. Spanish and Italian ten-year bonds also experienced increases in yields, 0.3% more (up 4.83%) in the case of Spain, and 0.28% higher (up 4.54%) for Italy. German bonds rose only 0.1% to 1.66%.
59. Some members of the FED came to the fore to clarify Bernanke's points, and appease the 'overreaction of markets'. Bill Dudley, president of the Federal Reserve Bank of New York, reiterated that future decisions of the FED would depend more on the outlook of the economy than the calendar. FT, 28 June 2013, p. 1.
60. Amar Bhidé and Edmund Phelps, 'Central Banking Needs Rethinking' WSJ, 18 July 2013, p. 16.

PART III The Legacy of the Crisis

Chapter 5 The Assault on the Welfare State

1. See Klaus Busch *et al.*, 'Eurocrisis, Austerity Policy and the European Social Model', Friedrich-Ebert-Stiftung, International Policy Analysis, February 2013.
2. Diego López Garrido, *The European Constitution*, 2005, p. 130.
3. 'Eurocrisis ...', op. cit.
4. See Dierk Hirschel, 'Beware of the German magic potion', *El País*, 30 May 2013, p. 31.
5. Sebastian Dullien, 'A German model for Europe?', European Council on Foreign Relations, July 2013, p. 3.
6. Severance pay has gone from 45–33 days per year worked with a maximum 24 months compared to 42 in the previous Socialist government regulation.
7. Diego López Garrido and Ricardo Peralta, 'An unconstitutional labour reform', El País, 8 March 2012.
8. 'Eurocrisis...', op. cit. p. 21.
9. Ibid, p. 26.
10. The remuneration of workers ccumulated between 2010 and 2012 a real cut (after inflation) of over 20% in Greece, 10% in Portugal and 6% in Spain and Ireland, compared to a rise of 1.5% in Germany (European Commission). Against this, the richest 500 in France were enriched by 25% in 2012 (Challenges, op. Cit., July 11, 2013). They represent 16% of the country's GDP, EUR 330 billion. The return to inequalities in recent years has been well exposed through compelling graphs in the work of Olivier Berruyer, *Les Faits sont Têtus*, 2013, especially pp. 145 et seq.
11. Published in Annals of Oncology, The Digital Country, 28 September 2013. Scientists especially investigated breast cancer.
12. Ben Casselman, 'Long-term jobless left out of recovery', WSJ, 4 September 2013, p. 7. The data provided by this article is illuminating, from the US Department of Labour.
13. In Ireland, Greece and Spain, the rate of long-term unemployment quadrupled between 2008 and 2012. For measures against youth unemployment, see Maria João Rodrigues, Youth unemployment, socio-economic divergences and tax capacity in the Euro area, Notre Europe, policy paper 101, November 2013. See also Education and Training Monitor 2013, European Commission.
14. In Spain, wages fell in real terms by 0.6% in the second quarter of 2013. In Portugal, they fell 0.10%. In Greece (in the first three quarters) they were down 10.1%. In Italy and Ireland wages fell 0.5% in the second quarter of 2013. In Germany, they rose 2%. American employees also suffered a decline in real income, according to the Bureau of Labor Statistics.
15. A. Bolaños, El País, 11 August 2013, p. 17.

16. Study cited in the article by Steve Johnson, 'Capital gobbles labour's share, but victory is empty', FT, 4 October 2013, p. 3.
17. Oxfam Report no. 174, September 2013, p. 13. Poverty in Italy in 2010 reached its highest rate in the last 16 years, according to the National Institute of Statistics of Italy (12.7% of the population lived in relative poverty, and 6.8% in absolute poverty, a figure that has doubled during the crisis).
18. See, for Spain, the annual report of Caritas, filed 10 October 2013. Data on average income of Spanish households are INE, Living Conditions Survey (LCS), 20 November 2013.
19. See Abraham F. Lowenthal, 'The US in the early 21st century: decline or renewal?' Real Instituto Elcano, 20 November 2013.
20. According to the World Bank's scorecard, the proportion of families in developing countries under the extreme poverty line (estimated at USD 1.25 per person per day) has decreased from 52% in 1980 to 43% in 1990 to 34% in 1999 and 21% in 2010 (in sub-Saharan Africa it was 49% in 2010). The same happened in child health and mortality. See Jeffrey Sachs, 'The end of poverty, soon', IHT, 26 September 2013.
21. The list of billionaires Forbes magazine is led by the USA, with 442, followed by China (122 billionaires from zero 1995), and Russia (110). Germany is the fourth country in billionaires (58), followed by India (55), Brazil (46), Turkey (44), Hong Kong (39) and the UK (38). Forbes uses a different approach to UBS on what it considers large fortunes.
22. Oxfam Report, op. cit., p. 16. For the evolution of inequality in developed countries, see Gottshalk and Smeeding, 'Empirical evidence on income inequality in industrialized countries', in Handbook of Income Distribution, 2000. Quoted in Taxing Working Families, A distributional Analysis, OECD Tax Policy Studies, no. 12, p. 24, 2005. The Oxfam report filed on 20 January, then delivered in Davos, contained data as chilling as that 1% of the population (the richest) holds half of world wealth; or that the 85 richest people have as much money as the poorest 3.570 million in the world. See also the recent book by Jean-Louis Servan-Schreiber, a very descriptive title: *Pourquoi les riches ont gagné*, 2014.
23. Stiglitz theorem on the distribution of income is explained in the work together with Mauro Gallegati (Universita Politecnica della Marche), presented in May 2013 at a workshop organized in a seminar in Rome by SIEDS (Societa Italiana di Economia). See Likewise P. Krugman, 'Why inequality matters' *International New York Times* (INYT), 17 December 2013, p. 9.
24. Some of these ideas were discussed at the Brookling Institute in November 2012, during the presentation of a book entitled *Inequality in America*, quoted by Chrystia Freeland, 'Inequality as a threat to growth', IHT, 30 November 2012, p. 2.
25. Demonstration of repression—shameful for European culture—is the Berlusconi-Bossi Act in which assisting an immigrant about to die at sea is punishable as a crime.
26. El País, 22 September 2013.
27. Data from Thomas Piketty and Emmanuel Saez, cited by Paul Krugman, 'The recovery of the rich', *El País*, 15 September 2013, 'Business', p. 21. Krugman warns how wealth in this case has little to do with culture. High income comes from the financial sector.
28. Paul Krugman, 'Free to be hungry' IHT, 24 Sept. 2013, p. 7. Paul Krugman has insisted in his columns, with particular emphasis in recent months, on the problem of inequality. I will cite a few: 'The populist imperative' INYT, 25–26 January 2014, p. 7; 'The rich unworthy' El País, 26 January 2014, 'Business', p. 3; 'Enemies of the poor' INYT, 14 January 2014, p. 7; 'The war over poverty' INYT, 11–12 January 2014, p. 7.

29. The Republicans have control of the Senate after the forthcoming mid-term elections of 2014, Obama will not be able to sign legislation regarding educational plans: universal access at preschool level and reform of higher education.
30. According to the US government, 50.5 million Americans are on Medicaid; 46.5 million in Medicare; 52 million on Social Security; 7.5 million on unemployment insurance, and 44.6 million in food programmes. These are the main programmes of social spending, which in 2010 accounted for 66% of the federal budget (in 1965 they accounted for 25%).
31. President Obama has suspended this duty for one year.
32. 'The Road to a Downgrade' WSJ, 29 July 2011, p. 16.

Chapter 6 Debt Crisis and Tax Evasion

1. Op. Cit., p. 9.
2. Jacques Sapir, *Faut-il sortir de l'euro?* 2010, p. 95.
3. See Alen Mattich, 'Investors Go Big in Europe Debt' WSJ, 1 October 2013, p. 15.
4. Eurostat, Euroindicators, 153/2013, October 2013. National debt in France is 92% of GDP; in Italy, 130%; in Greece, 160%. Outside the Eurozone, the debt at the end of 2013 in the UK was 93.6% of GDP; US, 108%; and Japan, 245%, where the bulk of the obligations is held by persons or domestic institutions. As for countries with bailout programmes, the debt of Cyprus gained 10.8 points, that of Greece, 8.6 points, and Portugal, 3.8 points. See Corsetti G., K. Kuester, A. Meier and G. Müller, 'Sovereign Risk and Belief-Driven Fluctuations in the Euro Area', IMF Working Paper, November 2013.
5. The IMF believes that 50% of corporate debt in Portugal, 40% of Spanish and 30% of Italian companies is comprised of debt on which interest repayments cannot be met. They cannot invest and grow. The Economist calls them 'zombie companies'. See 'Europe's other debt crisis', *The Economist*, 26 October 2013.
6. 'Dettes: la zone euro n'est pas tirée d'affaire', *Le Monde*, 25 October 2013, 'Economie et Entreprise', p. 3.
7. Elmar Altvater, 'The plagues of capitalism' in Financial, Economic and Systemic Crisis, op. cit., p. 137.
8. Paul de Grauwe, 'Pool debt, or face dangerous upheavals across Europe', Spring 2013.
9. Paul de Grauwe, 'The Creditors nations rule in the Eurozone', in The Future of Europe's Economy. Disaster or deliverance, Centre for European Reform, September 2013, pp. 19–22.
10. See the work of Ashoka Mody, former deputy director of the IMF, published by the think tank Bruegel in November 2013. Quoted in Gabriele Steinhauser, 'Flawed European Integration Risks More Divisions' WSJ, 22 October 2013, p. 4. See also the more complex work, a restructuring proposal by Daniel Alpert in his excellent *The Age of Oversupply*, 2013, pp. 191–193.
11. In an interview published in *Les Echos*, the 17 October 2011, the French Minister for the Civil Service, François Sauvadet said there has to be a 'redefinition of the perimeter of a modern state', referring, of course, to the unfailing aim of reducing public expenditure.
12. See in this respect the enlightening editorial of *The Times*: 'The Art of the Possible' (10 October 2013, p. 30), which praises the cultural change which has occurred because for the first time since the Second World War, 'a government has come to power with a mandate to spend less'.
13. See Bert Brys, Wage income tax reforms and changes in tax burdens: 2000–2009, OECD Taxation Working Papers, no. 10, 2010, pp. 24–25.

14. See Vanessa Houlder, Top rate tax cut defies global current, FT, 10 October 2013.
15. World Economic and Financial Surveys, Fiscal Monitor, 'Taxing Times', October 2013, International Monetary Fund.
16. This is Eurostat data, the 2013 edition of the publication Taxing Funds in the European Union. In Spain, revenues in 2010 were 32.1% of GDP, and in 2011, 31.4%. For a detailed study of the evolution of taxation in the EU until 2009: Ruiz-Huerta Agúndez, Garcimartín, Lopez and Rodriguez, Tax reform trends: towards a European, 2011 taxation.
17. See Graham Bowley, 'Tax debate pits big firms against small', *New York Times*, 25–26 May 2013, p. 11. In February 2014 an interesting project proposed by Republican Congressman Dave Camp was heavily criticized by private equity industry lobbyists, and which consisted of a tax increase on their earnings (from 23.8 to 35 met %).
18. Olivier Passet, 'Tax Concurrence in Europe: the Relaunch of Hostilities' Xerfi Synthèse, December 2013, pp. 12 and ss. In Austria, Finland and Germany, there are lower rates for SMEs in corporation tax. Chan Woon Nam, 'Comparison of reduced corporate tax rate in the EU, CESifo Forum, Spring 2013, p. 70.
19. For all see Piketty, Saez and Stantcheva, 'Optimal Taxation of Top Labor Incomes: A Tale of Three Elasticities' MBER, Working Paper 17616 (Cambridge, Massachusetts: National Bureau of Economic Research).
20. Eurosystem's Household Finance and Consumption Survey (Household Finance and Consumption Network, 2013). Quoted in 'Taxing Times' op. cit., p. 39.
21. 'Taxing Times' op. cit., p. 35.
22. Perhaps for that reason, and especially rising citizen protests against tax increases, Prime Minister Ayrault announced a complete rethinking of the French tax system, through a 'global debate' (November 2013). France, in contrast to its high taxation, doesn't withhold tax at origin, which reduces the taxation power of the state.
23. The low tax burden in Spain is compatible with it as it is one of the countries with the highest taxation for social security contributions paid by firms.
24. See a favourable increase in the tax burden in Japan in Takatoshi Ito, 'Japan must be brave—it is time to put up taxes', FT, 10 September 2013, p. 9. Against tax increases was Hiroko Tabuchi, 'Economists say a rise in sales tax may stifle Japan' IHT, 16 September 2013, p. 19. Abe's stimulus policy expressed in that of the USD 51 billion in investment in 2014, two-thirds come from tax increases.
25. Calculations by finance minister Chidambaram were that full tax reform would entail an additional income of 180 million rupees.
26. Credit Suisse estimated global wealth in 2011 to be USD 231 trillion, including financial and non-financial assets. James S. Henry, 'The price of off-shore revisited', Tax Justice Network, July 2012. According to Oxfam, tax havens that are legally under EU jurisdiction treasure EUR 9.5 trillion.
27. Friedrich Schneider, The Shadow Economy in Europe, Visa Europe, 2013.
28. It is a calculated by the most important Italian financial newspaper, *Il Sole 24 Ore*, from the ISTAT data given on the economy, 11 February 2013, pp figure. 1 and ss.
29. *El Mundo*, 19 August 2012, p. 37.
30. José Luis Escario, *Tax Havens: The Black Holes of the Global Economy*, 2011, pp. 96 et seq. Escario recommended a pan-European register of trusts. See fourth edition of the OECD Benchmark Definition of Foreign Direct Investment. Cited in OECD, Addressing Base Erosion and Profit Shifting, 2013, pp. 17 and 22.
31. The exact figures are contained in OECD, op. cit., p. 18. See table on classification of tax havens by the level of opacity in J. L. Escario, op. cit., pp. 78–79.
32. James S. Henry, op. cit., pp. 12–13. See also Nicholas Shaxson, *Treasure Islands. Uncovering the Damage of Offshore Banking and Tax Havens*, 2011.

33. It is an instructive article by C. Forelle and M. Stevis 'Money-Laundering Distrust Stalls Europe's Latest Bailout' published in WSJ, 6 March 2013, pp. 14–15.
34. It is a typical brokerage business. 90% of exports from developing countries disappear into the 'black hole of Geneva'. Why? Because there is total financial opacity and because there are very low taxes. This explains that between 2007 and 2010, developing countries have been able to lose up to EUR 578 billion in trade conducted through Switzerland. A higher figure than that devoted to development aid. Alex Prats, 'A black hole in Geneva' Blogs of El País, 16 May 2013.
35. Switzerland, followed by Hong Kong and Singapore, according to the 2013 report by the Boston Consulting Group's Global Wealth. See article by M. C. Kurapovna, 'Private Banking is Alive and Well in Switzerland', WSJ, 15–17 November 2013, p. 16.
36. This was recognized by Eveline Widmer-Schlumpf, Finance Minister and rotating president of the Swiss government (Federal Council). See the discussion of Julia Werdiger, 'Tradition of Switzerland as a US tax haven nears its end', IHT, 31 August–1 September 2013, p. 8.
37. Hervé Falciani is a former employee of HSBC in Geneva. He gave information to the police that enabled tax inspectors in France and Spain to pursue hundreds of tax evaders. His extradition was rejected by Spain in May 2013. The Swiss Federal Council agreed in principle, to help tax investigations from the data stolen by employees of Swiss banks. But in October 2013, it retracted under pressure from the right wing parties, banks and the Administrative Tribunal.
38. In April 2013, the International Consortium of Investigative Journalists, based in Washington, issued 2.5 million files detailing accounts in offshore banks opened by large fortunes and companies, mainly in the British Virgin Islands, Cook Islands and Singapore. See the discussion of Raphael Minder 'Swiss brace for scrutiny on bank secrecy', IHT, 24 May 2013, pp. 1 and 4.
39. From August 2008 to August 2009, public aid received by the 21 largest private banks was, in total, USD 393 billion in loans; USD 939 billion guaranteed toxic assets and USD 592 billion capital injections. 'The Price of Offshore Revisited', p. 33.
40. James S. Henry, op. cit., pp. 8, 19, 32 et seq. The loss of tax revenue is also produced in developing countries. They may be losing between USD 120 and 160 billion each year in tax revenue lost by evasion of taxes on anonymous wealth. It is more than all development aid coming from the OECD countries.
41. Interestingly, the OECD, which has been working on and trying to circumvent tax evasion and tax shelters, do not have any on their wish list. By just shamelessly collaborating with some kind of information, 'uncooperative jurisdictions' (as a euphemism) stop automatically being so for the OECD, which is what happened.
42. Catherine Boss, François Pilet and Titus Plattner, in their article 'Avocats suisses, levez-vous!' (Le Monde, 9 April 2013, p. 18), tells how the lawyer Peter Hafter has participated in assembling some of the largest fortunes in Europe.
43. The US tax system encourages investment more abroad than in the USA. Floyd Norris, 'Apple Finds a new dodge against taxes' IHT, 3 May 2013, p. 18.
44. In 2011, another unit of Ireland-based Apple, Apple Sales International, which sells iPhones, iPads and other products to distributors outside the US, had revenue of USD 22 billion, for which it paid the paltry sum of 10 million dollars in taxes, according to research by US Senate Representatives, a ratio of 0.05%.
45. Floyd Norris, 'Tax System hands firms carte blanche', IHT, 24 May 2013, p. 20.
46. M. Jiménez, El País, 31 October 2013. Jesús González, El País, 24 November 2013, p. 23.
47. See discussion of J. Ford, S. Gainsbury and V. Houlder, 'The Great Tax Fudge' in FT, 21 June 2013, p. 7. The title of the article makes a pun on fudge, which has a double meaning in English: 'sweet' and 'avoid the problem.'

48. See articles by Jamie Smith in FT, dated 6 February 2013 and 22 May 2013.
49. See 'Adobe gets creative with Ireland's tax rules' in FT, 13 September 2013, p. 15.
50. We recommend reading the diary of the sessions of the Joint Commission for the Spanish EU, session of 16 May 2013, wherein the content of the meeting of the European Council of 22 May 2013 was discussed on evasion and tax avoidance.
51. OECD Action Plan on Base Erosion and Profit Sifting, 2013.
52. 'Report on the fight against tax fraud, tax evasion and tax havens', 2 May 2013, p. 20.
53. The Joint Committee for the European Union (meeting of 21 January 2014) ruled favourably on the initiative of the Commission. The opinion, of which I was a rapporteur, reads:

> Multinational companies take advantage of the different existing regulation of corporate tax in the Union. In some countries, the interests of corporate debt are tax deductible. Meanwhile, in other countries, income a company has as interest on loans made to another are considered dividends, not taxable. So called 'hybrid loans'. Thus, a single transfer of funds is considered debt (the payer) in some countries and as the capital (the beneficiary) in others. And in both cases, taken out of the taxable income …
>
> The way to solve this problem the Commission in this proposal has been to force the state to which the payments will not be exempt from taxation (they can't qualify as deductible gains capital) if the State from which these payments come has deducted corporation tax when considered as financial costs (debt) of the payer company …
>
> This legislative proposal is ultimately an example of how the objectives thereof are not possible from the individual perspective of each State. It is also a sign that these objectives can only be achieved fully with a European tax harmonization of direct taxation, to avoid unfair competition among partner states of the Union and between multinational and national companies. Juncker came to accept this harmonization in November 2014.

54. 'Common Consolidated Corporate Tax Base' (CCCTB), in the terminology of the Plan of Action of the OECD.
55. Vanessa Houlder, 'Call for tax reform as Dutch lure corporate', FT, 29 April 2013, p. 1; Matt Steinglass, 'Dutch reform efforts focus on letterbox companies', FT, 29 April 2013, p. 2.
56. The US federal deficit in 2009 and 2010 exceeded one trillion dollars for the first and second time in history. According to Johnson and Kwak, this was due in part to the wars in Afghanistan and Iraq, but more important was the financial crisis that triggered the recession, which reduced tax revenues and increased social spending. Furthermore, the deficit was created by the incomprehensible tax cuts in 2001 and 2003, which were not accompanied by a decrease in expenses. S. Johnson and J. Kwak, White House Burning, 2012, op. cit., p. 8.
57. In 2010 and 2011, being Secretary of State for the European Union, I published articles in the newspaper *El País* on this topic. In the first one (4 August 2010), and I apologize for self-citation, I said:

> [...] since a few years ago the budgets of the most developed countries (OECD) have suffered fiscal failure. This has led to a starring role in public finances of these countries, such as the 'structural' and chronic indebtedness, i.e., the growth of sovereign debt. The blowing up of this debt has been about to destroy the Euro, the Euro area and therefore much of the European project'.

In the second of the articles, published a year later (4 October 2011), I stated: 'This is the debate today in the United States and Spain. The discussion of taxes. Without progressive taxes there will not be a fair way out of the crisis, nor will growth and employment be increased'. Diego López Garrido, 'The Welfare State: the return of taxation', *El País*, 4 August 2010; and 'The fiscal about-turn of the European Left', *El País*, 4 October 2011.

58. Katharine Pistor, 'La Dette contre la démocratie', *Le Monde*, 26 October 2013, p. 8.
59. Diego López Garrido, Constitutional Reform and Budgetary Stability. Article 135 of the Spanish Constitution, 2013, p. 15.
60. 'Taxing Times' op. cit., Executive Summary, p. 3.
61. Quoted in *Le Monde*, Journal Electronique.
62. In the case of Spain, the effect of an equivalent adjustment to 1% of annual GDP reduces by 0.5% the GDP, if financed with public revenue, and 1.1% if it is simply based on spending cuts. Quoted in *El País*, 28 October 2013.
63. Fiscal adjustment in an uncertain world, *Fiscal Monitor*, April 2013, International Monetary Fund, p. vii.
64. A team of researchers at the Swedish Institute for Social Research (SOFI), after analyzing welfare programmes of 18 OECD countries over 65 years (1930–1995) has concluded that the best way to organize these programmes is to provide universal coverage for the entire population. It applies to health, education, dependency, family, pensions, unemployment and so on. It strongly reduces poverty and demands, of course, a considerable fiscal effort greater than that required by welfare systems that only serve the poor, according to the American model. Quoted by Inés Calzada 'Is the legitimacy of the Welfare State at risk?' Eldiario.es, 'Public Agenda', 20 December 2013. In the latter article, it refers to the book of Bro Rothstein, *Just Institutions Matter*, which states that one of the conditions in order for the public to accept fiscally costly social programmes is the confidence that they have that all citizens pay taxes honestly.
65. *The Cost of Rights*: Why Liberty Depends on Taxes, 2011. The first edition entitled *The Cost of Rights* was published in 1999. The sentence of the World Bank President is taken from *El País*. Forum Latin America, 10 October 2013.
66. The IMF, in its report on Fiscal Surveillance 2013, said that, for most advanced economies, 'the greatest potential is in indirect taxes'. Michael Keen, director of fiscal affairs IMF recommends Spain expand the VAT base. He also believes that Spain has room to raise taxes on higher incomes.
67. According to data provided by Piketty, Saez and Landais, the richer French pay less taxes. In *Pour une révolution fiscale. Un impôt sur le revenu pour le siècle XXIème*, 2011. See Jean Gadrey, 'Impôts, fabrication du' ras-le-bol 'realite et de l'injustice' in *Le Monde* Diplomatique, 6 December 2013, pp. 12–13.
68. Quoted by Chrystia Freeland on 'Taxes, titans and the greater good' IHT, 3 May 2013, p. 2.

Chapter 7 The Hegemony of Financial Power

1. M. Albert, *Capitalism vs. Capitalism*, op cit., pp. 186 et seq.
2. Durant, op. cit., p. 86.
3. Ibid, p. 99.
4. Josep M. Bricall, *Five essays on the crisis*, op. cit., 2013, p. 70.
5. Ryan Tracy, 'FED Eyes Financial System's Weak Link', WSJ, 2 December 2013, p. 6.
6. *International New York Times*, 22 November 2013, p. 8. J.P. Morgan is also involved in the manipulation of the exchange rate and in the case of 'London Whale', for which it agreed to pay USD 920 million. INYT See 'J.P. Morgan deal may not be so punitive' 23 October 2013, p. 18, and Floyd Norris's article 'How a bank missed signs of vast

fraud', 10 January 2014, p. 19. The *Wall Street Journal* has stated a position on behalf of J.P. Morgan. It has done in several editorials: 'Robbery at J.P. Morgan', 3 September 2013, p. 12; 'J.P. Morgan and Its Victims', 21 November 2013, p. 12.

7. The Bank Secrecy Act, a 1970 law that requires banks to alert authorities of illegal activities appearance was applied. J.P. Morgan must pay compensation to victims of the Madoff fraud. For relationships between J.P. Morgan and Madoff see also Charles Ferguson, Inside Job, Barcelona, 2012, pp. 227 et seq.
8. Barclays was not penalized because it uncovered the cartel to the Commission.
9. UBS escaped punishment for revealing to the Commission the existence of collusion.
10. An example is the fine of USD 1.9 billion imposed on HSBC, the great British bank, for money laundering, which made it easier for Mexican drug cartels to move their money flows.
11. D. Schäfer, A. Ross and D. Strauss made a documented study of the possible manipulation of the global foreign exchange market in 'The big five', FT, 13 November 2013, p. 7.
12. For more extensive information, see the Life and Arts supplement of the *Financial Times*, December 7–8, 2013.
13. The American judiciary has contributed to the 'unveiling' of the pre-crisis years, full of fraudulent financial practices.
14. Quoted in 'Madoff trustee seeks opportunity to re-sue banks' The Global Edition of the *New York Times*, p. 17.
15. See 'Federal probe targets banks over bonds' WSJ, 9 January 2014, p. 1.
16. In the US, the difference between saving and spending of households reversed in less than a year: –2.1% of GDP in the last quarter of 2007 to 6.7% of GDP in the third quarter of 2008.
17. Quoted in D. Millet and E. Toussaint, Crise de la dette: la seule façon d'en sortir, op. cit., p. 50.
18. COM (2012) 0778. These amounts include the nationalization of Northern Rock by the British government in 2008.
19. Details of the Bank of International Settlements (BIS).
20. The most relevant are well collected and systematized by Alan S. Blinder in op. cit., Chapters 10 and 11, who we shall continue to follow in this section.
21. The proposal of the Treasury in June 2009 took the title 'Financial Regulatory Reform: A New Foundation: Rebuilding Financial Supervision and Regulation'.
22. The Dodd-Frank Act divided the Congress. In the House of Representatives the vote was 237 in favour and 192 against, and in the Senate, 60 in favour and 39 against, including in each house only three votes for from members of the Republican Party. It was the clearest partisan vote ever recorded in a major law on the financial system. Blinder, ibid., p. 306.
23. The factual application of this rule is complicated because it is difficult to discern when a bank is doing proprietary trading for a customer or for itself.
24. The Dodd-Frank Act gave 18 months to the Government Accountability Office (G-10) to make its report, and three years to the Securities and Exchange Commission (SEC).
25. The most important regulators in the US, and Treasury and the Federal Reserve are: the Office of the Comptroller of the Currency (OCC); the Financial Deposit Insurance Corporation (FDIC); the Securities and Exchange Commission (SEC); the Commodity Futures Trading Commission (CFTC); and the recent Consumer Financial Protection Bureau (CFPB), whose first president, Richard Cordray, did not take office until January 2012. In November 2010, Bernanke created within the Federal Reserve, the Office of Policy and Studies on Financial Stability, consisting of a group of renowned economists to advise the FED in its most important decisions, and especially the Federal Open

Market Committee (FOMC). This body, composed of the governors and regional FED presidents, adopts measures on interest rates and bond purchases.

26. The Senate tried to hinder all appointments of Obama to oversee the process in each of the regulatory authorities.
27. The New York Stock Exchange took the adoption of the Volcker Rules calmly. In Tuesday's session on 10 December, shares of Morgan Stanley rose by 1.5% and Goldman Sachs, by 1.4%.
28. Quoted in 'US Starts New Era in Bank Regulation', WSJ, 11 December 2013, p. 18.
29. See Randall S. Kroszner and Robert J. Schiller, Reforming US financial markets, 2011, p. 15.
30. Pricewaterhouse Coopers (in July 2012) evaluated at EUR 1.19 billion—of which 1 billion corresponded to the Eurozone—the dubious debts in the assets of European banks in 2012. It meant a multiplication by 2.3 since 2008. 60% of these loans are concentrated in Germany (EUR 179 billion), Spain (EUR 167 billion), Ireland and Italy. Quoted in 'The réforme de l'Union économique et monétaire: l'ambition politique on the fracture' Questions d'Europe, no. 297, 16 December 2013, p. 2 Fondacion Robert Schuman.
31. The initial position of the Commission expressed in its communication to the European Parliament and the Council: 'Roadmap towards a banking union', 12 September 2012, COM (2012) 510 final.
32. 'Proposal for a Regulation of the European Parliament and of the Council establishing uniform standards for resolving credit institutions and certain investment firms, established procedure in the context of a Single Resolution Mechanism and One Fund Banking Resolution and Regulation (EU) No. modified. 1.093/2010 of the European Parliament and the Council. Brussels', 10 July 2013. COM (2013) 520 final.
33. Tom Fairless, 'The unintended drawbacks of Europe's banking union', WSJ, 6–8 December 2013, p. 4. See also 'The Banking Union: progress and uncertainties 2014' A. Berges, E. Ontiveros and F. J. Valero, Working Paper No. Opex. 75/2014, Alternatives Foundation.
34. Economic and Financial Affairs, 10 December 2013, 17983/13, Press S96.
35. Pierre Moscovici, 'L'Union bancaire est une avancée politique pour tous les peuples d'Europe', *Le Monde*, 21 December 2013, p. 15.
36. According to the ECB, the states of the Eurozone kept in the bond market a maximum valuation of 6.5 million euros, equivalent to 70% of annual production in that area. See 'IMF wants investors to share pain of bailouts', 27 November 2013, pp. 1 and 15.
37. There is an interesting analysis of the Liikanen Report in the work of Juan Díez Gibson, op. cit.
38. In early January 2014, by leaks to the press, something more was learned about the idea of Commissioner Barnier—not by the Commission itself as a body—on the separation of activities with or without 'systemic risk' within a credit entity. It is a softer model in many elements than the Liikanen Report model. See A. Barker, 'Europe set to ease reform on bank splits', FT, 6 January 2014, p. 1.
39. See Philip Stafford, 'Fears grow over rules on derivatives trading', FT, 19 December 2013, p. 24.
40. The directive will reduce the frequency of transactions, negotiations and illuminate somewhat the dark transactions without any publicity so far, despite being conducted among institutional investors. It is hoped that this directive on financial markets and instruments will come into force in late 2016. Too long to keep its transformative effects.
41. See Roubini and Mihm, Economic Crisis, op. cit, pp. 204 et seq. André Lévy-Lang, *Il faut maîtriser la finance*, 2012, pp. 53 et seq.

42. Regulation 575/2013 of the European Parliament and of the Council of 26 June 2013 on prudential requirements for credit institutions and investment services companies; and Directive 2013/36 of the European Parliament and of the Council of 26 June 2013 on access to the activity of credit institutions and the prudential supervision of credit institutions and investment services companies. This legislation has been transposed into Spanish law by Royal Decree-Law 14/2013, of 29 November.
43. James Saft, 'Banks win, but growth suffer' IHT, 9 January 2013, p. 16.
44. Anat Admati and Martin Hellwig, *The Banker's New Clothes*, 2013, pp. 6 and ss. The authors explain the difference between 'required reserves' (ratio of cash deposits) and the 'minimum capital requirements' that are required by Basel III and the national or European legislation.
45. In July 2013, the Federal Deposit Insurance Corporation, the FED and the Comptroller of the Currency proposed to increase the ratio of capital to bank holding companies owning up to 5% and up to 6% in deposit banks within such companies. This is to increase the protection of taxpayers.
46. The FED estimated that banks subject to the new standard (with over 50 billion in assets) will add about USD 200 billion in assets of higher quality, for a total of two trillion dollars. R. Tracy and M. R. Crittenden, 'FED sets to bolster safety net at banks', WSJ, 25–27 October 2013, pp. 1 and 26.
47. The three main Irish banks' assets totalled 400% of GDP at the time of shock. The three major French banks had assets worth nearly three times the GDP.
48. Data from Bureau van Dijk Electronic Publishing Inc, quoted in 'Banking Business: Complexity Cubed' WSJ, 12–14 April 2013, p. 24.
49. Quoted in J. Saft, op. cit, INYT, 3 October 2013, p. 19.
50. On 4 November 2011, the Financial Stability Board (FSB) Basel published a list of 'Systemic ally Relevant Financial Institutions' SIF, by its English name). They are: Bank of America, Bank of China, Bank of New York Mellon, Banque Populaire CoE, Barclays, BNP Paribas, Citigroup, Commerzbank, Credit Suisse, Deutsche Bank, Dexia, Goldman Sachs Group Crédit Agricole, HSBC, ING Bank , J.P. Morgan Chase, Lloyds Banking Group, Mitsubishi UFJ FG, Mizuho FG, Morgan Stanley, Nordea, Royal Bank of Scotland, Santander, Société Générale, State Street, Sumitomo Mitsui FG, UBS, Unicredit Group, Wells Fargo.
51. WSJ, 20 January 2014, pp. 1 and 22. The other reasons for the increase in bank profits are less competition and the quantitative easing tranches, which have watered the financial system with liquidity.
52. In Spain, credit narrowed to EUR 45 billion in 2013, in the six major Spanish banks. However, deposits increased 5% in the first two semesters. Cinco Días, 1 November 2013, p. 19.
53. According to the European Commission, one-fifth of the short-term debt issued by governments and European companies is held by the money-market funds and 38% of the debt issued by banks. They give more interest than these depositor investors, and allow them immediate liquidity. The Commission proposes that these funds maintain capital reserves equal to 3% of their investments. Within the Union, there are divided opinions. France and Germany, in favour of regulation. Ireland and Luxembourg against. No prizes for guessing why.
54. Many European companies have decided and contact directly with private investors to raise funds at a cheaper price. Financial jargon calls it private placement market, which is already widespread in the US, where they go to look for money in European companies.

55. Jean-Michel Naulot, in his excellent book *Crise financière. Pourquoi les gouvernements rien ne font rien*, 2013, p. 42 et seq., is an exemplary exposure of all the most speculative financial innovations.
56. Ibid., p. 51.
57. Such transactions occur increasingly in markets without advertising, for that reason called 'dark pools'. The European Union will control this 'hiring in the dark' by tightening the Directive on markets in financial instruments. The agreement is that such contracts may not exceed 8% of those produced on European exchanges. Now they are estimated to account for 11%, and developed mainly in London. In the US, according to some reports, hiring outside official stock markets are 37% of those produced in the public markets. Quoted in 'Pressure grows for limits on dark pools', FT, 22 November 2013, p. 26.
58. The two business areas of derivatives that have continued to grow, the foreign exchange (forex) and interest rates are today dominated by 'over the counter' operations (OTC) by 50%, while banks are declining in the field.
59. The IMF raised the possibility in November 2012 in an internal report on capital movements, IMF Staff Paper, 'The liberalization and management of capital flows. An international view', published on 14 November 2012. Quoted by Jean-Michel Naulot, op. cit., p. 83.
60. In a survey by the consulting Kinetia Partners, 97% of financial services professionals thought in November 2013 that regulations were not enough to prevent another crash in financial markets. FT, 25 December 2013, p. 17. The pessimistic views of the British Prime Minister Gordon Brown were aired in an article in the *New York Times International*, which indicates the persistence of the problems that led to the crash, and the apathy of the EU. 'Stumbling toward the next crash' INYT, 19 December 2013, p. 12.
61. These few extremely useful pages Jean Michel Naulot dedicates to the necessary reforms for preventing speculation, and better distribution of credit. In op. cit., ch. 4 pp. 194–274. One of the reforms that has surfaced as possible in recent months is the proposal to cap abusive commissions by ATMs and credit cards.
62. The UK Financial Services Authority (FSA), in its report 'A regulatory response to the Global Banking Crisis', 2009, pp. 131 et seq., Echoed the bank 'ultra-activity' as the source of the crisis, and proposes the creation of 'restricted banks' (narrow banks), whose functions are essentially giving loans and payment services, while investment activity could only be carried out against 'safe' assets. It would be the way to avoid the too-big-to-fail scenario once more. Quoted by Gallino, op. cit., p. 284.
63. A. Admati and M. Hellwig, op. cit., pp. 222 et seq.
64. Gallino examines the strengths and weaknesses of the Dodd-Frank Act in relation to the essential objectives of the reforms necessary, in his judgment, in financial markets. Op. Cit., pp. 287–289.
65. Let me quote the statement supporting the tax on financial transactions, and the work of the European Commission's proposal, which I formulated as Secretary of State for the European Union in November 2010. *Cinco Días*, 27 October 2010.
66. Document COM (2011) 594, 'Proposal for a Council Directive on a common system of financial transaction tax and amending Directive 2008/7/EC'.
67. According to the Commission, in 2020, the share of EU ITF intended to constitute 23% of equity.
68. Formalized in the Ecofin of 9 October 2012, in Luxembourg. The initial Commission proposal was withdrawn and replaced by the 14 February 2013 one, Document COM (2013) 71 final, 'Proposal for a Council Directive establishing enhanced cooperation in the field of financial transactions tax'.

69. See C. Bastasin, 'Una tassa politica per la fiducia', *Il Sole 24 Ore*, 10 October 2012, p. 12.
70. See Larry Elliott, 'Bill Gates adds to his weight to case for Robin Hood tax', *The Guardian*, 3 November 2011, p. 28.
71. See Doc. 13017, 'Rapport de la Commission des questions sociales, de la santé et du developpement durable', presented by Hermine Naghdalyan.
72. K. Rogoff',Oublier la taxe sur les transactions financières' *Les Echos*, 17 October 2011, p. 15. Other economists have conducted technical reviews of the difficulty of discriminating by the monitoring body which trading activities are desirable and undesirable which not.
73. Articles—with very explicit headlines—published on the same day that the Commission presented its proposal for directives: R. Barley, 'Europe's FTT: A tax too far', WSJ, 15–17 February 2013. The *Wall Street Journal* editorial entitled artfully 'Europe Taxes the World', 15–17 February 2013. *The Economist*: 'Bin it. Plans for a transactions tax ought to be dropped', 23 February 2013.
74. S. Castle, 'British businesses bridle at planned EU tax on interbank transactions' IHT, 3 May 2013. A detailed critique of ITF from the UK can be seen in the report by London Economics: The effects of a financial transaction tax on European households' savings, City of London Corporation, February 2014.
75. These raucous demonstrations technical—not supported on a technical basis—were made by Noyer in a long interview in the *Financial Times*, 28 October 2013, pp. 1 and 3.
76. R. Atkins, 'ECB offers to recast "Robin Hood tax" amid fears over market impact', FT, 27 May 2013, p. 1.

Bibliography

Adda, E. J. 2004. *La mondialisation de l'économie. De la genèse à la crise*. París: Éditions de La Decouverte.

Admati, A. and Hellwig, M. 2013. *The Banker's New Clothes*. Oxford/New Jersey: Princeton University Press.

Albert, M. 1993. *Capitalism vs. Capitalism. New York: Four Walls Eight Windows.*

Alpert, D. 2013. *The Age of Oversupply*. London: Penguin.

Alvater, E. 2010. *Las plagas del capitalismo* [The plagues of capitalism], in S. Amin, E. Altwater, F. Morin and P. Gowan, *Crisis financiera, económica, sistémica*, [Financial, Economic and Systemic Crisis]. Madrid: Maia Editores.

Atkins, R. 2013. ECB offers to recast 'Robin Hood' tax amid fears over market impact. *Financial Times*, 27 May.

Attali, J. 2009. *La crise et après?* París: Fayard.

Barba Navaretti, G. 2013. Chi dovrà pagare il conto del supereuro. *Il Sole 24 Ore*, 8 February.

Barker, A. 2014. Europe set to soften bank split reforms. *Financial Times*, 6 January.

Barley, R. 2013. Europe's FTT: A tax too far?, *Wall Street Journal*, 15–17 February.

Bastasin, C. 2012. Una tassa politica per la fiducia. *Il Sole 24 Ore*, 10 October.

Bernanke Rides the Bull. *Wall Street Journal*, 20 June, 2013.

Berger, R. 2014. El modelo de negocio de Alemania, *El País*, 29 January.

Berges, A., Ontiveros, E. and Valero, F. J. 2014. *La Unión Bancaria: avances e incertidumbres para el año 2014*, Madrid, Fundación Alternativas, Documento de Trabajo, Opex núm. 75/2014.

Berruyer, O. 2013. *Les Faits sont Têtus*. Paris: Les Arènes.

Bhidé, A. and Phelps, E. 2013. Central banking needs rethinking. *Wall Street Journal*, 18 July.

Bibow, J. 2013. *Nadie ha ganado en la crisis del euro. El País*, 21 August.

Blackstone, B. 2013. Berlin dealt setback over austerity. *Wall Street Journal*, 23 July.

Blanchard, O. and Leigh, D. 2013. Errors in forecasts of growth and fiscal multipliers, IMF Working Paper, January.

Blyth, M. 2013. *Austerity. The History of a Dangerous Idea*. Oxford: Oxford University Press.

Blyth, M. 2013. The austerity delusion. *Foreign Affairs* May–June 2013.

Bolger, A. 2013. Private debt deals draw European enthusiasm. *Financial Times*, 11 December.

Boss, C., Pilet, F. and Plattner, T. 2013. Avocats suisses, levez-vous! *Le Monde*, 9 April.

Bowley, G. 2013. Tax debate pits big firms against small. *New York Times*, 25–26 May.

Bricall, J. M. 2013. *Cinco ensayos sobre la crisis* [Five essays on the crisis]. Barcelona: RBA.

Brown, G. 2013. Stumbling toward the next crash. *International New York Times*, 19 December.

Brys, B. 2010. Wage income tax reforms and changes in tax burdens: 2000–2009. OECD Taxation Working Papers, no. 10, OECD Publishing.

Busch, K., Hermann, C., Hinrichs, K. and Schulten, T. 2013. Eurocrisis, austerity policy and the European social model. Friedrich-Ebert-Stiftung, International Policy Analysis, February.

Calzada, I. 2013. *¿Está en riesgo la legitimidad del Estado de bienestar?* [Is the legitimacy of the Welfare State at risk?] eldiario.es, Agenda Pública, 20 December.

Casselman, B. 2013. Long-term jobless left out of recovery. *Wall Street Journal*, 4 September.

Castle, S. 2013. British businesses bridle at planned EU tax on interbank transactions. *International Herald Tribune*, 3 May.

Chan Woon Nam. 2013. Comparison of reduced corporate tax rate in the EU. CESifo Forum, Spring.

Charrel, M. 2013. Dettes: la zone euro n'est pas tirée d'affaire. *Le Monde*, 25 October.

Cohen, S. S. and De Long, J. 2010. *The End of Influence. What Happens when Other Countries have the Money*. New York: Basic Books.

Correa, R. 2013. L'Europe endettée reproduit nos erreurs. *Le Monde Diplomatique*, December.

Corsetti, G., Kuester, K., Meier, A. and Müller, G. 2013. Sovereign risk and belief-driven fluctuations in the euro area. IMF Working Paper, November.

Dalton, M. 2013. Europe's other brake: Private-sector debt. *Wall Street Journal*, 16 August.

December, R. 2014. Private equity firms enjoyed a record year. *Wall Street Journal*, 2 January.

Doncel, L. 2014. *Berlín y París incumplen con Grecia* [Berlin and Paris fail to comply with Greece]. *El País*, 1 February.

Dullien, S. 2013. A German model for Europe? European Council on Foreign Relations. London, July.

Duncan, R. 2012. *The New Depression. The Breakdown of the Paper Money Economy*. Singapore: John Wiley & Sons.

Duval, G. 2012. *La genèse d'une crise*, in *Comprendre la Crise, Alternatives Economiques* 58, December.

Eaglesham, J. 2014. Federal probe targets banks over bonds. *Wall Street Journal*, 9 January.

Eisinger, J. 2013. With banks, tough words aren't enough. *International New York Times*, 13 December.

Elliot, L. 2011. Bill Gates adds his weight to case for Robin Hood tax. *The Guardian*, 3 November.

Escario, J. L. 2011. *Paraísos Fiscales. Los agujeros negros de la economía globalizada* [Tax havens: the black holes of the global economy]. Madrid: Catarata.

Estefanía, J. 2013. *Errores que llevan al sufrimiento* [Errors that lead to suffering], *El País*, 7 January.

Erhel, C. *et al.* 2013. *Tendances de la qualité de l'emploi pendant la crise: une approche européenne comparative*. Paris: Centre d'Études de l'Emploi, March.

Ewing, J. 2013. No bounce for Europe in rebound by Germany. *International Herald Tribune*, 4 April.

Fairless, T. 2013. The unintended drawbacks of Europe's banking union. *Wall Street Journal*, 6–8 December.

Farlow, A. 2013. *Crash and Beyond*. Oxford: Oxford University Press.

Ferguson, N. 2013. The shutdown is a sideshow. Debt is the threat. *Wall Street Journal*, 7 October.

Ferguson, N. and Barbieri, P. P. 2013. The EU's feeble war on unemployment. *International Herald Tribune*, 4 April.

Ford, J., Gainsbury, S. and Houlder, V. 2013. The great tax fudge. *Financial Times*, 21 June.

Forelle, C. and Stevis, M. 2013. Money-laundering distrust stalls Europe's latest bailout. *Wall Street Journal*, 6 March.

Fratscher, M. 2013. The costs for Germany if the Eurozone collapses. *Europe's World*, 1 October.

Freeland, C. 2012. Inequality as a threat to growth. *International Herald Tribune*, 30 November.

Freeland, C. 2013. Taxes, titans and the greater good. *International Herald Tribune*, 3 May.

Fressoz, F. 2013. *François Hollande et l'exaspération des classes moyennes. Le Monde*, 6 November.

Gadrey, J. 2013. *Impôts, fabrication du 'ras-le bol' et réalité de l'injustice. Le Monde Diplomatique*, December.

Gallino, L. 2011. *Finanzcapitalismo. La civiltà del denaro in crisi*. Turín: Einaudi.

German Council Of Economic Experts. Against a backward-looking economic policy. Annual Economic Report 2013/14.

Giannuli, A. 2012. *Uscire della crisi è possible*. Milán: Ponte alle Grazie.

Gottshalk, P. and Smeeding, T. M. 2000. *Empirical Evidence on Income Inequality in Industrialized Countries. Handbook of Income Distribution*. Amsterdam: North-Holland.

Grauwe, P. de. 2013. Pool debt, or face dangerous upheavals across Europe. *Friends of Europe*, spring.

Grauwe, P. de. 2013. *The creditors nations rule in the Eurozone. The future of Europe's economy. Disaster or deliverance*. London: Centre for European Reform September.

Hannon, P. 2013. After crisis, US better off than Europe. *Wall Street Journal*, 6 October.

Henry, J. S. 2012. The price of off-shore revisited. *Tax Justice Network*, July.

Hirschel, D. 2013. *Cuidado con la poción mágica alemana* [Beware of the German magic potion]. *El País*, 30 May.

Holmes, S. and Sunstein, C. R. 2011. *El costo de los derechos. Por qué la libertad depende de los impuestos*. Buenos Aires: Siglo XXI.

Houlder, V. 2013. Call for tax reform as Dutch lure corporate. *Financial Times*, 29 April.

Houlder, V. 2013. Top rate tax cut defies global current. *Financial Times*, 10 October.

Hyman, L. 2012. *Borrow. The American Way of Debt*. New York: Vintage Books.

Irwin, N. 2013. *The Alchemists*. New York: Penguin.

Jiménez, A. and Martínez Prado, R. 2013. *La economía sumergida en España, Documentos de trabajo* 4, Fundación de Estudios Financieros.

Johnson, S. 2013. Capital gobbles labour's share, but victory is empty. *Financial Times*, 4 October.

Johnson, S. and Kwak, J. 2012. *White House Burning: The Founding Fathers, Our National Debt, and Why it Matters to You*. New York: Pantheon Books.

J.P. Morgan and its victims. *Wall Street Journal*, 21 November, 2013.

J.P. Morgan deal may not be so punitive. *International New York Times*, 23 October, 2013.

Kaletsky, A. 2013. Austerity is falling out of favour. *International Herald Tribune*, 26 July.

Keely, B. and Love, P. 2010. *De la crise à la reprise. Causes, déroulement et conséquences de la Grande Récession*. OCDE: Paris.

Kroszner, R. S. and Schiller, R. J. 2011. *Reforming US Financial Markets*. Cambridge: Massachusetts Institute of Technology.

Krugman, P. 2012. *¡Acabad ya con esta crisis!* Barcelona: Crítica.

Krugman, P. 2013. FED's interest in recovery seems to be tapering. *The Irish Times*, 25 June.

Krugman, P. 2013. Free to be hungry. *International Herald Tribune*, 24 September.

Krugman, P. 2013. How the case for austerity has crumbled. *The New York Review of Books* LX(10): pp. 67–73.

Krugman, P. 2013. *La recuperación de los ricos* [The recovery of the rich]. *El País*, 15 September.

Krugman, P. 2013. Looking for Mr. Goodpain. *International Herald Tribune*, 2–3 February.
Krugman, P. 2013. The market speaks. *International Herald Tribune*, 9–10 March.
Krugman, P. 2013. The urge to purge. *International Herald Tribune*, 6–7 April.
Krugman, P. 2013. Why inequality matters. *International New York Times*, 17 December.
Krugman, P. 2013. Zombie economics. *International Herald Tribune*, 16–17 February.
Krugman, P. 2014. Enemies of the poor. *International New York Times*, 14 January.
Krugman, P. 2014. The populist imperative. *International New York Times*, 25–26 January.
Krugman, P. 2014. *Los ricos indignos* [The rich unworthy]. *El País*, 26 January.
Krugman, P. 2014. The war over poverty. *International New York Times*, 11–12 January.
Kulish, N. 2013. Pressure builds on Merkel amid anti-austerity clamor. *International Herald Tribune*, 4–5 May.
Kurapovna, M. C. 2013. Private Banking is Alive and Well in Switzerland. *Wall Street Journal*, 15–17 November.
Landais, C., Piketty, T. and Saez, E. 2011. *Pour une révolution fiscale. Un impôt sur le revenue pour le XXIème siècle*. Paris: Seuil.
Laurent, S. and Parienté, J. 2013. *La réforme fiscale est-elle déjà engagée, comme le soutient François Hollande. Le Monde*, 21 November.
Lévy-Lang, A. 2012. *Il faut maîtriser la finance*. Paris: Eyrolles.
López Garrido, D. 1986. *Libertades Económicas y derechos fundamentales en el sistema comunitario europeo*. Madrid: Tecnos.
López Garrido, D. 1992. *El Tratado de Maastricht*. Madrid: Eurojuris.
López Garrido, D. 2005. *La Constitución Europea* [The European Constitution]. Albacete: Bomarzo.
López Garrido, D. 2010. *El Estado de bienestar: vuelta a la fiscalidad. El País*, 4 August.
López Garrido, D. 2011. *El giro fiscal de la izquierda europea. El País*, 4 October.
López Garrido, D. 2013. *Doce meses de desesperanza económica, Informe sobre el Estado de la Unión Europea*. Madrid: Fundación Alternativas and Friedrich-EbertStiftung.
López Garrido, D. and Peralta, R. 2012. *Una reforma laboral inconstitucional. El País*, 8 March.
López Garrido, D. (dir.) and Martínez Alarcón, M. L. (coord.). 2013. *Reforma constitucional y estabilidad presupuestaria. El artículo 135 de la Constitución Española*, Madrid, Centro de Estudios politicos.
López Garrido, D., Sartorius, N. and Carnero, C. 2003. *No podemos esperar a las elecciones alemanas* [We cannot wait for the German elections]. *El País*, 21 May.
Lowenthal, A. F. 2013. The US in the early 21st century: Decline or renewal? Madrid: Real Instituto Elcano, 20 November.
Lowrey, A. 2013. IMF talks of growth but pushes for austerity. *International Herald Tribune*, 16 April.
Malpass, D. 2013. FED Policy Is a Drag on Recovery. *Wall Street Journal*, 3 June.
Martín and Pérez De Nanclares, J. 2012. *El nuevo Tratado de Estabilidad, Coordinación y Gobernanza de la UEM: reflexiones a propósito de una peculiar reforma realizada fuera de los tratados constitucionales*. Revista de Derecho Comunitario Europeo, núm. 42, mayo-agosto.
Martínez Álvarez, J. A., *et al.* 2013. La economía española, su evolución y escenarios para la recuperación. Madrid: Instituto de Estudios Fiscales, 2 May.
Mathews, P. 2012. A politician's perspective on debt and default, in B. Lucey, Ch. Larkin, and C. Gurdgiev, *What if Ireland Defaults*? Dublin: Orpen Press.
Mattich, A. 2013. Investors go big in Europe debt. *Wall Street Journal*, 1 October.
Melloan, G. 2013. Bankers Haven't Gone Rogue—Regulators Have. *Wall Street Journal*, 27 August.

Millaruelo, A. and Río, A. del. 2013. Las medidas de política monetaria no convencionales del BCE a lo largo de la crisis. Boletín Económico del Banco de España, January.

Millet, D. and Toussaint, É. 2012. *AAA, Audit, Annulations, Autre Politique*. Paris: Seuil.

Milne, S. 2013. Ed Miliband will fail if he locks himself into Tory austerity. *The Guardian*, 1 May.

Milne, S. 2013. Europe's flesheaters now threaten to devour us all. *The Guardian*, 27 March.

Minder, R. 2013. Swiss brace for scrutiny on bank secrecy. *International Herald Tribune*, 24 May.

Morin, F. 2010. *La crisis financiera globalizada y las nuevas orientaciones del sistema*. In S. Amin, E. Altwater, F. Morin and P. Gowan, *Crisis financiera, económica, sistémica*. Madrid: Maia Editores.

Moscovici, P. 2013. *L'Union bancaire est une avancée politique pour tous les peuples d'Europe*. *Le Monde*, 21 December.

Münchau, W. 2013. Austerity obstructs real economic reform. *Financial Times*, 25 February.

Münchau, W. 2013. U.S. join misguised pursuit of austerity. *Financial Times*, 7 January.

Naulot, J.-M. 2013. *Crise financière. Pourquoi les gouvernements ne font rien*. Paris: Seuil.

Nixon, S. 2013. Financial innovation is suddenly back in fashion. *Wall Street Journal*, 9 September.

Nixon, S. 2013. U.S. treasury has it wrong on Germany. *Wall Street Journal*, 11 October.

Norris, F. 2013. Apple finds a new dodge against taxes. *International Herald Tribune*, 3 May.

Norris, F. 2013. Downturn takes hold far and wide. *International Herald Tribune*, 23–24 February.

Norris, F. 2013. Tax System hands firms carte blanche. *International Herald Tribune*, 24 May.

Ormerod, P. 2012. *The Death of Economics*. London: John Wiley & Sons, 1994.

Papadia, F. and Santini, C. 2012. *La Banca Centrale Europea*. Bolonia: Il Mulino.

Passet, O. 2013. Concurrence fiscal en Europe: la relance deshostilités [Tax concurrence in Europe: the relaunch of hostilities]. *Xerfi Synthèse*, December.

Patterson, S., Raice, S. and Barne, K. 2013. U.S. Starts New Era in Bank Regulation. *Wall Street Journal*, 11 December.

Piketty, Saez and Stantcheva, Optimal taxation of top labor incomes: A tale of three elasticities. MBER Working Paper No. 17616. Cambridge, Massachusetts: National Bureau of Economic Research.

Pistor, K. 2013. *La dette contre la démocratie*. *Le Monde*, 26 October.

Plender, J. 2012. Monetary policy: back under control. *Financial Times*, 11 December.

Pollin, R. and Ash, M. 2013. Why Reinhart and Rogoff are wrong about austerity. *Financial Times*, 18 April.

Posen, A. 2013. Germany is being crushed by its export obsession. *Financial Times*, 4 April.

Prats, A. 2013. *Un agujero negro en Ginebra* [A black hole in Geneva]. *Blogs de El País*, 16 May.

Rajan, R. G. 2011. *Grietas del sistema. Por qué la economía mundial sigue amenazada*. Barcelona: Deusto.

Rampini, F. 2013. *L'euro debole salva Italia*. *La Repubblica*, 10 February.

Reinhart, C. M. and Rogoff, K. S. 2011. *Esta vez es distinto: ocho siglos de necedad financiera*. Madrid: FCE.

Robbery at J.P. Morgan. *Wall Street Journal*, 3 September, 2013.

Rodrigues, M. J. 2013. Youth unemployment, socioeconomic divergences and fiscal capacity in the euro area. Notre Europe, policy paper 101, November.

Roger, P. 2013. Une fiscalité faiblement redistributive. *Le Monde*, 15 October.

Rogoff, K. 2011. *Oublier la taxe sur les transactions financières. Les Echos*, 17 October.
Rothstein, B. 1998. *Just Institutions Matter*. Cambridge: Cambridge University Press.
Roubini, N. and Mihm, S. 2011. *Crisis Economics. A Crash Course in the Future of Finance*. New York: Penguin.
Ruiz, A. 2013. *Economía sumergida: un lastre excesivamente oneroso*. Informe Mensual, La Caixa, Barcelona, September.
Ruiz Devesa, D. 2013. *El Banco Central Europeo en 2012*. En El Estado de la Unión Europea, El Fracaso de la Austeridad. Madrid: Fundación Alternativas y Friedrich-Ebert-Stiftung. Available at www.falternativas.org.
Ruiz-Huerta Agúndez, Garcimartín, López and Rodríguez. 2011. *Tendencias de reforma fiscal: hacia una fiscalidad europea*. Madrid: Fundación Alternativas, Opex.
Sachs, J. D. 2011. *The Price of Civilization*. New York: Random House.
Sachs, J. D. 2013. The end of poverty, soon. *International Herald Tribune*, 26 September.
Saft, J. 2013. Banks win, but growth suffer. *International Herald Tribune*, 9 January.
Sapir, J. 2010. *Faut-il sortir de l'euro?* Paris: Seuil.
Schäfer, D., Ross, A. and Strauss, D. 2013. The big five. *Financial Times*, 13 November.
Schneider, F. 2013. *The Shadow Economy in Europe*. Visa Europe, AT Kearney.
Servan-Schreiber, J. L., *Pourquoi les riches ont gagné*, París, Albin Michel, 2014.
Sevilla, J. V., El declive de la Socialdemocracia, Barcelona, RBA, 2011.
Shah, N. and Portlock, S. U.S. Economy Starts To Hit Growth Stride. *Wall Street Journal*, 31 January–2 February, 2014.
Shaxson, N. 2011. *Treasure Islands. Uncovering the Damage of Offshore Banking and Tax Havens*, New York: Palgrave Macmillan.
Skidelsky, R. 2009. *Keynes, the Return of the Master*, Barcelona: Crítica.
Stafford, P. 2013. Fears grow over rules on derivatives trading. *Financial Times*, 19 December.
Steinglass, M. 2013. Dutch focus reform efforts focus on letterbox companies. *Financial Times*, 29 April.
Steinhauser, G. 2013. EU Proposes Tourger. Fund Rules. *Wall Street Journal*, September.
Steinhauser, G. 2013. Flawed integration risks more European divisions. *Wall Street Journal*, 22 October.
Stevens, P. 2013. The new deal for Europe: More reform, less austerity. *Financial Times*, 26 April.
Stiglitz, J. E. 2010. *Le Rapport Stiglitz. Pour une vraie réforme du système monétaire et financier international aprés la crise mondiales* Paris: Les Liens qui Libèrent.
Stiglitz, J. E. 2011. *Caída libre. El libre mercado y el hundimiento de la economía mundial*. Madrid: Taurus.
Stiglitz, J. E. 2013. *Les illusions perdues des maîtres du monde. Les Echos*, 14 February.
Stolberg, S. G. and Mcintire, M. 2013. Republicans saw budget as a weapon. *International Herald Tribune*, 7 October.
Tabuchi, H. 2013. Economists say rise in sales tax may stifle Japan. *International Herald Tribune*, 16 September.
Takatoshi, I. 2013. Japan must be brave—it is time to put up taxes. *Financial Times*, 10 September.
Tracy, R. and Crittenden, M. R. 2013. FED sets to bolster safety net at banks. *Wall Street Journal*, 25–27 October.
Tracy, R. and Crittenden, M. R. 2013. FED Eyes Financial System´s Weak Link. *Wall Street Journal*, 2 December.
Tracy, R. and Crittenden, M. R. 2013. Financial system is stronger-treasury. *Wall Street Journal*, 18 December.

Vidal Folch, X. 2013. *Europa empieza a concretar su giro social. El País*, 29 June.
Vittori, J. M. 2012. *Lorsque la France réduisait sa dette publique. Les Echos*, 29 October.
Werdiger, J. 2013. Tradition of Switzerland as a US tax haven nears its end. *International Herald Tribune*, 31 August–1 September.
Wessel, D. 2012. Trying to calculate the cost of uncertainty. *Wall Street Journal*, 5 December.
Wolff, M. 2013. America's fiscal policy is not in crisis. *Financial Times*, 23 January.
Wolff, M., 2013. Britain's austerity is indefensible. *Financial Times*, 26 April.
Wolff, M. 2013. Germany's strange parallel universe. *Financial Times*, 25 September.
Wolff, M. 2013. Germany is a weight on the world. *Financial Times*, 6 October.

Further Reading

A cross ideology that threatens America, *The Observer*, 31 July, 2011.
A GOP shutdown strategy. *Wall Street Journal*, 3 October, 2013.
An Obama-Cruz shutdown. *Wall Street Journal*, 1 October, 2013.
Action plan on base erosion and profit sifting, OECD Publishing, 2013.
Addressing base erosion and profit shifting. OECD Publishing, 2013.
Adobe gets creative with Ireland's tax rules. *Financial Times*, 13 October, 2013.
Apple CEO pushes back against US tax probe. *Wall Street Journal*, 22 May, 2013.
Austerity. An idea on trial. *The Guardian*, 22 April, 2013.
Banco Central Europeo. 2012. Opening statement at Deutscher Bundestag, 24 October.
Bin it. Plans for a transactions tax ought to be dropped. *The Economist*, 23 February, 2013.
Business analysis. *The Guardian*, 25 January, 2013.
CESifo World Economic Survey, Múnich, April, 2013.
Congressional Budget Office. 2013. The 2013 long-term budget outlook. CBO, September.
Consensus builds against austerity. *International Herald Tribune*, 10 May, 2013.
Debt and Growth. *Wall Street Journal*, 1 May, 2013.
Ecofin Brief, 2 March, 2013. Available at www.europa.eu/economy-finance/publications.
Economic Policy Reforms 2013. Going for growth, OECD Publishing.
Economies en transition. Paris: OCDE, 1989.
Editorial. *Financial Times*, 7 February, 2013.
Education and training monitor 2013, European Commission, 2013.
Entrevista con Michael Keen. El País Negocios, 22 December, 2013.
EU leaders and IMF closer on crisis cures. *International Herald Tribune*, 22 April, 2013.
European Commission. Alert mechanism report 2014. Brussels, COM, 2013.
European stagnation. *International Herald Tribune*, 6 May, 2013.
European economic forecast. European Economy 7/2013, European Commission, autumn, 2013.
European economic forecast. European Economy 2/2014, European Commission, winter, 2013.
Europe's austerity fable. *Wall Street Journal*, 24 April, 2013.
Europe's bitter tonic. *International Herald Tribune*, 16 April, 2013.
Europe's other debt crisis. *The Economist*, 26 October, 2013.
Europe taxes the world. *Wall Street Journal*, 15–17 February, 2013.
Eurostat. 2013. Euroindicators, 153/2013, October, 2013.
Eurosystem's household finance and consumption survey. *Household Finance and Consumption Network*, 2013.
Fiscal adjustment in an uncertain world. *Fiscal Monitor*, International Monetary Fund, April, 2013.
Fondacion Robert Schuman. 2013. *La réforme de l'Union économique et monetaire: l'ambition politique, la fracture. Questions d'Europe* 297, 16 December.

Hoja de ruta hacia una unión bancaria. COM, 510 final, 12 September, 2012.
IMF World Economic Outlook, 2013. Transitions and Tensions. IMF.
Informe sobre la lucha contra el fraude fiscal, la evasión fiscal y los paraísos fiscales, 2 May, 2013.
Intermon Oxfam, 2012. Crisis, desigualdad y pobreza. Available at www.oxfamintermon.org/es/documentos, quoted in *El País*, 14 December.
Intermon Oxfam, 2013. Informe Oxfam 174, September.
International Labour Office, 2009. 8th European Regional Meeting, Lisbon.
Les Économistes Atterés, L'Europe maltraitée, Paris: Les Liens qui Libèrent, 2012.
London Economics, 2014. The effects of a financial transaction tax on European households. Savings, City of London Corporation, February.
Memoria Anual de Cáritas, presentada el, 10 October, 2013.
OECD Economic Outlook, Vol. 2013/2. OECD Publishing. Preliminary version, 2013.
Osservatorio di Politica Internazionale. 2012. *L'Europa verso un political compact: opzioni per uscire dalla crisi*, 58, June.
Posición del Consejo de Asuntos Europeos sobre el Consejo Europeo de los días 14–15 March, Fundación Alternativas, 2013. Available at www.falternativas.org.
Pressure grows for limits on dark pools. *Financial Times*, 22 November, 2013.
Propuesta de directiva del Consejo por la que se establece una cooperación reforzada en el ámbito del impuesto de transacciones financieras. Documento COM, 71 final, 2013.
Propuesta de directiva del Consejo relativa a un sistema común del impuesto sobre las transacciones financieras y por la que se modifica la directiva 2008/7/CE. Documento COM, 594, 2011.
Propuesta de Reglamento del Parlamento Europeo y del Consejo por la que se establecen normas uniformes y un procedimiento uniforme para la resolución de entidades de crédito y de determinadas empresas de inversión, en el marco de un Mecanismo Único de Resolución y un Fondo Único de Resolución Bancaria, y se modifica el Reglamento (UE) núm. 1.093/2010 del Parlamento Europeo y del consejo. Bruselas. 10 de julio de 2013, COM, 520 final, 2013.
Rapport de la Commission des questions sociales, de la santé et du developpement durable. Presentado por Hermine Naghdalyan, Comisión Europea, Doc. 13017.
Regional Economic Prospect in EBRD Countries of Operations, January. EBRD Office of the Chief Economist, 2013. Available at www.ebrd.com.
Spending review. Vital, body and pointless. *The Guardian*, 1 May, 2013.
Statement of the Eurogroup, Greece, 16 November, 2010.
Taxing Funds in the European Union. Eurostat, 2013.
Taxing Working Families, A distributional Analysis, OCDE, Tax Policy Studies, no. 12, 2005.
The art of the possible. *The Times*, 10 October, 2013.
The liberalization and management of capital flows. An international view. International Monetary Fund Staff Paper, 14 November, 2012.
The road to a downgrade. *Wall Street Journal*, 29 July, 2011.
US Financial Services Authority. 2009. A regulatory response to the global banking crisis. London: FSA.
U.S. Budget Gap stimulating than expected. *International Herald Tribune*, 16 May, 2013.
VV.AA. *El Estado de la Unión Europea. El fracaso de la austeridad, Fundación Alternativas y Friedrich-Ebert-Stiftung*, Madrid, Exlibrís, 2013. Available at www.falternativas.org.
World Economic and Financial Surveys. 2013. Taxing times, fiscal monitor, International Monetary Fund, October.